MPLS

Technology and Applications

MPLS

Technology and Applications

Bruce Davie

Yakov Rekhter

MORGAN KAUFMANN PUBLISHERS

AN IMPRINT OF ACADEMIC PRESS

A Harcourt Science and Technology Company

SAN FRANCISCO   SAN DIEGO   NEW YORK   BOSTON
LONDON   SYDNEY   TOKYO

Senior Editor	Jennifer Mann
Senior Production Editor	Edward Wade
Editorial Coordinator	Karyn Johnson
Cover Design	Ross Carron Design
Cover Images	© Yoav Levy/Phototake/PictureQuest
Text Design	Side By Side Studios, Mark Ong
Technical Illustration & Composition	Technologies 'N Typography
Copyeditor	Jennifer McClain
Proofreader	Ken DellaPenta
Indexer	Ty Koontz
Printer	Courier Corporation

Designations used by companies to distinguish their products are often claimed as trademarks or registered trademarks. In all instances where Morgan Kaufmann Publishers is aware of a claim, the product names appear in initial capital or all capital letters. Readers, however, should contact the appropriate companies for more complete information regarding trademarks and registration.

ACADEMIC PRESS
A Harcourt Science and Technology Company
525 B Street, Suite 1900, San Diego, CA 92101–4495, USA
http://www.academicpress.com

Academic Press
Harcourt Place, 32 Jamestown Road, London, NW1 7BY, United Kingdom
http://www.academicpress.com

Morgan Kaufmann Publishers
340 Pine Street, Sixth Floor, San Francisco, CA 94104–3205, USA
http://www.mkp.com

04 03 02 01   5 4 3 2

Library of Congress Cataloging-in-Publication Data

Davie, Bruce S.
 MPLS : technology and applications / Bruce Davie, Yakov Rekhter.
  p. cm.
 Includes bibliographical references and index.
 ISBN 1-55860-656-4
 1. Internet (Computer network) 2. Telecommunication—Switching systems. 3. Computer network protocols. 4. Asynchronous transfer mode. 5. Routers (Computer networks) I. Rekhter, Yakov. II. Title.

TK5105.875.I57 D35 2000
004.6'6—dc21   00-036537

This book is printed on acid-free paper.

Contents

Preface

The concept of "Internet time" as shorthand for the rapid rate of technological innovation in the Internet is by now well established. There can be few technologies that exemplify this high rate of change more than Multiprotocol Label Switching—MPLS. When our book on label switching technologies, *Switching in IP Networks* (the first book on the subject), appeared two years ago, we could speak only about the likely future direction of MPLS, which was then in the early stages of its definition and standardization. We could not even imagine putting the term *MPLS* on the cover for fear that too few people would know what we meant.

MPLS has now become a fundamentally important technology in the Internet, and the time is clearly right (if not overdue) to devote a book to the subject. Several of the largest Internet service providers have deployed MPLS in their production networks to solve problems such as traffic engineering and to offer IP services efficiently over ATM backbone networks. Virtual private network (VPN) services based on MPLS technology are now available, and the first customers of those services have enthusiastically adopted the new technology. The majority of high-end routers now shipping support MPLS, and multivendor interoperability has been demonstrated.

In spite of these successes, much confusion surrounds MPLS. Some people mistakenly believe that the chief attraction of label switching is that it can be implemented efficiently and thus improve forwarding performance; others point to the success of high speed IP lookup algorithms and hardware to argue that MPLS provides no value at all. In this book, we explain exactly what MPLS is and how it works, and we carefully examine the benefits that it provides. While these benefits do not necessarily imply that MPLS should be deployed in every network in the world, they are significant enough to warrant consideration by the operators of most large networks and by those who must buy networking services from service providers.

We have tried to make this book accessible to a wide audience. We have assumed most readers have a certain amount of knowledge of IP routing, but we have provided some background in this area where appropriate. More advanced readers should not hesitate to skim sections that look like standard discussions of routing. By the same token, the last two chapters discuss some fairly advanced routing capabilities, and readers with a less strong background in routing should not feel ashamed to skip through some of this material. Similarly, the discussion on quality of service (QoS) may be too brief for those looking for a complete tutorial on the subject, while some more experienced readers may find they can skip the overview of this topic.

We hope the book will be of value to network designers and engineers, in both service provider and enterprise environments, who need to understand enough about MPLS to determine whether it is a possible candidate for deployment in their networks. You should find enough here to gain an understanding of the strengths and weaknesses of label switching compared to other techniques, such as conventional routing and layer 2 switching, and to weigh the different options against one another. This will enable you to make informed decisions about what role, if any, MPLS should play in your network. The book should also provide a useful introduction to the field for engineers developing MPLS products. The information here will make it easier to understand the detailed technical material that can be found in Internet drafts, Requests for Comments (RFCs), and literature provided by various MPLS vendors. In those areas where the standards are not yet complete, you may also gain a sense of whether to go with one proposed approach now or to wait for the standards to solidify in the future.

Organization of This Book

The chapters of this book divide into three groups:

- Introduction and overview: Chapters 1 and 2
- Details of two predecessor technologies: Chapters 3 and 4
- MPLS protocols and applications: Chapters 5 through 8

In the first chapter we examine why it was necessary to invent label switching in general and MPLS in particular. We discuss the numerous problems that label switching aims to solve. We also give a brief history of the inventions and announcements that made this topic the focus of so much attention. Chapter 2 describes the overall architectural issues that pertain to the whole area of label switching. There are certain fundamental similarities between MPLS and the label switching technologies that preceded it, such as the forwarding algorithm and use of IP control protocols. In addition, the designers of any label switching approach must make some of the same key architectural choices, for example, between control-driven and data-driven label assignment. We examine the ramifications of some of these choices.

Chapters 3 and 4 provide detailed descriptions of two of the most important technologies that led up to the creation of MPLS. The first of these is Ipsilon's IP Switching, which was largely responsible for making label switching known in the networking industry. The second is Cisco's Tag Switching, from which many of the basic concepts of MPLS were derived. By looking at these two technologies in detail, we see a broad spectrum of different design choices and shed some light on the factors that shaped the design of MPLS.

In Chapter 5 we begin our detailed description of MPLS by examining the fundamentals of the MPLS architecture and the core protocols, notably the Label Distribution Protocol (LDP). Chapter 6 describes the role of MPLS in supporting quality of service and explains how both of the main QoS approaches in the Internet—Integrated Services and Differentiated Services—can be supported in an MPLS network. Chapter 7 explains the application of MPLS to constraint-based routing and examines the range of protocols that may be used in this application. Finally, Chapter 8 describes one approach to building VPNs using MPLS.

Throughout the book we have made comments about the strengths and weaknesses of different approaches and the wisdom of the various design decisions that have been made. As much as possible, we have tried to be objective and unbiased in our analysis. Because we have also been involved as designers of some of the protocols and participants in the standards process, it is inevitable that we favor some design choices over others. Probably no author could be completely neutral when discussing such matters. However, we have endeavored to present the different approaches and comparative arguments in a way such that you can draw your own conclusions. We have also worked hard not to "oversell" MPLS. It is a technology with plenty of capabilities, but it is not the panacea that some analysts would have us believe. Our reviewers helped enormously in keeping our exposition as objective as possible.

Acknowledgments

We are greatly indebted to those who reviewed all or part of this book. Our thanks go to those who reviewed the initial book proposal: Fred Baker, John Brassil, Juha Heinanen, Mike Minnich, Greg Minshall, and Peter Newman. Greg and Peter (both, at the time, with Ipsilon) also reviewed Chapter 3, "IP Switching." Bart Burns and H. Jonathan Chao slogged through the entire manuscript, and Pratip Banerji and Ranjeet Sudan read most of it. We appreciate all the helpful suggestions and corrections provided by these people; they have greatly enhanced the quality of the book.

Paul Doolan, our coauthor on *Switching in IP Networks*, generously agreed to let us draw on material from that book for our discussions of IP Switching and the MPLS core protocols. Our colleagues Francois le Faucheur, Stefano Previdi, George Swallow, and Dan Tappan contributed material for some of the figures.

We also wish to thank everyone at Morgan Kaufmann Publishers who made this book possible. The encouragement of our editor, Jennifer Mann, and the considerable support of her assistant, Karyn Johnson, made the whole process almost enjoyable at times. The entertainment budget of MKP, as administered by Jennifer, continues to be a bright spot in many a dull conference.

The fact that we were able to write this book at all is in large part due to the flexibility and generosity of our employers, Cisco Systems. As well as providing us with "day jobs" during the writing of the book, they gave us the chance to work together on the development of label switching technology. We thank them for this opportunity.

Finally, neither of us could have survived the challenge of writing a book in our spare time without the support and understanding of our families, for which we heartily thank them.

Introduction

The Internet has long provided fertile ground for technological innovation. As new networking technologies spring up, some manage to attract a remarkable level of attention. Multiprotocol label switching—MPLS—is one such technology. This book provides a thorough and balanced examination of MPLS and aims to answer some fundamental questions about the technology. First, what is MPLS? Second, how does it work? And finally, what benefits does it provide? In answering this last question, we hope to show that the benefits offered by MPLS justify the attention it has received in the networking industry.

MPLS evolved from several similar technologies that were invented in the mid-1990s. The most well known of these (although not the first to be publicly disclosed) was dubbed *IP Switching* by its inventors at the start-up company Ipsilon. Toshiba had previously described a similar scheme, implemented in their *Cell Switching Router* (CSR), and several other approaches were soon published, notably Cisco's *Tag Switching* and IBM's *Aggregate Route-based IP Switching* (ARIS). All of these approaches share some common traits. They all use a simple label swapping technique for forwarding data. They all use the control paradigm of the Internet protocol suite. That is, they use IP addresses and standard Internet routing protocols such as OSPF and BGP.

However, the various approaches differ significantly in their goals as well as in the details of their implementation.

With all this activity, it was not too surprising that the Internet Engineering Task Force (IETF) chartered a working group to standardize a common approach drawing on these ideas. Not wanting to pick a name that would imply endorsement of any one company's product, the IETF picked a neutral (and slightly cumbersome) name for the group: Multiprotocol Label Switching (MPLS). MPLS technology is now well on its way to becoming an industry standard.

This book provides a detailed description and analysis of MPLS technology and the set of problems that it addresses. It describes the architectural issues and the details of the MPLS protocols, explores the design choices that have been made, and discusses the pros and cons of those choices. It also describes some of the key concepts that were developed by the predecessors of MPLS. This helps to explain some of the design decisions behind MPLS and to illustrate the wide range of requirements that MPLS must address. Finally, we discuss some of the main applications of MPLS and address the question of when it is and is not appropriate to deploy MPLS.

It is important that we define some terms at this early stage. One word that we have already used several times is *forwarding*. We use this to refer to the common operation that both switches and routers perform on packets: they receive a packet on an input, determine where it needs to go by examining some fields in the packet, and send it to the appropriate output.

The set of approaches described in this book will be referred to collectively as *label switching* technologies. A *label* is simply a relatively short, fixed-length identifier that is used to forward packets. Label values are normally local to a single link (more precisely, a single datalink layer subnet) and thus have no global significance. They are also unstructured; that is, they are not made up of distinct components. A label switching device will usually replace the label in a packet with some new value before forwarding it on to the next hop. For this reason we call the forwarding algorithm *label swapping*. Forwarding decisions based on labels use the *exact match* algorithm to decide where to send the packets; we describe this algorithm in detail in Chapter 2. And, by our definition, a label switching device, which we will call a *Label Switching Router* (LSR), runs standard IP control protocols (e.g., routing protocols, RSVP, etc.) to determine where to forward packets.

We examine several predecessors of MPLS in this book. All of them are label switching technologies by the above definition, and each has its own terminology. The vendor-specific terms for LSRs are *Cell Switching Router* (CSR), *IP Switch, Tag Switching Router* (TSR) or *Tag Switch,* and *Integrated Switch Router* (ISR). There are other approaches that we have not covered, either because they did not differ significantly enough from these four to add much to the discussion, or because they were not label switching approaches. In particular, we have not covered *switch-based routers,* which behave externally like a conventional router but which are built internally around a switching fabric. Such devices are interesting pieces of hardware, but address a different set of problems than LSRs. They focus primarily on performance, which is only a small part of the problem space addressed by label switching.

Before looking at the details of any of these approaches, however, it will be helpful to consider the set of factors that led to the focus of attention in this area.

1.1 How Did We Get Here?

Many factors led to the development of label switching. It is often assumed that there was just one factor—the need for fast, cheap IP routers. This may be true for one or two of the predecessors of MPLS, but, as we will see in the following sections, the label switching field as a whole was driven by much more than just the need for speed. In the following discussion, each factor may have been important in the development of only a subset of the label switching approaches. However, it is the combination of all these factors that has caused the field to develop to the point where MPLS seems certain to be part of the networking landscape for the foreseeable future.

1.1.1 Growth and Evolution of the Internet

It is by now something of a cliché to talk about the "explosive" or "exponential" growth of the Internet, but the fact remains that it has experienced remarkable growth. The Internet is clearly getting bigger in almost any dimension that can be measured, and this growth has created a wealth of technical challenges. Label switching is in part a response to these challenges.

The growth in both the number of users of the Internet and in their bandwidth requirements has placed increasing demands on the Internet service providers' (ISPs') networks. To meet the growing demand for bandwidth, ISPs need higher performance switching and routing products. We discuss the role of performance in motivating the label switching effort in the next section.

As well as getting faster, networks need to deal with increased numbers of nodes, more routes in routing tables, more flows passing through a given point, and so forth. In general, network providers need to be concerned with *scalability,* which we can define loosely as the ability to grow the network in all these dimensions without finding some insurmountable problem. Label switching has been in part motivated by the need for scalability, which we discuss further in Section 1.1.3.

Perhaps the most important motivating factor behind label switching, and certainly one that is not well appreciated in the networking community, is the need to evolve the routing functionality of the Internet and of IP networks in general. The growth of the Internet is continually placing new demands on the routing protocols, and there is an ever-growing need for new routing functionality—both to deal with the growth itself and to meet the evolving needs of the growing user population.

In the past, routing functionality was notoriously difficult to evolve, and part of the reason is the close coupling between routing and forwarding in IP networks. As an example, consider the process of deploying Classless Interdomain Routing (CIDR). The effect of CIDR is to say that IP network prefixes, which had previously been 8, 16, or 24 bits long, could now be of any length. This greatly enhanced the efficiency with which addresses could be assigned in the Internet and also helped enable more scalable aggregation of addressing and routing information. However, making this change also required a change in the forwarding algorithm of virtually all IP routers, because prefixes could now be of any length. These algorithms are crucial to the performance of a router and are implemented in either hardware or very finely tuned software. Making changes to the forwarding algorithms is typically an expensive and time-consuming proposition.

One of the attractions of label switching is that the forwarding algorithm is fixed and that new control paradigms can be deployed without making any changes to it. As we will see in the next chapter, a wide variety of control modules can be used to control the label switching process, and they all use exactly the same forwarding algorithm. Thus, it is entirely feasible to put the forwarding algorithm in hardware or to tune the fast path software once without concern that it will need to be re-optimized every time a new piece of routing functionality is required. This has significant potential to shorten the time it takes to develop and deploy new routing functionality in IP networks. It is our belief that this is the most significant benefit of label switching and that as a result label switching is likely to form the foundation for the next generation of routing architecture.

Some readers may at this point be wondering what happened to IP version 6 (IPv6). Wasn't it supposed to be the basis of the next generation of IP networks? The reality is that IPv6 serves a very specific purpose: extending the IP address space so that a greater number of IP nodes can be uniquely addressed. IPv6 actually makes no change to the routing architecture that was developed for IP version 4 (IPv4). Other new functionality, such as resource reservations, security, and so on, while often discussed in the same breath with IPv6, is largely independent of it.

Interestingly, label switching has the potential to simplify the deployment of IPv6, because it would require no change to the forwarding algorithms. All of the label switching techniques described in this book could operate with IPv6, given the availability of routing protocols that carry IPv6 addresses.

1.1.2 Price and Performance

In any network based on the Internet protocol suite, whether it is part of the global Internet or a private internetwork,[1] one of the key components is the router. The most fundamental task of a router is to forward IP packets (or datagrams) across the network. As we will see in more detail in the next chapter, forwarding IP datagrams is a rather complex operation. Furthermore, routers often perform a wide range of functions in addition to just forwarding packets, such as filtering the flow of packets between different parts of a network. Indeed, the most important characteristic of a router for many applications is not how fast it can forward packets but how rich a set of functionality it provides.

Another important network component is the switch. Whereas routers are layer 3 devices (they forward IP packets, and IP is a layer 3 protocol in the 7-layer protocol model), switches are layer 2 devices—

---

1. In this book we follow the convention of using the term *Internet* (spelled with a capital *I*) to refer specifically to the well-known global network with which most readers are familiar, whereas we use the generic term *internetwork* to refer to an arbitrary network based on the Internet protocol suite.

they forward layer 2 protocol packets. Compared to routers, switches tend to be rather simple. They do not provide the same rich set of features, and they normally support a very limited number of protocols and interface types. By contrast, routers usually support dozens of protocols and a wide range of interface types and speeds. The forwarding algorithm of a switch is invariably very simple. Some types of switches, notably ATM switches and Frame Relay switches, use a forwarding algorithm based on label swapping.

Given the different complexity of the tasks performed by routers and switches, it is not surprising that they tend to exhibit different price/performance characteristics. First, we should define what we mean by *performance*. Characterizing the performance of a switch or a router can be quite complex because it tends to depend on many factors, such as the exact traffic pattern presented to the inputs of the device. However, it is normally possible to come up with a reasonably representative performance number either in terms of the packets per second that the device can forward between inputs and outputs or in terms of its total bandwidth capacity. For example, if a switch has 10 inputs, each of which can accept data at 150 Mb/sec (150×10^6 bits/second), and it can switch data from all of those inputs simultaneously, we might say it has a total capacity of 1.5 Gb/sec ($10 \times 150 \times 10^6 = 1.5 \times 10^9$ bits/second).

When we look at the price/performance characteristics of switches and routers, we usually find that switches come out ahead. By this we mean that, for a given performance level, the price of the router tends to be higher than the equivalent switch. Conversely, for a given cost, a switch tends to offer a higher performance level than a router. This is not too surprising when you consider that the router has to forward packets and perform various other services, while the switch, in essence, does very little but forward packets. This performance difference is exacerbated by the fact that the actual forwarding operation of a router is more complex than that of a switch, for reasons discussed in the next chapter.

Related to this observation is the fact that the highest level of performance at any given time has usually been found in switches rather than routers. Thus, for example, switches capable of handling 10 Gb/sec of total capacity were available well before routers of similar capacity.

There remains considerable room for debate about whether the observed price/performance differences between switches and routers are fundamental or are just historical artifacts resulting from different design goals, marketing strategies, and any number of other factors. However, it is very hard to dispute the observed price/performance differences at the point in time when the various label switching schemes were proposed.

This leads directly to one of the key motivations for the development of all the label switching approaches. What if you could build a device that did the most important job of a router—forwarding IP packets—using hardware that looks like a switch? You would have a product that has the price/performance characteristics of a switch, but the functionality of a router. Of course, you might not get all the more esoteric router features, but in some situations, those features aren't really necessary. This has become even more attractive as the success of the Internet has increased the number of situations in which IP is the only protocol that a router needs to handle. It was the desire to provide IP forwarding at the price/performance level of a switch that motivated much of the work described in this book.

1.1.3 Integration of IP over ATM

Another factor motivating much of the work described in this book is the desire to integrate IP and ATM (Asynchronous Transfer Mode). ATM switches started to appear on the market in the late 1980s and promised to provide great performance improvements over earlier network technologies. However, as the standards for ATM networks evolved, driven by bodies such as the International Telecommunications Union (ITU; the primary standards-setting body for telecommunications equipment, formerly known as CCITT) and the ATM Forum, ATM acquired an architectural model that differed significantly from the IP architecture. Notably, whereas IP is based on a datagram or connectionless model of data delivery, ATM is based on a connection-oriented or virtual circuit model. IP and ATM also have completely separate addressing schemes and a host of other differences, including different models of multicast communication and resource allocation. These different architectural models presented a significant challenge, and the label switching efforts were in part a response to that challenge.

In the early stages of ATM's development, it seemed possible (to some observers, at least) that ATM would "conquer the world," that is, become the dominant networking technology. Many hard-core ATM advocates imagined the development of native ATM-based applications and new protocol stacks designed to take advantage of the features of ATM. However, it soon became apparent that a major function of many ATM networks would be the forwarding of IP datagrams. This was in large part the result of the success of the Internet, and of the fact that TCP/IP-based applications, such as Web browsers, had become entrenched. Thus, the ATM and IP standards bodies were faced with the problem of how to "map" the IP architecture onto ATM networks.

A factor making this problem even more pressing was the difference in performance between ATM switches and commercially available routers. The relatively high performance of ATM switches, and the fact that ATM had been designed to operate over wide area links, made ATM an attractive technology with which to build the backbone of an internetwork. Some large parts of today's Internet are built out of ATM switches surrounded by relatively low speed routers. An example of such a network design is shown in Figure 1.1.

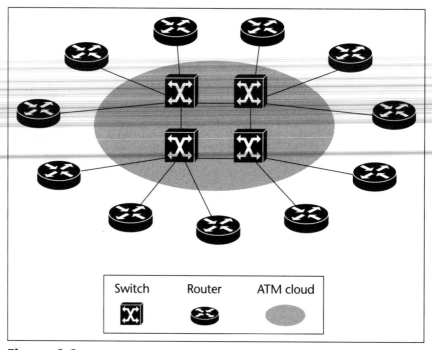

Figure 1.1
An IP over ATM network. Routers connect to a "cloud" of ATM switches.

The type of network shown here is often said to use the *overlay model*. The idea is that the IP network is overlaid onto an ATM network. The ATM network provides a core of high speed connectivity, and the IP network, which is composed of a set of routers interconnected by ATM virtual circuits, provides the intelligence to forward IP datagrams, which is the main job of the network.

The problem of mapping IP onto ATM was taken up by a number of standards bodies, primarily the ATM Forum and the IETF. The complexity of the problem can be appreciated to some extent just by counting the number of different working groups that have tackled aspects of this mapping problem. These include

- The IP over ATM (IPATM) working group, which defined encapsulations for IP datagrams when carried inside ATM adaptation layer PDUs and an address resolution protocol (ATMARP) for mapping IP addresses to ATM addresses, which was later extended to handle multicast

- The IP over Large Public Data Networks (IPLPDN) and later Routing over Large Clouds (ROLC) working groups, which defined the Next Hop Resolution Protocol (NHRP) to enable widely separated hosts and routers to establish direct virtual circuits across an ATM network

- The LAN emulation working group (LANE), which defined procedures to make an ATM network appear to behave more like a multiaccess LAN

- The Multiprotocol over ATM (MPOA) working group, which combined and extended the work of many of the other groups to support multiple network layer protocols (as opposed to just IP)

- The Integrated Services over Specific Link Layers (ISSLL) working group, which is defining procedures to map the resource reservation model of IP onto that of ATM (along with other link layers)

As this quick survey suggests, mapping between IP and ATM involves considerable complexity. Most of the above groups have defined some sort of server (ATMARP, MARS, NHRP, BUS, to name a few) to handle one of the mapping functions, along with the protocols necessary to interact with the server. A continuing problem is dealing with the fact that servers represent a single point of failure, and thus there is a desire to make redundant servers, which of course require synchronization protocols to keep them consistent with each other.

Where did all this complexity come from? In essence, it all derives from the fact that the Internet protocols and the ATM protocols were developed with virtually no regard for each other and happened to end up in very different places. This realization has prompted a lot of people to wonder if ATM switches could be used with a different set of protocols than those defined by the ATM Forum and the ITU—a set of protocols that are more consistent with the Internet architecture and that would eliminate the need for the plethora of complex mappings. Several label switching efforts described in this book are in fact attempts to define such a set of protocols, which can control an ATM switch in such a way that it naturally forwards IP packets without the help of half a dozen servers mapping between IP and ATM.

As we will see in the following chapters, the various schemes to forward IP packets using label switching all do away with the overlay model and the complexity it brings. Instead of having two different protocol architectures with different addressing, routing protocols, resource allocation schemes, and so on, all of the proposals enable IP control protocols to run directly on ATM hardware. The ATM switches still forward packets using label swapping, but the mechanisms by which they set up the forwarding tables and allocate resources are all driven by IP control protocols. From a control point of view, the ATM switches effectively *become* IP routers, thus removing the need to map between IP and ATM control models.

Scalability Issues

There is a little-known but important scaling problem that arises whenever an IP network is built as an overlay on a layer 2 mesh, as might be done with a Frame Relay backbone as well as an ATM one. By "scaling problem," we mean that some measure of complexity in the network grows much faster than the number of nodes in the network, so that at some point it just becomes unfeasible to make the network any bigger.

Consider the network in Figure 1.2. If the ATM network in the middle is to provide high speed connectivity among all the routers, a full mesh of virtual circuits (VCs) must interconnect all the routers. Anything less would mean that there would be an extra router hop between some pairs of routers, which could cause the extra router in the middle of the path to become a bottleneck. However, a full mesh of

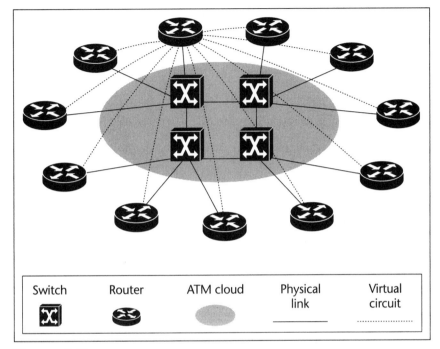

Figure 1.2
Virtual circuits between routers over an ATM network.

VCs means that all the routers are, in effect, directly connected to each other. In Figure 1.2, to avoid cluttering the diagram, we have shown only the VCs that originate at one of the routers; in reality, a full mesh would consist of $n(n-1)/2$ VCs, or 55 VCs, in this example.

To appreciate the problem here, it is necessary to know a little about how routing protocols work. A router is normally configured to have an *adjacency* with each of its directly connected neighbors. The adjacencies enable the router to keep track of who it is directly connected to and whether any links have gone down and are used to exchange routing information with those neighbors.

When the routers are connected by a full mesh of virtual circuits, the number of immediate neighbors any router has is equal to the number of routers around the cloud minus 1 (itself). The fact that there are ATM switches between the routers doesn't prevent them from appearing to be directly connected at the network layer—the switches are effectively invisible at this layer. So, in Figure 1.2, the number of adjacencies any router has is 10—the number of other routers connected to the cloud. Thus, the lines in the figure represent not only VCs but also routing adjacencies.

It can be shown that the amount of routing information that is transmitted in such a network in the presence of a topology change in the core of the network can be as much as the order of n^4, where n is the number of routers around the core. (The derivation of this result is too involved to present here.) Because the amount of information grows so quickly with increasing n, it can reach a point where routing traffic alone can overload a router, leading to very poor performance. Thus, we conclude that such a design is poor from a scaling perspective.

Several approaches can be taken to alleviate this scaling problem. One place to start is to eliminate the full mesh of VCs. As we observed, this means that the path between some pairs of routers will now involve an extra router hop, which may be acceptable if the performance of the intermediate router is adequate to handle the extra traffic. Alternatively, the Next Hop Resolution Protocol (NHRP) allows routers to establish VCs over which they can send data without needing to establish a routing adjacency over the VC. This approach has its own set of problems, including the need to run a number of NHRP servers and the possibility of introducing persistent forwarding loops. NHRP is also suitable only for unicast traffic; it is not defined for multicast.

Another approach to solve this scaling problem involves label switching. First, recall that an LSR by definition runs IP control protocols, including IP routing protocols, and may be implemented using unmodified ATM hardware. Thus, without changing the physical topology or devices in Figure 1.2, we can dramatically reduce the number of adjacencies that any one router has by running IP routing protocols on the ATM switches. This is illustrated in Figure 1.3.

Because the ATM switches are able to run IP routing protocols, the notion of an immediate neighbor has now changed from the router on the other end of a VC to the device—router or LSR—at the other end of a physical link. Thus, the maximum number of adjacencies that any one router has is greatly reduced and no longer grows with the size of the network, which results in a much more scalable design. Note that the router that had ten adjacencies in Figure 1.2 now has only one and that the LSRs (which used to be ATM switches) have no more than five adjacencies each—one with each directly connected

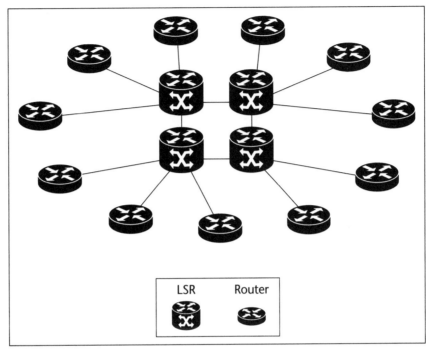

Figure 1.3

Eliminating a full mesh of adjacencies using label switching. Each router or LSR has an adjacency with its immediate neighbor. Unlike Figure 1.2, in this figure there is just one adjacency on each physical link.

router, whether it is a conventional router or an ATM switch functioning as an LSR.

This is not the only situation in which scalability can be improved with label switching. We consider another situation that is not specific to ATM in Section 4.1.2.

1.1.4 Extending Routing Functionality

It is important to emphasize that label switching is not just about making ATM hardware behave more like an IP router. Nor is it just about making faster, cheaper IP routers. Label switching also enables new functionality that could not readily be provided with existing IP routing techniques. The ability to offer new routing capabilities has been another motivating factor behind the development of label switching. In this section we are discussing something slightly different from the routing evolution described in Section 1.1.1. The issue here is that label switching enables routing capabilities that conventional routing is unable to support.

The most notable example of an area where label switching promises to expand the capabilities of conventional IP routing is the area of destination-based routing. Virtually all routing today in IP networks is destination-based; that is, the decision about where to forward a packet is made based only on its destination address. In principle, other fields in the IP header (e.g., source address, Type of Service bits) could be used when deciding where to forward a packet, but various design considerations have led to router designs that almost always forward based on destination address alone. By contrast, network technologies that rely on label swapping techniques, such as Frame Relay and ATM, can provide different functionality.

To understand how label switching enables new functionality, consider the network shown in Figure 1.4. This is a classic example of a type of function that is hard to provide with conventional routing. It is sometimes called "the fish picture" because the network resembles a fish in profile. Consider the case where router B is a conventional router that forwards packets using only the IP destination address. When a packet arrives at B from one of its neighbors, the forwarding

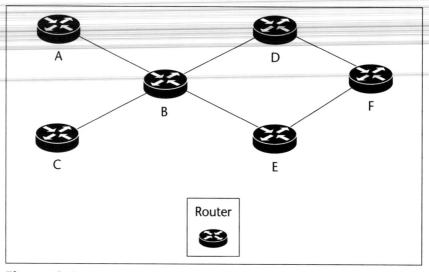

Figure 1.4
Label switched paths.

decision is not affected by any factor other than destination address. Now suppose we wanted router B to implement the simple policy "packets arriving from A that are going to router F should go via router D, while all other packets destined for F should go via router E." A forwarding mechanism that looks only at destination clearly cannot implement this policy.

By contrast, it is rather easy to implement such a policy at B if B forwards packets based on label switching. The main reason is that A and C are under no obligation to use the same label for all packets going to router F. Suppose A uses a label value of 5 for packets destined for F, while C uses the label value 12. Thus, when the packets arrive at router B, it can forward packets with label 5 to router D and packets with label 12 to router E.

Although this brief example glosses over the details, it should be clear that label switching enables new routing functionality to be deployed in devices that are also able to function as IP routers. This example is actually one of the simplest cases of *traffic engineering*, which is discussed in Chapter 7. Other examples of how label switching enables new types of routing functionality are discussed in Chapter 8.

1.2 A Brief History

Now that we have seen some of the reasons why the inventors of the various approaches to label switching felt the need to invent them, it is worth taking a brief look at the sequence of events that led up to the current situation. As we noted in the previous section, label switching tries to solve a wider range of problems than just the integration of IP and ATM; nevertheless, it is fair to say that the problems that existed in mapping between the protocol models of IP and ATM were significant drivers in the development of label switching. Thus, we start our historical overview by briefly reviewing the IP over ATM situation prior to the arrival of the first label switching techniques.

1.2.1 IP over ATM

Attempts to standardize ATM protocols have been going on since the 1980s, and a need was soon recognized in the IP community (at least the part of it that wasn't just hoping ATM would go away) to figure out how to carry IP datagrams over ATM networks. A number of IETF working groups tackled this problem, and two notable Requests for Comments (RFCs)[2] were produced in 1993 and 1994.

The first IP over ATM standard, described in RFC 1483, addresses the apparently simple problem of how to encapsulate IP datagrams (and packets of other protocols) on an ATM link. The second, RFC 1577, defines "classical IP over ATM" and ATMARP. The classical model assumes that ATM networks are used much like other subnet technologies, which means that IP routers and hosts can communicate over a subnet if they are on the same subnet, that is, if the network and subnet parts of their addresses are the same. If they are on different subnets, then one or more routers need to be involved to forward the packet from the source subnet to the sink subnet.

In defining the classical IP over ATM model, it was recognized that IP devices could be connected to a common ATM network (e.g., a large ATM network offered by a public carrier) yet be on different subnets. Thus, the idea of a logical IP subnet (LIS) was introduced. A LIS consists of the set of IP hosts and routers that are connected to a common ATM network and that share a common IP network and subnet address. RFC 1577 only addresses communication within a LIS and assumes that to get a packet from one LIS to another, it needs to go through a router that is connected to both LISs. This is illustrated in Figure 1.5.

The first thing to notice about the classical model is that it implies that two IP devices connected to the same ATM network but on separate LISs will not be able to use a single VC across the ATM network to send IP datagrams to each other. Instead, they need to send packets through a router. This approach seemed unattractive to many people, especially given the high performance of commercially available ATM switches relative to routers at the time of this work. Although it might appear that this problem could be solved by decreeing that the ATM network must be a single LIS, this is often difficult for administrative reasons. For example, two unrelated organizations connected to a single public ATM network are unlikely to want to administer their IP addresses from a common subnet address space.

Having defined the concept of the LIS, RFC 1577 defines the key mechanism needed for two IP devices on the same LIS to establish communication: ATMARP. The Address Resolution Protocol (ARP) is used on conventional media (such as Ethernet) to enable IP devices to

---

2. The RFC series is a collection of documents archived by the IETF, almost all of which are kept on-line, and which includes all Internet standards. However, by no means are all RFCs standards; some have even been April Fools' jokes.

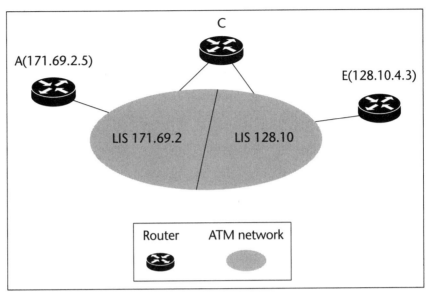

Figure 1.5
Logical IP subnets. A single ATM network is divided into two logical IP subnets. Routers A and E are on different LISs and so must communicate through router C in the classical model.

learn the address information needed to communicate, for example, the Ethernet address. Similarly, ATMARP allows two IP devices to learn each other's ATM addresses. Because conventional ARP depends on link layer broadcast, which ATM does not support, ATMARP introduced the concept of an ARP server, a single node on a LIS that provides IP-address-to-ATM-address resolution for the LIS. Each IP device on a LIS registers with the ARP server and provides its ATM address and its IP address. Any device on the LIS can then ask the ARP server to resolve an IP address to an ATM address. Equipped with the ATM address, the device can then set up a virtual circuit to that address using ATM signalling, and then send data.

The problem of establishing an ATM virtual circuit to an IP device on a different LIS, which RFC 1577 does not address, was taken up by the Routing over Large Clouds (ROLC) group of the IETF. The proposed approach to solving the "extra router hop" problem described above was the Next Hop Resolution Protocol (NHRP). NHRP enables an IP device on one logical IP subnet to learn the ATM address of another IP device on a different subnet through the use of one or more "next hop servers." The details of this protocol are rather complex and not strictly relevant to this discussion; it is sufficient to note here that, as with ATMARP, NHRP enables an IP device to learn the ATM address of another IP device with which it wants to communicate, and thus it can set up an ATM VC to that device using ATM signalling.

1.2.2 Toshiba's Cell Switching Router (CSR)

All of the work just described makes the basic assumption that routers do routing and ATM switches do ATM switching and never the twain shall meet. The work embodied in Toshiba's CSR proposal represents one of the first publicly described pieces of work that called that assumption into question. The CSR architecture introduced the idea that an ATM switching fabric could be controlled by IP protocols (such as IP routing and RSVP) rather than ATM signalling protocols such as Q.2931. Such an approach, if carried to its logical conclusion, could do away with the need for virtually all ATM signalling and all the mapping functions between IP and ATM. Also, as the CSR proponents noted, a mixture of conventional ATM switches and CSRs could be used; for example, CSRs could interconnect LISs to remove the need for NHRP.

The CSR ideas were presented first to an IETF working group meeting and later at a "Birds of a Feather" (BOF)[3] session of the IETF in 1994 and early 1995. It is probably fair to assume that many other organizations were developing similar ideas at the time. However, the BOF did not result in a clear definition of a problem that the IETF needed to address, and the level of public activity in the field remained fairly low.

1.2.3 IP Switching

For a variety of reasons, including more complete technical specifications, better timing, the existence of a production quality product (as opposed to a prototype), and effective marketing, IP Switching, as defined by the start-up company Ipsilon, made a much larger impact in the marketplace and the trade press than the CSR approach. Ipsilon announced their approach in early 1996. Technically, the two

---

3. Birds of a Feather sessions are the necessary precursor to forming a working group. They are held to determine whether there is a problem that needs a standards-based solution and to establish the level of interest in the IETF community. Not all BOFs lead to working groups.

approaches have considerable similarities. However, the advantages claimed by the proponents of IP Switching over other well-known approaches can be clearly stated and understood:

- IP Switching enables a device with the performance of an ATM switch to perform the job of a router.

- Fast routers (not ATM switches) are what's needed today because IP, the protocol of the Internet, is the dominant protocol and existing routers are too slow.

- ATM signalling and mapping IP to ATM has become so complex that, for the purposes of IP forwarding, we're better off without ATM control protocols altogether.

These arguments are in fact brief versions of some of the motivations described in Section 1.1 for the whole label switching effort. Many people found them very compelling.

Ipsilon documented their approach in a number of informational Internet RFCs. As already noted, not all RFCs are standards (informational RFCs are not), but this nevertheless enabled Ipsilon to legitimately claim that theirs was an "open" approach because the basic protocols were publicly available. Another significant contribution was the specification of a simple switch control protocol (GSMP) that could enable virtually any ATM switch to be turned into an "IP switch" with the addition of an external controller.

For the sake of clarity, we will use the term *IP Switching* to refer specifically to the Ipsilon approach, even though it is often used elsewhere to refer to a wider range of approaches. When a generic term is needed, we will use the term *label switching*.

1.2.4 Tag Switching

A few months after Ipsilon's announcement, Cisco Systems announced another approach to label switching, which they named *Tag Switching*. As we will see in the following chapters, Tag Switching was a significant technical departure from IP Switching and the CSR approach. For example, it did not rely on the flow of data traffic to set up forwarding tables in the switch, and it was specified for a number of link layer technologies other than ATM.

Like Ipsilon, Cisco produced an informational RFC describing the approach. Unlike Ipsilon, however, Cisco announced its intention to pursue the standardization of Tag Switching through the IETF. In this vein, a large number of Internet drafts were produced, describing many aspects of Tag Switching, including operation over ATM, PPP and 802.3 links, support for multicast routing, and support for resource reservation using RSVP. The standardization effort that Cisco started became known as the Multiprotocol Label Switching (MPLS) working group, and MPLS is now widely used as the generic term for label switching.

1.2.5 IBM's ARIS

Shortly after Cisco's announcement of Tag Switching and the effort to standardize it in the IETF, a number of Internet drafts were submitted by authors from IBM describing another label switching approach called *Aggregate Route-based IP Switching,* or *ARIS*. ARIS has more in common with Tag Switching than with the other approaches mentioned so far—both use control traffic rather than data traffic to set up forwarding tables—but ARIS also differs from Tag Switching in some significant ways. Many of the ARIS ideas made their way into the MPLS standardization effort.

1.2.6 The Multiprotocol Label Switching (MPLS) Working Group

When Cisco made its announcement about Tag Switching, it also announced its intention to standardize the technology. Following the publication of the first set of Tag Switching Internet drafts, a BOF session was held in December 1996, with presentations made by Cisco, IBM, and Toshiba (who had, by this time, produced a new set of Internet drafts on the CSR approach). The BOF session was one of the most well attended in IETF history.

The level of interest in the BOF, and the fact that so many companies had produced fairly similar proposals to solve a problem, made it clear that a standardization effort was in order. Even though some doubt existed as to whether the problem being solved was an important one (for example, some people made the argument that faster routers would make the whole problem irrelevant), there was no doubt that, without a standards group, there would be a proliferation of incompatible label switching techniques. Thus, an effort to charter a working group began, and a charter was successfully accepted by the IETF in early 1997. The first meeting of the working group was held in April 1997.

As noted above, the name *Multiprotocol Label Switching* was adopted primarily because the names *IP Switching* and *Tag Switching* were each associated with the products of a single company, and a vendor-neutral term was required. In spite of the decision to use the word *multiprotocol* in the name, there has been little interest so far in considering any network layer protocol other than IP. At the time of writing (January 2000), the working group has made considerable progress, the details of which are described in the latter chapters of this book.

1.3 Summary

The label switching area, which includes various flavors of IP Switching, Tag Switching, and Multiprotocol Label Switching (MPLS), has become a focus of great attention. This area has become important as designers seek to solve several related problems:

- The need to evolve the routing architecture of IP networks
- The need for greater performance, or better price/performance characteristics, in routers
- The seemingly ever-increasing complexity of mapping IP to ATM
- Scalability
- The need to add new routing functionality

There has been a tendency to view label switching as only addressing one or two of these areas and thus to underestimate its impact. Although other solutions that address some of these areas may appear, we believe that the ability of label switching to address all of them makes it likely that label switching will provide a foundation for the next generation of routing architecture.

A wide variety of techniques have been proposed to address the above problems. All the techniques use label swapping as the forwarding algorithm, and all run IP control protocols. Consequently, any of the approaches can turn an ATM switch into a device that behaves exactly like a router from a control point of view. It is not, however, required to use ATM hardware to build a label switching router. For example, a standard software-based router can also implement label switching.

There are many important differences between the various label switching techniques, and each has made different contributions to the IETF's standardization efforts. The IETF label switching standard, MPLS, combines many of the best ideas for the preceding approaches and thus promises to provide a solution that will have a significant impact on networks of the future.

1.4 Further Reading

We will provide references to publications describing IP Switching, Tag Switching, and MPLS at the end of the relevant chapters. For this chapter, we provide references to the other approaches that preceded MPLS: CSR and ARIS. We also list the IP over ATM standards that helped to motivate the label switching effort. Here and throughout the book we will include on-line references; note that all RFCs referenced can be found at

www.rfc-editor.org/rfc.html

CSR is documented in

Katsube, Y., K. Nagami, and H. Esaki. *Toshiba's Router Architecture Extensions for ATM: Overview*. RFC 2098, April 1997.
Nagami, K., et al. *Toshiba's Flow Attribute Notification Protocol (FANP) Specification*. RFC 2129, April 1997.

Toshiba also maintains an ftp site with numerous papers on the CSR at

ftp://ftp.wide.toshiba.co.jp/pub/csr/

ARIS documentation can be found in

Feldman, N., and A. Viswanathan. *ARIS Protocol Specification*. IBM Technical Report TR 29.2368, March 1998.

For more information on ARIS and CSR, see

Davie, B., P. Doolan, and Y. Rekhter. *Switching in IP Networks: IP Switching, Tag Switching, and Related Technologies*. San Francisco: Morgan Kaufmann, 1998.

The standards for classical IP over ATM and the Next Hop Resolution Protocol are

Heinanen, J. *Multiprotocol Encapsulation over AAL5*. RFC 1483, July 1993.
Laubach, M. *Classical IP and ARP over ATM*. RFC 1577, January 1994.
Luciani, J., D. Katz, D. Piscitello, B. Cole, and N. Doraswamy. *NBMA Next Hop Resolution Protocol (NHRP)*. RFC 2332, April 1998.

Further information on IP addressing, routing, and forwarding can be found in any number of introductory texts, such as

Comer, D. E. *Internetworking with TCP/IP. Vol. 1: Principles, Protocols, and Architecture.* 3rd ed. Englewood Cliffs, NJ: Prentice Hall, 1995.

Peterson, L., and B. Davie. *Computer Networks: A Systems Approach.* San Francisco: Morgan Kaufmann, 2000.

CHAPTER

2

Fundamental Concepts

In this chapter we describe the fundamental concepts of label switching. Although there are differences among various approaches to label switching, certain concepts are common to all of these approaches—such concepts form the fundamental building blocks of label switching. A solid grasp of these concepts will help you understand and compare the individual approaches to label switching, and lays the groundwork for understanding the design decisions behind the MPLS standards.

We begin this chapter with a description of the functional decomposition of network layer routing into control and forwarding components. We then proceed to describe label switching forwarding and control components. While describing the label switching control component, we present and compare various design alternatives. We then describe the type of devices that are needed to support label switching, followed by a brief discussion of the relationship between label switching and network layer routing and addressing. The chapter concludes with a brief summary.

2.1 Network Layer Routing Functional Components: Control and Forwarding

Network layer routing can be partitioned into two basic components: control and forwarding. The forwarding component is responsible for the actual forwarding of packets from input to output across a switch or router. To forward a packet the forwarding component uses two sources of information: a forwarding table maintained by a router and the information carried in the packet itself. The control component is responsible for construction and maintenance of the forwarding table.

Each router in a network implements both control and forwarding components. The actual network layer routing is realized as a composition of control and forwarding components implemented in a distributed fashion by a set of routers that forms the network.

The control component consists of one or more routing protocols that provide exchange of routing information among routers, as well as the procedures (algorithms) that a router uses to convert this information into a forwarding table. OSPF, BGP, and PIM are examples of such routing protocols.

The forwarding component consists of a set of procedures (algorithms) that a router uses to make a forwarding decision on a packet. The algorithms define the information from the packet that a router uses to find a particular entry in its forwarding table, as well as the exact procedures that the router uses for finding the entry. As an illustration, we consider three cases: (1) forwarding of unicast packets, (2) forwarding of unicast packets with Types of Service, and (3) forwarding of multicast packets.

For unicast forwarding, the information from a packet that a router uses to find a particular entry in the forwarding table is the network layer destination address, and the procedure that the router uses for finding the entry is the longest match algorithm.

For unicast forwarding with Types of Service, the information from a packet that a router uses to find a particular entry in the forwarding table is the network layer destination address and the Type of Service value, and the procedure that the router uses for finding the entry is the longest match algorithm on the destination address and the exact match algorithm on the Type of Service value.

For multicast forwarding, the information from a packet that a router uses to find a particular entry in the forwarding table is a combination of the network layer source and destination addresses and the incoming interface (the interface that a packet arrives on), and the procedure that the router uses for finding the entry uses both the longest match and the exact match algorithms.

2.1.1 Forwarding Equivalence Classes

We may think about procedures used by the forwarding component as a way of partitioning the set of all possible packets that a router can forward into a finite number of disjoint subsets. From a forwarding point of view, packets within each subset are treated by the router in the same way (e.g., they are all sent to the same next hop), even if the packets within the subset differ from each other with respect to the information in the network layer header of these packets. We refer to such subsets as Forwarding Equivalence Classes (FECs). The reason a router forwards all packets within a given FEC the same way is that the mapping between the information carried in the network layer header of the packets and the entries in the forwarding table is many-to-one (with one-to-one as a special case). That is, packets with different content of their network layer headers could be mapped into the same entry in the forwarding table, where the entry describes a particular FEC.

One example of an FEC is a set of unicast packets whose network layer destination address matches a particular IP address prefix. A set of multicast packets with the same source and destination network layer addresses is another example of an FEC. A set of unicast packets whose destination addresses match a particular IP address prefix and whose Type of Service bits are the same is yet another example of an FEC.

An essential part of a forwarding entry maintained by a router is the address of the next hop router. A packet that falls into an FEC associated with a particular forwarding entry is forwarded to the next hop router specified by the entry. Therefore, the construction of a forwarding table by the control component could be modeled as constructing a set of FECs and the next hop for each of these FECs.

One important characteristic of an FEC is its forwarding granularity. For example, at one end of the spectrum, an FEC could include all the packets whose network layer destination address matches a particular address prefix. This type of FEC provides coarse forwarding granularity. At the other end of the spectrum, an FEC could include only the packets that belong to a particular application running between a pair of computers, thus including only the packets with the same source and destination network layer addresses (these addresses identify the computers), as well as the transport layer port numbers (these ports identify a particular application within a computer). This type of FEC provides fine forwarding granularity.

You could observe that coarse forwarding granularity is essential for making the overall system scalable. On the other hand, supporting only coarse granularity would make the overall system fairly inflexible, as it wouldn't allow differentiation among different types of traffic. For example, it would not allow different forwarding or resource reservations for traffic that belongs to different applications. These observations suggest that to build a routing system that is both scalable and functionally rich would require the system to support a wide spectrum of forwarding granularities, as well as the ability to flexibly intermix and combine different forwarding granularities.

2.1.2 Providing Consistent Routing

A correctly functioning routing system requires consistent forwarding across multiple routers. This consistency is accomplished via a combination of several mechanisms.

The control component is responsible for consistent distribution of routing information used by the routers for constructing their forwarding tables. The control component is also responsible for the consistency of the procedures that the routers use to construct their forwarding tables (and thus FECs and associated next hops) out of the routing information. Combining these two factors—consistent information distribution and consistent local procedures—results in consistency among forwarding tables, and therefore FECs and associated next hops, across routers that form a network.

The forwarding component is responsible for consistent procedures for extracting the information from packets, as well as for a consistent way of using this information to find an appropriate entry in a forwarding table, resulting in a consistent mapping of packets into FECs across multiple routers. Consistent mapping of packets into FECs, combined with the consistent forwarding tables across multiple routers, provides a correctly functioning routing system.

As an illustration, consider an example of unicast forwarding with OSPF as a routing protocol. The OSPF procedures guarantee (by means of reliable flooding) that the link-state information is consistent among a set of routers. The OSPF procedures also guarantee that all these routers will use the same procedure (the shortest path first algorithm) for computing their forwarding tables based on the link-state information. Combining these two factors results in consistent forwarding tables (consistent set of FECs and their next hops) among the routers. The forwarding component guarantees that the only information carried in the packets that will be used for making the forwarding decision will be the destination network layer address and that all the routers will use the longest match algorithm to find an appropriate entry in their forwarding tables.

2.2 Label Switching: The Forwarding Component

Decomposition of network layer routing into control and forwarding components could be applied not only to the "conventional" routing architecture but to the label switching approach as well. In this section we describe some of the fundamental concepts associated with the label switching forwarding component.

The algorithm used by the label switching forwarding component to make a forwarding decision on a packet uses two sources of information: the first one is a forwarding table maintained by a Label Switching Router (LSR), and the second is a label carried in the packet.

2.2.1 What Is a Label?

A label is a short, fixed-length entity, with no internal structure. A label does not directly encode any of the information from the network layer header. For example, a label does not directly encode network layer addresses (neither source nor destination addresses). The semantics of a label are discussed in Section 2.2.4.

2.2.2 Label Switching Forwarding Tables

Conceptually, a forwarding table maintained by an LSR consists of a sequence of entries, where each entry consists of an incoming label, and one or more subentries, where each subentry consists of an outgoing label, an outgoing interface, and the next hop address (see Figure 2.1). Different subentries within an individual entry may have either the same or different outgoing labels. There may be more than one subentry in order to handle multicast forwarding, where a packet that arrives on one interface would need to be sent out on multiple outgoing interfaces.

Incoming label	First subentry	Second subentry
Incoming label	Outgoing label Outgoing interface Next hop address	Outgoing label Outgoing interface Next hop address

Figure 2.1
Forwarding table entry.

The forwarding table is indexed by the value contained in the incoming label. That is, the value contained in the incoming label component of the Nth entry in the table is N.

In addition to the information that controls where a packet is forwarded (next hop), an entry in the forwarding table may include the information related to what resources the packet may use, such as a particular outgoing queue that the packet should be placed on.

An LSR could maintain either a single forwarding table or a forwarding table per each of its interfaces. With the latter option, handling of a packet is determined not just by the label carried in the packet but also by the interface that the packet arrives on. With the former option, handling of a packet is determined solely by the label carried in the packet. An LSR may use either the first or the second option, or a combination of both.

2.2.3 Carrying a Label in a Packet

Essential to the label switching forwarding component is the ability to carry a label in a packet. This can be accomplished in several ways.

Certain link layer technologies, most notably ATM and Frame Relay, can carry a label as part of their link layer header. Specifically, with ATM the label could be carried in either VCI or VPI fields of the ATM header. Likewise, with Frame Relay the label could be carried in the DLCI field of the Frame Relay header.

Using the option of carrying the label as part of the link layer header allows support of label switching with some but not all link layer technologies. Constraining label switching to only the link layer technologies that could carry the label as part of their link layer header would severely limit the usefulness of label switching (as it would immediately exclude the use of label switching over such media as Ethernet or point-to-point links).

A way to support label switching over link layer technologies where the link layer header can't be used to carry a label is to carry the label in a small "shim" label header. This shim label header is inserted between the link layer and the network layer headers (see Figure 2.2) and thus could be used with any link layer technology. Use of the shim label header allows support of label switching over such link layer technologies as Ethernet, FDDI, Token Ring, point-to-point links, and so on.

2.2.4   Label Switching Forwarding Algorithm

The forwarding algorithm used by the forwarding component of label switching is based on label swapping. The algorithm works as follows. When an LSR receives a packet, the router extracts the label from the packet and uses it as an index in its forwarding table. Once the entry indexed by the label is found (this entry has its incoming label component equal to the label extracted from the packet), for each subentry of the found entry the router replaces the label in the packet with the outgoing label from the subentry and sends the packet over the outgoing interface specified by this subentry to the next hop specified by this subentry. If the entry specifies a particular outgoing queue, the router places the packet on the specified queue.

In the previous paragraph, our description assumes that an LSR maintains a single forwarding table. However, an LSR may also maintain a distinct forwarding table for each of its interfaces. In this case, the only modification to the algorithm is that after the LSR receives a packet, the LSR uses the interface on which the packet was received to select a particular forwarding table that will be used for handling the packet.

Link layer header	"Shim" label header	Network layer header	Network layer data

Figure 2.2
Carrying label in the shim label header.

Readers familiar with ATM will notice that when an LSR maintains its forwarding tables on a per-interface basis, the forwarding algorithm just described corresponds to the algorithm used to forward cells in ATM switches. This fact is key to some (but not all) of the label switching approaches we will discuss in the following chapters.

A label always carries forwarding semantics and may also carry resource reservation semantics. A label always carries forwarding semantics because a label carried in a packet uniquely determines a particular entry in the forwarding table maintained by an LSR and because that particular entry contains information about where to forward a packet. A label may optionally carry resource reservation semantics because the entry determined by the label may optionally include the information related to what resources the packet may use, such as a particular outgoing queue that the packet should be placed on. When a label is carried in the ATM or Frame Relay header, the label has to carry both forwarding and resource reservation semantics. When a label is carried in the shim label header, then the information related to what resources the packet may use may be encoded as part of that header, rather than being carried by a label (so that the label will carry just forwarding semantics). Yet another option is to use both the label and the (nonlabel) part of the shim header to encode this information. And, of course, even with the shim header, the label may carry both forwarding and resource reservation semantics.

Simplicity of the forwarding algorithm used by the label switching forwarding component facilitates inexpensive implementations of this algorithm in hardware, which, in turn, enables faster forwarding performance without requiring expensive hardware.

One important property of the forwarding algorithm used by label switching is that an LSR can obtain all the information needed to forward a packet as well as to decide what resources the packet may use in just one memory access. This is because (a) an entry in the forwarding table contains all the information needed to forward a packet as well as to decide what resources the packet may use, and (b) the label carried in the packet provides an index to the entry in the forwarding table that should be used for forwarding the packet. The ability to obtain both forwarding and resource reservation information in just one memory access makes label switching suitable as a technology for high forwarding performance.

It is important to understand that the use of label swapping forwarding combined with the ability to carry labels on a wide range of link layer technologies means that many different devices can be used to implement LSRs. For example, carrying the label inside the VCI field of ATM cells enables unmodified ATM switch hardware to function as an LSR, given the addition of suitable control software. Similarly, the shim header described above appears in packets in a place where most conventional routers can process it in software. Thus, with the addition of suitable software, a conventional router can also become an LSR.

2.2.5 Single Forwarding Algorithm

In the "conventional" routing architecture, different functionality provided by the control component (e.g., unicast routing, multicast routing, unicast routing with Types of Service) requires multiple forwarding algorithms in the forwarding component (see Figure 2.3). For example, forwarding of unicast packets requires longest match based on the network layer destination address; forwarding of multicast packets requires longest match on the source network layer address plus the exact match on both source and destination network layer addresses, whereas unicast forwarding with Types of Service requires the longest match on the destination network layer address plus the

Routing function	Unicast routing	Unicast routing with Types of Service	Multicast routing
Forwarding algorithm	Longest match on destination address	Longest match on destination + exact match on Type of Service	Longest match on source address + exact match on source address, destination address, and incoming interface

Figure 2.3
Conventional routing architecture.

Routing function	Unicast routing	Unicast routing with Types of Service	Multicast routing
Forwarding algorithm	Common forwarding (label swapping)		

Figure 2.4
Label switching architecture.

exact match on the Type of Service bits carried in the network layer header.

One important property of label switching is the lack of multiple forwarding algorithms within its forwarding component; the label switching forwarding component consists of just one algorithm—the algorithm based on label swapping (see Figure 2.4). This forms one important distinction between label switching and the conventional routing architecture.

You may think that constraining the forwarding component to a single forwarding algorithm would significantly limit the functionality that could be supported with label switching. However, as we will see in later chapters, this is not the case. The ability to support a wide range of routing functionality with just one forwarding algorithm is one of the key assumptions behind label switching, and so far this assumption has proven to be correct. In fact, as we'll see later, the functionality that could be supported with label switching (using a single forwarding algorithm) could be richer than the functionality that could be accomplished with the conventional routing architecture (which uses multiple forwarding algorithms).

2.2.6 Forwarding Granularity

The label switching forwarding component, by itself, doesn't place any constraints on the forwarding granularity that could be associated with a particular FEC, and therefore with a label. The spectrum of forwarding granularities that could be associated with FECs, and therefore with labels, as well as the ability to intermix different forwarding granularities, is determined solely by the label switching control component. It is completely up to the control component to decide whether and how to exploit this.

2.2.7 Multiprotocol: Both Above and Below

From the previous description of the label switching forwarding component we can make two important observations. First of all, the forwarding component is not specific to a particular network layer. For example, the same forwarding component could be used when doing label switching with IP as well as when doing label switching with IPX. This makes label switching suitable as a multiprotocol solution with respect to the network layer protocols (see Figure 2.5).

Moreover, multiprotocol capabilities of label switching go beyond the ability to support multiple network layer protocols; label switching is also capable of operating over virtually any link layer protocol. This makes label switching a multiprotocol solution with respect to the link layer protocols.

These properties of label switching explain the name given to the IETF working group that is currently working to standardize this technology: Multiprotocol Label Switching (MPLS).

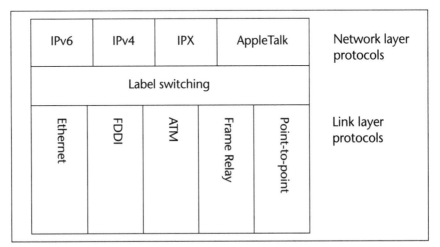

Figure 2.5
Multiprotocol: above and below.

2.2.8 Label Switching Forwarding Component: Summary

As we discussed at the beginning of this section, the forwarding component of network layer routing defines (a) the information from a packet that a router uses for finding a particular entry in its forwarding table, as well as (b) the exact procedures that a router uses for finding the entry. The label switching forwarding component defines a label carried in a packet as the information that an LSR uses to find a particular entry in its forwarding table. The label switching forwarding component defines the exact match on the label as the procedure for finding an entry in a forwarding table.

The following summarizes the rest of the key properties of the label switching forwarding component:

- The label switching forwarding component uses a single forwarding algorithm based on label swapping.
- The label carried in a packet is a short, fixed-length unstructured entity that has both forwarding and resource reservation semantics.
- The label switching forwarding component by itself doesn't place any constraints on the forwarding granularity that could be associated with a label.
- The label switching forwarding component can support multiple network layer protocols as well as multiple link layer protocols.

2.3 Label Switching: The Control Component

As we mentioned before, decomposition of network layer routing into control and forwarding components could be applied not only to the conventional routing architecture but to label switching as well. In this section we describe some of the fundamental concepts associated with the label switching control component.

The control component of label switching is responsible for (a) distributing routing information among LSRs and (b) the procedures (algorithms) that these routers use to convert this information into a forwarding table that is used by the label switching forwarding component. Just like a control component of any routing system, the label switching control component must provide for consistent distribution of routing information among LSRs as well as consistent procedures for constructing forwarding tables out of this information.

There is a great deal of similarity between the control component of the conventional routing architecture and the label switching control component. In fact, the label switching control component includes all the routing protocols (e.g., OSPF, BGP, PIM, and so forth) used by the control component of the conventional routing architecture. In this sense the control component of the conventional routing architecture forms a part (subset) of the label switching control component.

However, the control component of the conventional routing architecture is not sufficient to support label switching. This is because the information provided by the control component of the conventional routing architecture isn't sufficient to construct forwarding tables used by the label switching forwarding component, as these tables have to contain mappings between labels and next hops.

To fill the void we need procedures by which an LSR can

   a. Create bindings between labels and FECs
   b. Inform other LSRs of the bindings it creates
   c. Utilize both (a) and (b) to construct and maintain the forwarding table used by the label switching component

The overall structure of the label switching control component is shown in Figure 2.6.

The network layer routing protocols provide LSRs with the mapping between FECs and next hop addresses. Procedures for creating label binding between labels and FECs, and for distributing this binding information among label switches, provide LSRs with the mapping

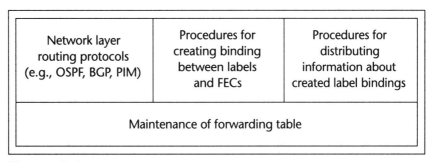

Figure 2.6
The label switching control component.

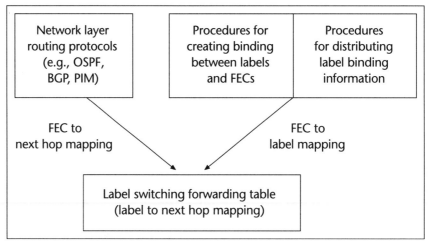

Figure 2.7
Construction of a label switching forwarding table.

between FECs and labels. The two mappings combined provide the information needed to construct the forwarding tables used by the label switching forwarding component (see Figure 2.7).

2.3.1 Local versus Remote Binding

Recall that each entry in a forwarding table maintained by an LSR contains one incoming label and one or more outgoing labels. Corresponding to these two types of labels in the forwarding table, the label switching control component provides two types of label bindings. The first type of label binding occurs when the router creates the binding with a label that is chosen and assigned locally. We refer to such binding as local. The second type of label binding is when the router receives from some other LSR label binding information that corresponds to the label binding created by that other router. We refer to such binding as remote.

An important difference between a local and a remote binding is that with the local binding the label associated with the binding is chosen locally, by the LSR itself, whereas with the remote binding the label associated with the binding is chosen by some other LSR.

2.3.2 Upstream versus Downstream Binding

The label switching control component uses both local and remote bindings to populate its forwarding table with incoming and outgoing labels. This could be done in two ways. The first method is when labels from the local binding are used as incoming labels and labels from the remote binding are used as outgoing labels. The second is exactly the opposite—labels from the local binding are used as outgoing labels, and labels from the remote binding are used as incoming labels. We examine each option in turn.

The first option is called *downstream* label binding because binding between a label carried by a packet and a particular FEC that the packet belongs to is created by an LSR that is downstream (with respect to the flow of the packet) from the LSR that places the label in the packet. Observe that with downstream label binding, packets that carry a particular label flow in the direction opposite to the flow of the binding information about that label.

The second option is called *upstream* label binding because binding between a label carried by a packet and a particular FEC that the packet belongs to is created by the same LSR that places the label in the packet; that is, the creator of the binding is upstream with respect to the flow of packets. Observe that with upstream label binding, packets that carry a particular label flow in the same direction as the label binding information about this label.

The names *upstream* and *downstream* seem to have caused considerable confusion, but no attempt to come up with less confusing names has yet succeeded. We have found that it helps to consider the flow of data packets—they flow toward the downstream end of the link—and then ask the question "At which end of the link were the bindings created: upstream or downstream?" Figure 2.8 illustrates flow of both data packets and label binding information for the downstream and upstream label binding modes. In each case data packets flow "down" to the right. In downstream allocation, binding is generated at the downstream end of the link; with upstream allocation, binding is generated at the upstream end.

2.3.3 "Free" Labels

An LSR maintains a pool of "free" labels (labels with no bindings). When the LSR is first initialized, the pool contains all possible labels

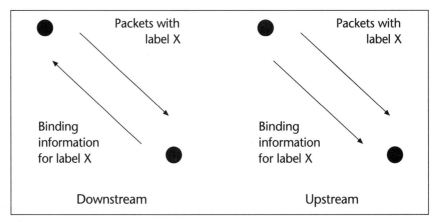

Figure 2.8
Downstream versus upstream label binding.

that the LSR can use for local binding. The size of this pool ultimately determines how many concurrent label bindings the LSR will be able to support. When the router creates a new local binding, the router takes a label from the pool; when the router destroys a previously created binding, the router returns the label associated with that binding to the pool.

Recall that an LSR could maintain either a single forwarding table or multiple forwarding tables—one per interface. When the router maintains a single label switching forwarding table, the router maintains a single pool of labels. When the LSR maintains a label switching table on a per-interface basis, the LSR maintains pools of labels on a per-interface basis as well.

2.3.4 Creating and Destroying Label Binding: Control-Driven versus Data-Driven Label Binding

An LSR creates or destroys a binding between a label and an FEC as a result of a particular event. Such an event could be triggered either by data packets that have to be forwarded by the LSR or by control (routing) information (e.g., OSPF routing updates, PIM JOIN/PRUNE messages, RSVP PATH/RESV messages) that has to be processed by the LSR. When the creation or destruction of bindings is triggered by data packets, we refer to it as *data-driven* label binding. When the creation or destruction of bindings is triggered by control information, we refer to it as *control-driven* label binding.

There is a wide range of options within both data-driven and control-driven approaches. For example, a data-driven approach might create a binding to an application's flow as soon as it sees the first packet for a flow, or it might wait until it has seen several packets, suggesting that the flow is long enough to warrant creation of a binding.

The choice between these methods for establishing bindings will clearly have some impact on performance and scalability, that is, how well the approach works as networks grow. We might also expect to see some effect on robustness, in the sense of how well the approach works in widely different conditions. We will discuss each of these areas of impact in turn.

Performance

The first thing to notice about the performance is that, under ideal conditions, an LSR can forward data at whatever speed the label switching forwarding component runs, regardless of whether the LSR uses control- or data-driven label binding. In many cases, this is determined by the speed of the underlying hardware. Thus, for example, if a label switching scheme runs on an ATM switch, then the *best-case* forwarding performance will be that of the ATM switch. Most ATM switches can forward traffic at "wire speed" on all of their interfaces, provided the traffic pattern is such that no interface is congested. Thus, for example, a 16 OC-3 port switch will have a capacity close to 16×155 Mb/sec $= 2.5$ Gb/sec. Under ideal conditions, any label switching scheme using this switch would achieve the same throughput.

The key phrase here is "under ideal conditions." The question is how close to ideal will the real operating environment be. This question has proven quite difficult to answer, especially for data-driven schemes. For example, the ideal condition for a data-driven scheme where labels are associated with individual application flows is when all flows are infinitely long-lived. In this case, the cost of setting up a label switched path for a flow is amortized over the (infinite) length of the flow, becoming negligible.

Considerable research has been performed to determine how far from ideal the conditions in real networks are. Part of the challenge of such research is finding reasonable traffic statistics, since most network operators are not very keen on making the details of their traffic traces publicly available. Furthermore, even when you can get real trace data, there are no guarantees that it will accurately reflect a "typical" network at the time it was collected, much less that it is an accurate predictor of the sort of traffic that will be found in networks in the near future.

Data-driven label binding assumes that an LSR supports both the label switching forwarding component and the conventional routing forwarding component. Supporting the conventional routing forwarding component is needed because label binding is created as a side effect of conventional forwarding of a packet.

The major performance issue for data-driven schemes when conditions deviate from ideal is the fact that every packet that is not label switched must be handled by the conventional routing forwarding component. Almost by definition, it has much less forwarding capacity than the label switching forwarding component; otherwise, why bother with label switching? So the concern is how much load can be placed on this conventional forwarding component.

If we are very aggressive in creating label bindings with data-driven schemes by, for example, creating label binding on the first packet of a new flow, we might be able to get away with using the conventional forwarding component to forward only one packet per flow. Because of the adverse impact this would have on scalability (as we discuss below), plus the delay associated with distributing and setting up bindings at remote LSRs, the conventional forwarding component is much more likely to forward several packets at the start of each flow. We can conclude that the packet forwarding capacity that is required of the conventional forwarding component is dependent on the rate at which new flows arrive and the number of packets in each flow that are not label switched. The rate of flow arrival equals the offered load in packets per second divided by the average number of packets per flow.

PPS required = (Packets forwarded per flow) × (PPS offered) / (Packets per flow)

The hard part of this to get a handle on is the packets forwarded per flow. Even if the flow identifier has a simple rule such as "Create label binding for any flow longer than 10 packets," there may be many flows that are only 1 packet long, which puts much more load on the conventional forwarding component than flows that are 9 packets long. A number of papers (which appear in Section 3.6, Further Reading, at the end of Chapter 3) have tried to address this issue. Note that the packet forwarding capacity of the conventional forwarding component is crucial to the performance of data-driven schemes. If the component is unable to keep up with the packet forwarding, flow classification, routing, and label binding work that is required, something has to give: either it drops data packets, stops doing flow identification and label distribution (which only makes matters worse), or stops processing routing updates (which could make matters much worse).

The consensus of the research is that performance of data-driven schemes under real traffic loads can be quite good, with a high fraction (70–80%) of the traffic label switched and thus achieving the performance of the underlying hardware. The main concerns with data-driven approaches are really scalability and robustness in the face of changing traffic patterns, subjects we will return to shortly.

Another performance issue that arises with data-driven schemes (and, to a lesser extent, with control-driven ones as well) is the capacity required by the label switching control component. Every time an LSR decides that a flow should be label switched, it needs to exchange label binding information with its neighboring LSRs, and it may also need to make some changes to the state of its local label binding. All of these things involve control traffic needed to distribute label binding information and therefore consume resources of the label switching control component. Moreover, all these things consume more resources as a higher percentage of flows are selected to be label switched. It is hard to quantify how expensive the operation of setting up and distributing label binding is, but it is clear that the performance of data-driven schemes is sensitive to this factor. If the LSR cannot set up and distribute label binding state at the rate required by the flow detection algorithm, then a lower percentage of flows will have to be label switched, and performance will suffer.

What about control-driven schemes? Like data-driven schemes, they too can perform at the level of the underlying hardware under ideal conditions, but the definition of ideal is very different. For example, when providing destination-based routing functionality, the ideal conditions for a control-driven scheme are simple: as long as the topology is stable, all traffic that arrives at a (nonedge) LSR can be label switched without a single packet having to pass through the control processor. Unlike in the data-driven schemes, you can imagine networks in which these ideal conditions might prevail for long periods.

When topology changes, it still may be possible for control-driven schemes to achieve ideal performance. Recall that a control-driven scheme may learn bindings for routes from neighbors who were not next hops for those routes; in the event of a topology change making those neighbors become next hops, label switching can continue uninterrupted. (It is possible that, on some hardware platforms, a few packets might be lost while the label switching tables are modified; this is highly implementation dependent.)

Note that a topology change also affects the performance of data-driven schemes. In general, if the path of a flow changes, then for new LSRs on the path it is as if a new flow has been created. Any such flow must be forwarded conventionally at first. Thus, a topology change might place a very high burden on an LSR that has just become the new next hop for some other LSR. First, it suddenly receives a large number of flows that used to travel over some other path. Also, the normal process of new flow arrival due to new applications being started does not go away at this time. All of these flows need to be forwarded and analyzed by the flow detection algorithms. That, in turn, creates additional load on both the conventional forwarding component and the label switching control component. During such transients, the forwarding capacity of an LSR could approach the forwarding capacity of its conventional forwarding component—potentially an order of magnitude less than its best-case performance.

A significant performance issue for control-driven schemes arises in situations where aggregation of routes occurs. As is so often the case, we find a conflict between scalability and performance.

Figure 2.9 illustrates a situation where routing aggregation may occur. LSR X is able to reach network prefix 10.0.1/24 (the /24 means

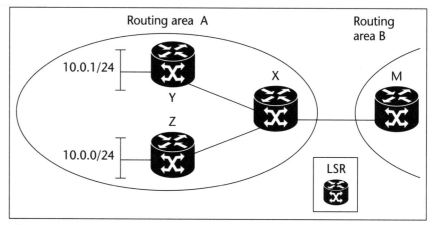

Figure 2.9
Effect of route aggregation.

that this prefix is 24 bits long) via LSR Y and network prefix 10.0.0/24 via LSR Z. These prefixes have the same high order 23 bits and thus can be aggregated as 10.0.0/23. Consequently, LSR X can advertise the single, aggregated prefix to LSR M. This means that, if LSRs X and M are binding labels to prefixes in their routing tables, X should only advertise a single label to LSR M for the aggregated prefix. When LSR X receives packets from LSR M that contain this label, it is not possible for LSR X to completely determine the correct forwarding for such packets from the label. Thus, LSR X would need to perform some amount of conventional forwarding using the layer 3 header. Note that LSR X may still be able to label switch many packets, for example, those going from LSR Y to LSR Z and vice versa.

This situation is the most nonideal for control-driven LSRs. Scalability dictates that aggregation of addresses is a good thing, but at the same time aggregation creates situations where conventional forwarding must be performed rather than label switching. The effect on performance of course depends on what fraction of traffic cannot be label switched and on the relative performance of the label switching forwarding path and the conventional forwarding component.

It should be noted that address aggregation does not happen by accident; it is deliberately chosen by network designers to improve network scalability. Thus, it is possible to predict where it will have an effect, and even to design the network such that the places where most aggregation happens are not the places where label switching is most needed, such as in the core of a high speed backbone network. Still, a network designer needs to take some care to make sure that if an LSR is placed at an aggregation point, it has enough conventional forwarding capability to handle the fraction of traffic that cannot be label switched.

Scalability

As we have already seen, performance and scalability are closely related and are often in conflict with each other. One way to assess the scaling properties of a label switching scheme is to consider how many labels need to be assigned in various scenarios.

As with performance, it is hard to get good data that enables the scalability of data-driven schemes to be determined. In general, steps to improve performance, such as increasing the sensitivity of the flow detection algorithm, have a negative impact on scalability by increasing the total number of labels that are required at any given time.

To provide a feel for the relationship between performance and scalability of data-driven approaches, we will examine some traffic data collected in September 1995 at an Internet exchange point in the San Francisco Bay Area. This data was analyzed by some researchers at Ipsilon to produce the graphs shown in Figures 2.10 and 2.11. We note that the total volume of traffic flowing through the point of collection was rather small—on the order of 30–40 Mb/sec—so the relevant information here is more in the trends than in the absolute numbers.

Figure 2.10 shows both the number of instantaneous labels (connections) and the number of exchanges of label binding information (connection setup) per second required as a function of the number of packets in a flow examined before establishing a label switched path. It is clear that decreasing the flow detection sensitivity quickly reduces the total number of labels that are needed.

Figure 2.11 shows the percentage of bytes and packets that end up being label switched, again as a function of the number of packets examined at the start of each flow before it is label switched. The good news here is that the amount of data that can be switched, measured either in bytes or packets, drops much more slowly than the number of labels required as flow detection sensitivity is decreased. This means that there is a net benefit in examining more packets before deciding to label switch a flow—within limits, of course. Note that the main benefit is in setting the number of packets examined to about 10, getting us to the "knee" of the connections curve while only reducing the percentage of bytes switched by about 10%. Note also that in this case, the total number of labels needed (on the particular day that this trace was collected at one particular place) was about 15,000. The problem is in extrapolating from the available trace data to other places in the Internet on other days, or other times of day. Other points in the Internet have much larger traffic volumes and may also carry a different mixture of flows. We return to this issue in the next section. However, just the shape of the curves is encouraging, because it means that there is some hope of tuning the system to provide a good trade-off between number of labels and percentage of label switched traffic. Such tuning will obviously be much easier if traffic patterns do not change very often.

With control-driven schemes, the scaling properties depend not on the nature of the data traffic but on the properties of the control traffic, which in turn depend on factors such as the topology and design of the network. For example, in a control-driven scheme that binds a label to each prefix in the routing table, the number of labels is easy to calculate. At the time of writing, the largest routing tables—those in the Internet backbone—contain about 60,000 address

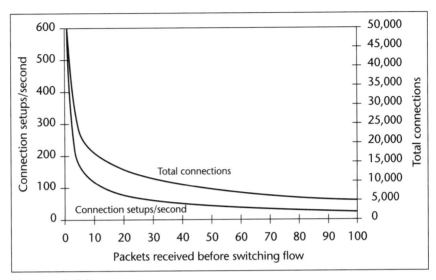

Figure 2.10
Effect of flow detection sensitivity on label requirements.

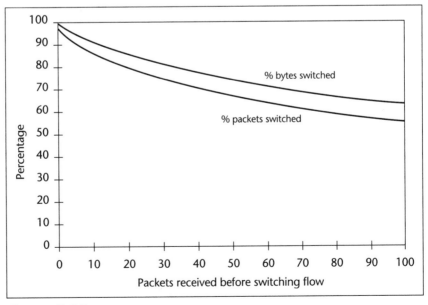

Figure 2.11
Effect of flow detection sensitivity on switched traffic.

prefixes. Of course, there is no necessity to bind one label to every entry in the routing table. As we'll see in Section 4.1.2, for example, an LSR at the core of the Internet could bind one label to each border router of the domain it is in—on the order of a few hundred labels. Such flexibility gives control-driven approaches an edge in terms of scalability.

Robustness

In comparing the robustness of the different approaches, we are trying to address the question "How sensitive is the performance or scalability of each scheme to changes in the network environment?" As some of the discussion in the previous sections has indicated, data-driven schemes do not seem to rate as well as control-driven schemes in this regard. The reason for this is rather intuitive: changes in the flow of data are much harder to predict than changes in the flow of control information. All that is needed to make a big change in the flow of data is a new application or a change in the usage pattern of an existing application. For example, suppose a new Web site that provides some sort of transaction service such as stock quotes is attached to the Internet. Suddenly, the traffic flowing to that site will consist of many short flows that cannot be flow switched, so that what might have been a small increase in total traffic could represent a large increase in load on the conventional forwarding component, perhaps driving it beyond the point where it has enough bandwidth to cope.

It is not hard to think of many different scenarios where changes in user behavior or application characteristics could have a serious impact on a data-driven scheme. By contrast, it is hard to imagine the sort of change that would be required to cause a surprising degradation in the performance of a control-based scheme. For example, an Internet service provider is unlikely to find that the rate of change of routing information has become radically different over a short period of time. (If such a dramatic change did happen, it would most likely be a sign of some sort of error condition, and it would have bad effects whether or not label switching was used.) Only a truly radical change in the way networks are built, such as widespread deployment of mobile networking nodes, could cause a major surprise for a control-driven scheme.

One way to understand this major difference between data-driven and control-driven schemes is to think about data-driven schemes as a form of caching. A new flow represents a cache miss; once it has been identified as worthy of label switching, and the label switched path is established, all subsequent packets in the flow generate cache hits. In processor design, caching can provide significant performance gains if the usage pattern matches that expected by the designer. However, in the worst case, the performance of the system degrades to the performance it would have had without the cache. The challenge of designing a good caching system for the Internet is that the usage pattern is so dynamic that it almost defies characterization, and a system designed to perform well today offers no guarantees of adequate performance in the future.

To summarize, it is not clear whether you could build a system that is robust enough with respect to changes in traffic pattern and at the same time able to exploit the potential advantages of data-driven label binding.

You could also observe that the use of data-driven label binding complicates the overall system behavior, because the operations of the control component are controlled by a mix of control and data traffic, whereas with control-driven label binding the operations of the control component are controlled solely by the control traffic. More complex system behavior, in turn, is likely to contribute negatively to the overall system robustness.

2.3.5 Distributing Label Binding Information: What Are the Options?

Once an LSR creates or destroys a binding between a locally chosen label and an FEC, the LSR needs to inform other LSRs of that binding; this will provide other LSRs with the remote label binding information. Distributing label binding information can be accomplished in several ways.

Piggyback on Top of Routing Protocols

One way to distribute label binding information is to piggyback this information on top of the routing protocols. This approach is only possible in control-driven schemes, because it ties label distribution to the distribution of control (routing) information, and has some attractive properties. First of all, it makes the distribution of label binding information consistent with the distribution of routing information. It also allows race conditions to be avoided, where either the label binding information (binding between labels and FECs) would be available, but the associated routing information (and, more specifically, the binding between FECs and next hops) would not, or vice versa. Finally, it simplifies the overall system operation, as it eliminates the need for a separate protocol to distribute label binding information.

However, this approach has drawbacks as well. First of all, the routing information that is distributed by a particular protocol may not be suitable for distributing label binding information—only the protocols where distributed routing information explicitly contains mapping between FECs and next hops would be suitable for piggybacking label binding information. For this reason Link-State Routing Protocols (e.g., OSPF) make a rather poor match for what is required to distribute label binding information. On the other hand, for precisely the same reason, protocols such as BGP and PIM seem to be quite suitable for distributing label binding information as well.

Even if the routing information distributed by a protocol makes the protocol suitable for the distribution of label binding information, extending the protocol to carry this information may not always be feasible. This is because extending the protocol may involve changes to the format of the messages used by the protocol, which, in turn, may result in backward incompatibility. So, even if you view the option of piggybacking the label binding information on top of the routing protocol as desirable, it may not always be feasible.

You also have to be concerned about the possibility that a label, piggybacked in a protocol message, might be received by a device that does not understand labels. Either this must be prevented or the piggybacking must be done in a way that non–label switching devices are easily able to ignore label bindings received in this way.

Label Distribution Protocol

Constraining label switching to only the cases where the routing protocols can piggyback label binding information is undesirable. A way to circumvent this limitation is by distributing label binding information via a separate protocol.

The ability to support label switching with routing protocols that can't be used for piggybacking label binding information is perhaps the major advantage of using a separate label distribution protocol. But it is likely to be the only advantage of this approach.

On the negative side, this approach makes it more difficult to avoid race conditions—you may end up in a situation where an LSR would have label binding information (label to FEC binding), but not the routing information (FEC to next hop binding) needed to use the label binding information, or vice versa.

Another drawback of this approach is that it introduces yet another protocol into the system, which increases the overall complexity of the system.

If the label switching control component uses only one label distribution protocol, then this approach also makes it hard to make the distribution of label binding information consistent with the distribution of routing information. To see why this is true, observe that while some of the routing protocols exchange routing information based on the technique of incremental updates and explicit acknowledgments (e.g., BGP), other routing protocols use periodic refreshes of complete routing information (e.g., PIM).

A way to avoid this mismatch is to have more than one label distribution protocol. With this method you could make one label distribution protocol that will be used in conjunction with OSPF and will rely on incremental updates and explicit acknowledgments, while making another label distribution protocol that will be used in conjunction with PIM and will rely on periodic refreshes of complete binding information. But though this approach would solve the problem of consistent distribution of label binding information, it would introduce even more protocols into the system, which in turn would result in an even more complex system.

Based on the above discussion, the option of piggybacking label binding information on top of routing protocols should be viewed as preferred whenever possible or feasible; a separate label distribution protocol should be used only when piggybacking is not possible or feasible. By limiting the scope where a label distribution protocol is needed, you could hope to either reduce or avoid mismatch between the distribution of label binding information and the distribution of routing information while at the same time being able to stay with a single label distribution protocol.

2.3.6 Multicast Considerations

Supporting multicast forwarding with label switching places certain requirements on the label switching control component. In this section we look at some of these requirements.

Multicast routing uses spanning trees[1] for forwarding of multicast packets, where a tree could be associated either with a combination of a particular source and multicast group (source-based tree) or just with

---

1. The spanning trees we refer to in this section should not be confused with spanning trees constructed by bridges. The former are constructed by network layer multicast procedures (e.g., PIM); the latter are constructed by link layer procedures (e.g., IEEE 802.1).

a particular group (shared tree). We refer to such trees as *multicast distribution trees*.

To provide consistent forwarding of multicast packets with label switching, an LSR, when it receives a packet, must be able to unambiguously identify a particular multicast distribution tree that the LSR should use to forward the packet. To identify a particular multicast distribution tree, the only information provided by a packet to an LSR is (a) a label carried in a packet and (b) an interface that the packet arrived on. Relying on just a combination of a label and an incoming interface for identifying a particular tree requires that an LSR maintains its label switching table on a per-interface basis.

When a multiaccess link layer technology has native multicast capabilities (e.g., Ethernet), label switching must be able to utilize these capabilities. Such utilization requires that a group of LSRs that are all connected to a common multiaccess subnetwork with native multicast capabilities and are part of a common multicast distribution tree agree on a common label to use for that particular tree. To support this, the label switching control component must include (a) procedures for electing one particular LSR within the group that will be responsible for creating label binding and (b) procedures for distributing this label binding information to the rest of the LSRs in the group.

When an LSR connected to a multiaccess subnetwork (e.g., Ethernet) receives a multicast packet, the LSR has to identify a particular multicast distribution tree that should be used to determine how to handle the packet. To identify the tree, the LSR has to identify the previous hop LSR that sent the packet. This, in turn, requires that no two LSRs connected to a common multiaccess subnetwork can use a combination of the same label and the same interface for creating label bindings for different multicast distribution trees. One way to accomplish this is to partition the set of labels that can be used for multicast by a set of LSRs connected to a common multiaccess subnetwork into disjoint subsets and to give each LSR its own subset. The LSR would use such a subset as its pool of free labels that is associated with the interface that connects the router to the subnetwork. We will see an example of this approach in Chapter 4.

2.3.7 Handling Routing Transients

We use the term *routing transient* to refer to episodes in a network where routing information across a network is changing. At such times, information stored at different nodes may be temporarily inconsistent. These episodes most commonly occur as a result of failures of links or routers or both.

Although all of the routing protocols used by conventional routing guarantee loop-free paths in a steady state, almost all of them (with the exception of EIGRP[2]) can't guarantee loop-free paths during routing transients. Clearly, using these protocols as part of the label switching control component does nothing to alter this situation. Therefore, label switching, just like conventional routing, needs to have mechanism(s) to deal with the adverse effects of forwarding loops during routing transients.

The major adverse effect caused by a forwarding loop is excessive consumption of networking resources (e.g., buffers on routers, CPU on routers, bandwidth) by packets that are forwarded along the loop. This, in turn, may result in the lack of resources needed to handle other packets. Especially detrimental to the overall system could be the lack of resources needed to handle packets that carry routing information (control traffic). At the minimum this would slow down the convergence of the routing system, thus prolonging the duration of routing transients and therefore forwarding loops caused by these transients. Even worse, the lack of resources needed to handle packets that carry routing information may cause routing instabilities. Also detrimental to the overall system, although to a lesser degree, is the lack of resources needed to handle noncontrol traffic for which non-looping paths are available.

One way to deal with the adverse effects of forwarding loops during routing transients is to make sure that when a forwarding loop is formed, no traffic enters such a loop. In this book we refer to this as *loop prevention*. Another alternative is to allow traffic to enter the loop but to constrain the amount of resources that can be consumed by such traffic. In this book we refer to this as *loop mitigation*.

All other factors being equal, loop prevention may be viewed as more desirable than loop mitigation. However, all other factors aren't equal. When comparing loop prevention and loop mitigation mechanisms, we need to look at such issues as (a) the overhead in terms of additional control traffic, (b) scalability, (c) negative impact (if any) introduced by such mechanisms on the nonlooping traffic, and (d) the

---

2. EIGRP (Enhanced Interior Gateway Routing Protocol) is a Cisco proprietary intra-domain routing protocol that employs the "DUAL" algorithm for loop avoidance.

ability to contain the negative impact of the looping traffic on the nonlooping traffic (and especially on the control traffic).

Conventional routing employs loop mitigation as the way to deal with the adverse effects of forwarding loops during routing transients. Loop mitigation is achieved via the time-to-live mechanism, where the network layer header contains a field, called time-to-live (TTL). A router that forwards a packet decrements this field by 1. If a router receives a packet whose time-to-live value is 0, the router discards the packet. This way, even if a packet enters a forwarding loop, the number of times the packet would be able to circle the loop is bounded—eventually the time-to-live field in the packet will reach 0, and the packet will be discarded.

Because the forwarding path taken by a packet may include both LSRs and conventional routers, it is important that the mechanisms used by the LSRs to deal with forwarding loops during routing transients be able to coexist and interoperate with the mechanisms used by the conventional routers. In practical terms that means that the mechanisms used by the LSRs must be able to coexist and interoperate with the time-to-live mechanism.

A way to make the mechanisms used by the LSRs to deal with forwarding loops during routing transients coexist and interoperate with the time-to-live mechanism is to have the LSRs use the time-to-live mechanism as well. Unfortunately, this may be fairly difficult to achieve when label switching is used over certain link layer technologies, most notably ATM and Frame Relay. This is because neither the ATM nor the Frame Relay header contains the TTL field, and neither ATM nor Frame Relay switches are capable of handling the TTL field carried in the network layer header. On the other hand, if a label isn't carried in the link layer header, but in a shim label header, you could add the TTL field to the shim header, thus making it possible for label switching to use the time-to-live mechanism to deal with forwarding loops during routing transients.

The alternative to using TTL for loop mitigation is to use additional control mechanisms in LSRs either to prevent or to mitigate loops. We will see examples of all these approaches in the following chapters.

Important to realize is that, in the absence of misconfiguration, loops are a transient phenomenon. They are also a fact of life with IP routing protocols, such as RIP, OSPF, IS-IS, and BGP. Thus, you may consider accepting that transient loops could happen and try to ensure that the consequences are not too severe, just as conventional IP does.

2.4 Edge Devices

So far we have described how LSRs forward packets that carry labels. But how do these packets get their labels in the first place? Turning "unlabeled" packets into "labeled" ones and vice versa is performed by the edge LSRs.

You can think of an edge LSR as a device that implements the control and forwarding components of both label switching and conventional routing. When an edge LSR receives a packet without a label, the LSR uses the conventional forwarding component to determine the FEC that this packet belongs to and the next hop that the packet should be sent to. If the next hop is an LSR, then the LSR uses the label switching forwarding component to determine the label that should be added to the packet. Likewise, when an edge LSR receives a packet with a label, the LSR uses the label switching forwarding component to determine the FEC that this packet belongs to and the next hop that the packet should be sent to. If the next hop is not an LSR, then the LSR just strips the label from the packet and hands the packet to its conventional forwarding component, which, in turn, sends the packet to the next hop.

The fact that both LSRs and conventional routers use the same set of routing protocols makes interworking between the conventional and the label switching control components trivial. The only thing that is required of the label switching control component is the ability to determine whether a particular (next hop) router is an LSR or not.

In some cases, a host may function as the edge device. Because hosts do not generally run routing protocols, there are some additional challenges to making a host capable of applying labels to packets. We return to this subject in the next chapter.

2.5 Relationship between Label Switching and Network Layer Addressing and Routing

Label switching replaces forwarding algorithms used by various routing functions with a single forwarding component. At the same time, label switching doesn't replace procedures for establishing and maintaining routing information—label switching assumes the use of the existing procedures, such as OSPF, BGP, and so forth. Likewise, label switching doesn't replace the need for network layer (e.g., IP) addressing, as the network layer addressing information forms an essential part of routing information, and this information is used by the label switching control component.

How does label switching fit into the ISO 7-layer reference model? To answer this question observe that label switching doesn't fit into layer 2 (link layer), as label switching is independent of a particular link layer technology (we can use label switching over ATM, over Ethernet, over point-to-point links, etc.). Label switching doesn't form a layer 3 (network layer) on its own either, for the reasons outlined in the previous paragraph (as it doesn't have its own routing and addressing). Moreover, the ISO reference model assumes that a given link or a network layer uses a single format for the transport of the data from the layer above. Label switching clearly violates this assumption, as over ATM it uses the ATM header to carry the label information, while over Ethernet or point-to-point links it uses the "shim." So perhaps the answer to the question we asked at the beginning of this paragraph is that label switching just doesn't fit into the ISO reference model. The fact that at the time of this writing label switching has been already deployed suggests that there is a clear distinction between the reference model and the referenced reality, and moreover that this distinction has no impact on reality.

2.6 Summary

All approaches to label switching, as we have defined it in this book, have certain common characteristics, and all must make some common design choices. This chapter has introduced the common ground on which the rest of the book builds.

An LSR implements a control component and a forwarding component. The forwarding component is based on a simple label swapping algorithm and uses fixed-length labels. These labels are used as an index to the label switching table, which identifies where a packet should be forwarded and perhaps some local resource assignment as well. In contrast to conventional routing, the LSRs use the same algorithm no matter what control components are in use.

The control components consist of conventional network layer routing protocols and one or more label binding mechanisms. It is in the area of creating and distributing label bindings that the various approaches show the most diversity. Label bindings may be created by upstream or downstream LSRs; they may be created in response to data or control traffic; and the bindings may be distributed in a stand-alone protocol or piggybacked on an existing one.

2.7 **Further Reading**

For an overview of various routing protocols used in the Internet (OSPF, RIP, BGP, PIM, etc.), we recommend

Halabi, B. *Internet Routing Architectures.* Indianapolis: Cisco Press, 1997.

Huitema, C. *Routing in the Internet.* Englewood Cliffs, NJ: Prentice Hall, 1995.

The protocols OSPF, PIM, BGP, and RSVP are all specified in Internet RFCs:

Braden, R., L. Zhang, S. Berson, S. Herzog, and S. Jamin. *Resource ReSer-Vation Protocol (RSVP): Version 1 Functional Specification.* RFC 2209, September 1997.

Estrin, D., et al. *Protocol Independent Multicast-Sparse Mode (PIM-SM): Protocol Specification.* RFC 2117, June 1997.

Moy, J. *OSPF Version 2.* RFC 1583, March 1994.

Rekhter, Y., and T. Li. *A Border Gateway Protocol 4 (BGP-4).* RFC 1771, March 1995.

The DUAL algorithm for loop prevention is described in

Garcia-Luna-Aceves, J. J. "A Unified Approach to Loop-Free Routing Using Distance Vectors or Link States." *Computer Communications Review* 19, no. 4, September 1989.

IP Switching

I n this chapter we examine the label switching approach known as IP Switching. An individual device that implements the IP Switching architecture is, of course, an IP Switch. As noted previously, we use these terms specifically to describe the approach developed by Ipsilon, even though they are sometimes used generically elsewhere.

One of the significant innovations of the Ipsilon approach to label switching was to define not only a label distribution protocol (which all approaches do) but also a switch management protocol. This protocol, known as GSMP (General Switch Management Protocol), allows an ATM switch to be controlled by an "IP Switch controller" and thus turned into an IP Switch. This protocol takes the separation of control and forwarding, discussed in Section 2.1, to its logical conclusion: it enables control and forwarding to reside in separate physical boxes connected by a link, over which GSMP runs.

GSMP provides a range of technical, business, and economic benefits. In particular, at the time that Ipsilon was founded, ATM switches with capacities of around 2.5 Gb/sec (16 × OC-3) were becoming "commodity" items, in the sense that they were being manufactured by many vendors and were differentiated more by price than by features. In such an environment, an approach that could turn any vendor's ATM switch into something with the capabilities of a router with only a modest increase in total cost was likely to have considerable market appeal. This is exactly what GSMP enabled Ipsilon to do.

GSMP is a rather simple master/slave protocol, with the slave running on the ATM switch and the master running on an IP Switch controller (which is really a general-purpose computing engine with an ATM interface to allow it to talk to the switch). Only the slave portion has to know anything that is specific to the ATM switch hardware.

In addition to GSMP, Ipsilon also defined a label binding protocol, called Ipsilon Flow Management Protocol (IFMP), the details of which we discuss in Section 3.2. In order to spur acceptance of their approach, Ipsilon published these as informational RFCs. Without going through a lengthy standardization process, this made the relevant specifications accessible to anyone who wanted to see them.

Having specified and published the protocol specifications, Ipsilon set about finding ATM switch vendors with whom they could form partnerships. Ipsilon would provide the IP Switch controller, some "port-ready" GSMP slave code, and engineering assistance to any interested vendor.

The open approach and the successful establishment of partnerships with many well-established switch vendors almost certainly helped speed the acceptance of IP Switching in the marketplace. For example, buying a switch from an established vendor and controlling it with software from a start-up that uses radically new protocols seems less risky than buying a complete product (with the same new protocols) from a start-up. This philosophy was apparently quite successful. The expression that seemed to be constantly applied to Ipsilon in the months following the announcement of their products was "they have gained a lot of mindshare"; that is, they had the attention of the marketplace.

We now turn to look more closely at the technology of IP Switching. We begin with an examination of the overall approach, followed by a discussion of each of the main protocols, IFMP and GSMP.

3.1 IP Switching Overview

One of the basic premises underlying the IP Switching architecture is that the alternative IP over ATM models are complex and inefficient. Recall from Chapter 1 that those models involve running two control planes: first, ATM Forum signalling and routing and then, on top of that, IP routing and address resolution. IP Switching, like other label switching approaches, uses just the IP component plus a label binding protocol (IFMP in this case) to allow forwarding of IP on ATM switch hardware. This approach completely removes the ATM control plane, and the need to adapt between IP and ATM control planes, from the picture.

Figure 3.1 illustrates the removal of the ATM control plane and the layers mapping between IP and ATM control planes. In Figure 3.1(a), we see the layers of control software necessary to control the ATM hardware and some of the protocols needed to map between IP and ATM control planes. Figure 3.1(b) shows a simple model of the IP Switching architecture: IP, supplemented with a label binding protocol (IFMP), directly controls the ATM hardware. Note that this figure is equally applicable to other label switching approaches such as Tag Switching and MPLS.

The basic goal of IP Switching is thus to integrate ATM switches and IP routing in a simple and efficient way. A number of subgoals follow from this, including the ability to build IP routing products with high performance at relatively low cost. This in turn helps address some of the scaling issues discussed in Chapter 1. IP Switching also aims to leverage the quality of service capabilities of ATM switches, which we address in Section 3.3.1.

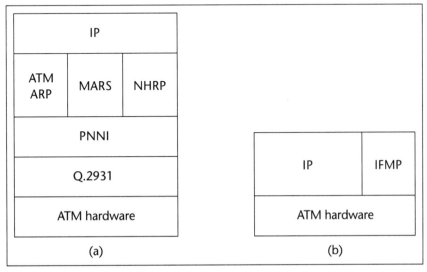

Figure 3.1
Removing the ATM control plane: IP over standard ATM (a); IP Switching (b).

One consequence of removing all ATM control plane functions is that IP Switches peer directly with other IP Switches. They can also be interconnected across "clouds" of conventional ATM switches using virtual paths (VPs); we discuss the details at the end of this section.

We begin our discussion of the IP Switching architecture by considering a single IP Switch. Figure 3.2 is a simplified illustration of the major hardware and software components of an IP Switch and of the data and control flows between switches. The switch controller is the control processor of the system. It communicates with the ATM switch itself using GSMP. Observe that the switch controller runs IP routing and forwarding code (the functions of a conventional router) as well as IFMP, GSMP, and flow classification.

Before any IP Switching can be performed, there has to be a way to get control traffic, including routing protocols and IFMP messages, between switches. A "default VC" is defined for this. It uses a well-known

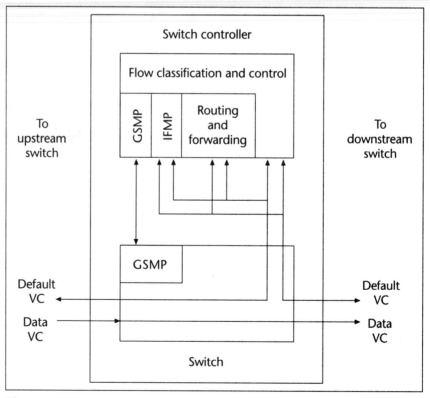

Figure 3.2
IP Switch architecture.

VCI/VPI value, so that two adjacent IP Switches will be able to communicate without first signalling for a VC. It is a VC in the sense that it connects a pair of adjacent IP Switch controllers through their attached ATM switches, but no ATM procedures (e.g., signalling) are used to establish it. Traffic that flows on the default VC is encapsulated in accordance with RFC 1483 (using LLC/SNAP, as is common for data on ATM VCs) and is sent to the switch controller and reassembled. The default VC is also used for data that does not yet have a label associated with it. Such data is forwarded in software by the switch controller.

Like all label switching approaches, IP Switching relies on IP routing protocols to establish a routing information base from which the next hop for a packet can be determined. Only after this has been done, that is, only after the next hop has been identified, does the separate process of negotiating label bindings with that next hop take place.

The IFMP and GSMP modules implement the respective protocols. We have briefly discussed the role of the protocols in the introduction; they are described in more detail in Sections 3.2 and 3.3.

In very simple terms, the flow classification and control module inspects the IP traffic arriving at the switch and selects from it *flows* that are likely to benefit from being label switched. (A precise definition of a flow is provided in Section 3.2.2. For now, we can think of it as the set of packets sent from one host to another.) The module then uses IFMP to inform neighboring switches about its decisions. This ultimately enables traffic to be moved on to a label switched path, so that IP packets are forwarded by the label switching (ATM) hardware.

In common with the publicly available documentation for other label switching approaches, IP Switching specifies the interswitch label binding protocol (IFMP in this case) but not the internal mechanisms that use it. There are good reasons for this. Flow classification is to some extent a matter of local policy—it doesn't greatly matter if different switches use slightly different policies, although performance will certainly suffer if the policies of neighboring switches are significantly different. This is an area where a vendor can differentiate its products by providing capabilities superior to some other vendor. It is also likely that a user will want to tune these policies to match local conditions. Thus, there is much less incentive to specify this part of the architecture in detail, as compared to the protocols.

While flow classification and detection approaches may not need to be specified, there are several that have been described in the literature and analyzed. One is sometimes called the *X/Y* classifier: if *X* packets matching the definition of the flow arrive in *Y* seconds, then the flow is eligible to be label switched. Another algorithm looks at TCP or UDP port numbers and tries to label switch the long-lived flows. For example, queries to the Domain Name System (DNS) are usually one or two packets long, while File Transfer Protocol (FTP) sessions tend to be much longer. Because these classification policies are local, the network administrator can select and tune the algorithms according to local conditions.

IP Switching uses the term *flow redirection,* or just *redirection,* to describe the process of binding labels to flows and establishing label switched paths. One IP Switch tells another to redirect a particular flow to it. The semantics are simply "use label *x* to send traffic from flow *y* to me." Recall that a label is just a locally significant identifier that will be used to switch some class of packets. Because IP Switching is designed to run on ATM hardware, labels represent VPI/VCI values.

If we consider a network of three IP Switches, we can see how the redirection process results in the establishment of a label switched path for a flow. In Figure 3.3 data is flowing from A via B to C on a default VC. Imagine that switch B decides that a particular flow *y* is a suitable candidate for switching. It sends a redirect to switch A specifying flow *y* and the label (VPI/VCI) on which it expects to receive it. At this point no switched path has been established through B, but A may commence sending traffic on the advertised label to B.

When B receives data from A with this new label, it must initially forward it to C over the default VC. (Note that to prevent interleaving of packets from different flows, B must reassemble the datagrams before forwarding them.) If C then decides to issue a REDIRECT message

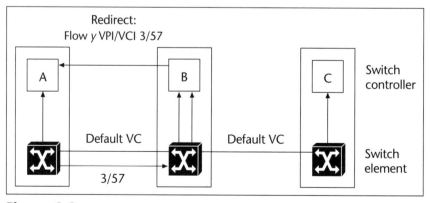

Figure 3.3

Flow redirection. Switch B issues a REDIRECT message to switch A.

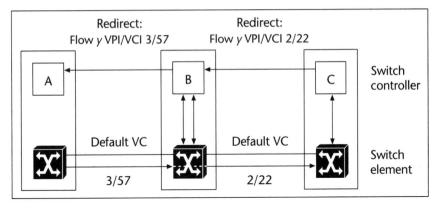

Figure 3.4
Flow redirection and switching. Switches B and C redirect the same flow, allowing it to be switched at B.

for the flow *y*, the situation depicted in Figure 3.4 results. Switch B can now forward traffic on the VPI/VCI specified in the REDIRECT message from C. It can also recognize that this same flow is arriving from A on the VPI/VCI that was specified in the REDIRECT message it issued to A (see Figure 3.3). Because the same flow arrives at B on one VC and leaves on another, it now becomes possible to switch it. To do this B uses GSMP to inform its switching element to set up the appropriate switching path. In the example in Figure 3.4, B uses GSMP to set up the switch so that traffic on VPI/VCI 3/57 on the incoming port from A leaves on VPI/ VCI 2/22 on the port leaving B toward C.

An important point to notice is that A and C need not necessarily be switches in this example. In the terminology of Chapter 2, they are acting as *edge* LSRs—the devices that apply the first label to a packet. An edge LSR might be implemented as a conventional router with an ATM interface to enable non-ATM (or non–IP Switching) networks to connect to an IP Switching network. Furthermore, a host with an ATM interface could apply the label to a packet, given suitable software. Thus, IP Switches can directly interconnect hosts. This is much easier to do in a data-driven model than in a control-driven one, and in fact IP Switching is unique among label switching techniques in its ability to fully support host attachment.

Although we have not described the CSR approach in detail, we note that there are many similarities between IP Switching and the CSR. In the taxonomy of Chapter 2, they are both data-driven approaches. By contrast, Tag Switching, ARIS, and MPLS are all control-driven approaches. The choice of control- or data-driven models is probably the most significant differentiating factor among different label switching approaches.

Although the example above showed IP Switches directly connected to each other, there is no particular reason why they could not be connected together using ATM virtual paths. This would enable them to be connected across a public ATM network that used standard ATM switches. The only requirement is that the labels used in REDI-RECT messages must be contained in the VCI field, since the VPI field is used for the VP switching across the public network.

We can now see where IP Switching fits into the taxonomy defined in Chapter 2. Note that each IP Switch's decision to switch a flow is made independently of the other switches and without waiting for other label bindings (REDIRECT messages) to arrive. Thus, in our taxonomy, independent label binding is used. As already noted, IP Switching is a data-driven approach. Because binding is data-driven, bindings are not piggybacked on an existing protocol, but are distributed independently. Finally, the bindings are assigned at the downstream end of a link with respect to data flow.

3.2 Ipsilon Flow Management Protocol (IFMP)

IFMP runs on a point-to-point link between two IP Switches and is designed to communicate flow to label binding information between them. The protocol operates using the downstream label allocation model discussed in Chapter 2. Although the downstream node is in charge of label allocation and advertisement, it does so in a purely advisory way; that is, the upstream node is free to use the labels or ignore them as it sees fit. Decisions on how and when to assign labels is a matter of local policy, in the sense that each switch can make its own assignment decisions. However, it makes sense for all the switches in a domain, or at least for ones adjacent to each other, to have a coherent view of what this policy is to enable the establishment of switched paths as described above.

IFMP is a *soft state* protocol, by which we mean that the state that it installs will automatically *time out* (i.e., be deleted after some interval) unless refreshed.[1] In the case of IFMP, this means that flow binding

---

1. While this definition of soft state is fairly well accepted, it is overly simplistic to divide protocols into "soft" and "hard." Instead, most protocols lie somewhere on a spectrum between the two extremes.

information has a limited life once it is learned by an upstream switch and must be refreshed periodically as long as it is required. The messages that install flow state contain a lifetime field, which indicates for how long that state is to be considered valid. If the flow binding is not refreshed by the downstream IP Switch, it is timed out and will no longer be used by the upstream switch to forward traffic. The fact that flow information is continually refreshed by IFMP means that the protocol can run directly over IP using best-effort data delivery. If a message gets lost, some flow state synchronization between two IP Switches may be temporarily lost. However, as soon as the state is refreshed (i.e., the message is resent) the flow state will again be synchronized, and all will be well. There is of course a trade-off to be made between the desire to reduce the period in which two switches might have inconsistent state and the desire to minimize the control traffic load that is generated by sending the refreshes at short intervals.

Another thing to note about the soft state approach is that there is no need to explicitly remove state information, since it will time out eventually, although an explicit removal mechanism may improve efficiency by causing faster response.

There are two constituent parts to IFMP, an adjacency protocol and the main redirect protocol. We discuss these in turn.

3.2.1 IFMP's Adjacency Protocol

Adjacency protocols are common in networking, and the name gives a good hint as to the function. Such protocols are used to communicate and discover information about immediate neighbors. They are also commonly used to make sure that a neighbor doesn't disappear silently, because of link failure or system reboot, for example, or at least to make sure a system recognizes a neighbor's reappearance.

IP Switching relies on cooperation between switches. It is important that a consistent view of the state of label assignation is maintained between switches. The IFMP adjacency protocol enables cooperating switches to exchange an initial set of information so that they acquire enough shared state to begin label exchange.

The IFMP adjacency protocol allows the switches at the ends of a link to learn each other's identity. The ADJACENCY message is encapsulated into an IP datagram and sent to the limited broadcast address. It is a convention in IP that the limited broadcast address (255.255.255.255) is listened to by all hosts on a network, and thus the IP Switches at either end of the link can send messages to each other before each knows the other's address. When an IP Switch receives an ADJACENCY message from one of its neighbors, it deduces the identity of the remote IP Switch by inspecting the source address in the IP encapsulation of the ADJACENCY message. In keeping with the soft state model, adjacency protocol messages are resent periodically.

The adjacency protocol also allows switches to agree on an instance number for the link between them and to learn the sequence number of the next message they expect to see from each other. Link instance and packet sequence numbers are used to detect loss of synchronization between two IP Switches. In the event that one switch detects some sort of error condition, the protocol enables the link to be reset: all previous flow state information learned across it is discarded, and the two parties attempt to resynchronize. In the meantime, data would be forwarded over that link using the default VC.

3.2.2 IFMP's Redirection Protocol

There are five message types defined in the IFMP redirection protocol. All have the common header format illustrated in Figure 3.5. All of the protocol messages are encapsulated into IP datagrams, which are sent to the unicast IP address of the peer system, learned via the IFMP adjacency protocol. The message body itself may contain more than one message element with the restriction that multiple messages, if present, must all be of the same type as indicated by the Opcode field in the header. The five message types are

- REDIRECT: The message used to bind a label to a flow and thus redirect it for switching.
- RECLAIM: Enables a label to be unbound for subsequent reuse.
- RECLAIM ACK: Acknowledgment that a RECLAIM message was received and processed.
- LABEL RANGE: Enables the acceptable range of labels for a switch to be communicated to its neighbors.
- ERROR: Used to deal with various error conditions.

The fields in the common message header are mostly self-explanatory. The purpose of instance and sequence number has already been touched upon in the description of the adjacency protocol. For example, an IP Switch expects to see the sequence number in messages from its peer increase by one with each message. The sequence number is used by the redirection protocol to help process messages in order.

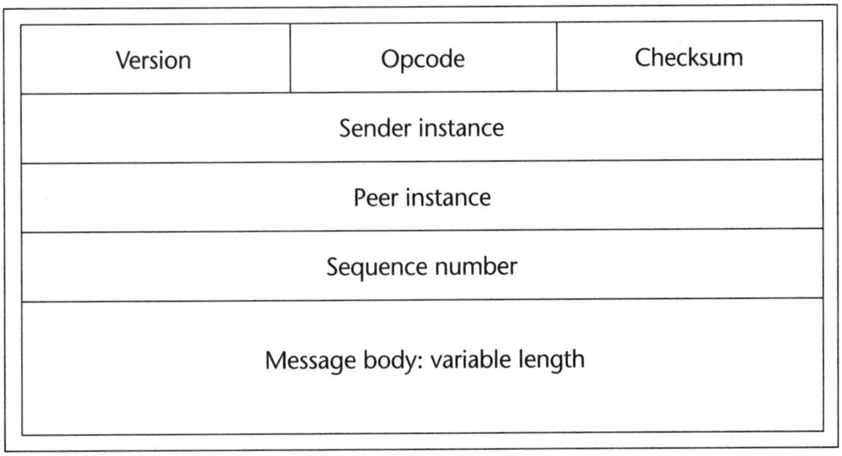

Version	Opcode	Checksum
Sender instance		
Peer instance		
Sequence number		
Message body: variable length		

Figure 3.5
IFMP REDIRECT *protocol message format.*

Strict in-order processing is not always required, however. For example, if message number 2 establishes a binding between a label and a flow, and message number 1 establishes a binding between a different label and a different flow, the recipient can process them in any order.

We will confine ourselves to detailed inspection of just one message type: the REDIRECT message. (The other message formats can be found in the IFMP specification, RFC 1953.) We focus on REDIRECT not just because it is so central to IP Switching but also because it introduces in a concrete way something that we have glossed over until now, the precise definition of a flow.

The REDIRECT message body format is illustrated in Figure 3.6. Looking at the message we see *flow type* and *flow identifier* for the first time. At this point in our discussion of IP Switching, the general term *flow*, which has sufficed in our description up until now, will no longer do. Flow identifiers in IP Switching are a little more complicated than a general familiarity with label switching concepts might lead us to expect.

An IP *flow* is often understood to refer to a sequence of datagrams from one source IP address to another destination IP address. Such a flow, which we can call a host-to-host flow, can be described or identified by an ordered pair of the form <source address, destination address>. Roughly speaking, this is called a Type 2 flow in IP Switching.

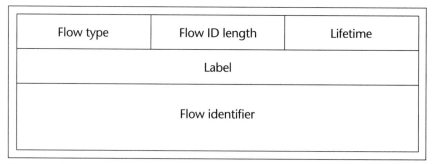

Flow type	Flow ID length	Lifetime
Label		
Flow identifier		

Figure 3.6
IFMP REDIRECT *message body.*

We can also specify a flow at a finer granularity by including transport layer port addresses, so the flow would be identified by <source address, source port, destination address, destination port>. This enables different applications between the same pair of machines to be distinguished. Ipsilon calls these Type 1 flows. These flow definitions are fairly common; for example, the Resource Reservation Protocol (RSVP) uses similar definitions. Ipsilon's definitions of flows build on these but also include a number of other fields from the IP datagram header in the flow identifier. The reason for including these fields will become clear as we discuss the usage of flow identifiers.

The IP Switching architecture allows for a variety of flow types to be defined, and there are two such types at the time of writing. The formats of the Type 1 and Type 2 flow identifiers are illustrated in Figure 3.7 and Figure 3.8, respectively.

The flow Type 1 identifier is used to identify application flows and thus includes the source and destination protocol port numbers. In addition, it includes five fields from the IP version 4 (IPv4) header. These are the version, the IP header length (IHL), the Type of Service byte (ToS), the time-to-live field (TTL), and the protocol ID. The meanings of these fields are not particularly important at this point; we simply note that they are exact replicas of fields in the IPv4 header. Note also that at a given point in the network, these fields should remain constant for all the packets belonging to the same application flow. The precise definition of a flow is simply this: a set of packets that have the same value in all the header fields is included in the corresponding flow identifier.

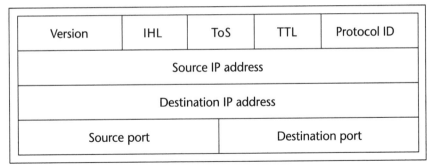

Figure 3.7
IFMP flow Type 1 identifier.

Version	IHL	Reserved	TTL	Reserved
Source address				
Destination address				

Figure 3.8
IFMP flow Type 2 identifier.

The flow Type 2 identifier corresponds to the host-to-host flow mentioned above. It includes all the same fields from the IPv4 header as a Type 1 identifier except for the protocol number and ToS byte. The reason to exclude these fields is that they are not likely to be the same for all packets between a pair of hosts.

The apparent complexity of these flow types when compared with the simple model just described arises from two capabilities provided by the IP Switching architecture. As we will see in Section 3.2.5, it handles TTL "correctly"; it also provides some protection against *spoofing*. Spoofing is a general term for a number of techniques used for gaining unauthorized access to network or computer resources. Label switching offers some particular opportunities for spoofing attacks. The IP Switching architecture includes some features to make such attacks more difficult. The flow identifiers are only one component involved in providing this antispoofing protection. The other is the encapsulation used on the redirected VCs. We will examine this first and will return to the issue of spoofing in Section 3.2.4.

3.2.3 Encapsulation of Redirected Flows

In our discussion of redirection in Section 3.1, we glossed over the details of encapsulation, that is, the representation of IP packets on redirected VCs. A significant detail is that when data is sent on a redirected VC the encapsulation is changed from the one used on the default VC. Figure 3.9 illustrates the encapsulations used on both default and redirected VCs for Type 2 flows. We will consider the simpler case of Type 2 flows in detail before explaining the slight differences when Type 1 flows are used.

The important differences between the two encapsulations are that when a flow is moved onto its own redirected VC from the default VC

- The LLC and SNAP fields disappear.
- The IP header gets transformed into an IFMP flow type header. (With Type 1 flows, the TCP or UDP header would also be affected, for reasons explained below.)

The disappearance of the LLC/SNAP fields is not very significant, as they were not doing much apart from indicating that the layer 3

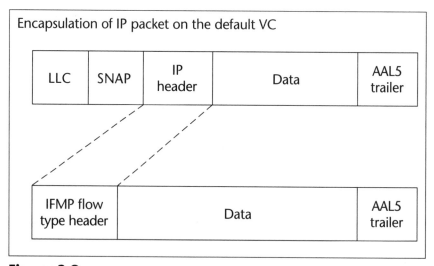

Figure 3.9
Encapsulation on default and redirected VCs (flow Type 2).

protocol is IP. What happens in transforming the IP and TCP/UDP headers is more complex and interesting. The header is actually compressed, in that some fields are removed. It should be apparent that such a compression process needs to be reversible.

Figure 3.10 illustrates the transformation in more detail. The figure shows a standard IPv4 header, a flow Type 2 identifier, and the encapsulation (or header) used for datagrams of flow Type 2 on a redirected VC. In addition to the fields described above, the IPv4 header contains

- Total length of the datagram
- Identification, flags, and fragment offset, which are used for IP fragmentation
- A header checksum, used to check for corruption of the header

Note that all of these fields appear in the flow Type 2 encapsulation, along with the Types of Services field and the protocol number. Every other field from the IP header is included in the flow Type 2 identifier. That is, given a flow identifier and the matching flow encapsulation, all the fields of the original IP header can be reconstructed. Using the labels of the three parts of Figure 3.10, we observe that a = b + c. We now examine how this works in practice.

Recall that the sequence of events leading up to the appearance of a redirected flow on a certain VC is as follows:

1. An IP Switch selects a flow by inspection of its IP header (Figure 3.10(a)).

2. The switch sends a REDIRECT message containing a flow identifier (Figure 3.10(b)) and a VCI/VPI to use for the selected flow to its upstream neighbor.

3. The upstream IP Switch sends the flow on the VC specified in the REDIRECT message using the appropriate flow type encapsulation. In this case it is flow Type 2 (Figure 3.10(c)).

Now consider an IP Switch receiving a redirected flow. The flow arrives on the VPI/VCI, which the switch selected and communicated to its upstream neighbor using a REDIRECT message. The switch keeps a copy of all REDIRECT messages it has sent. Thus, it can use the VPI/VCI of the incoming flow to obtain the corresponding flow identifier. Now it has both the flow identifier and the arriving flow itself. As we observed, it is possible to generate the original IPv4 header by combining these two together.

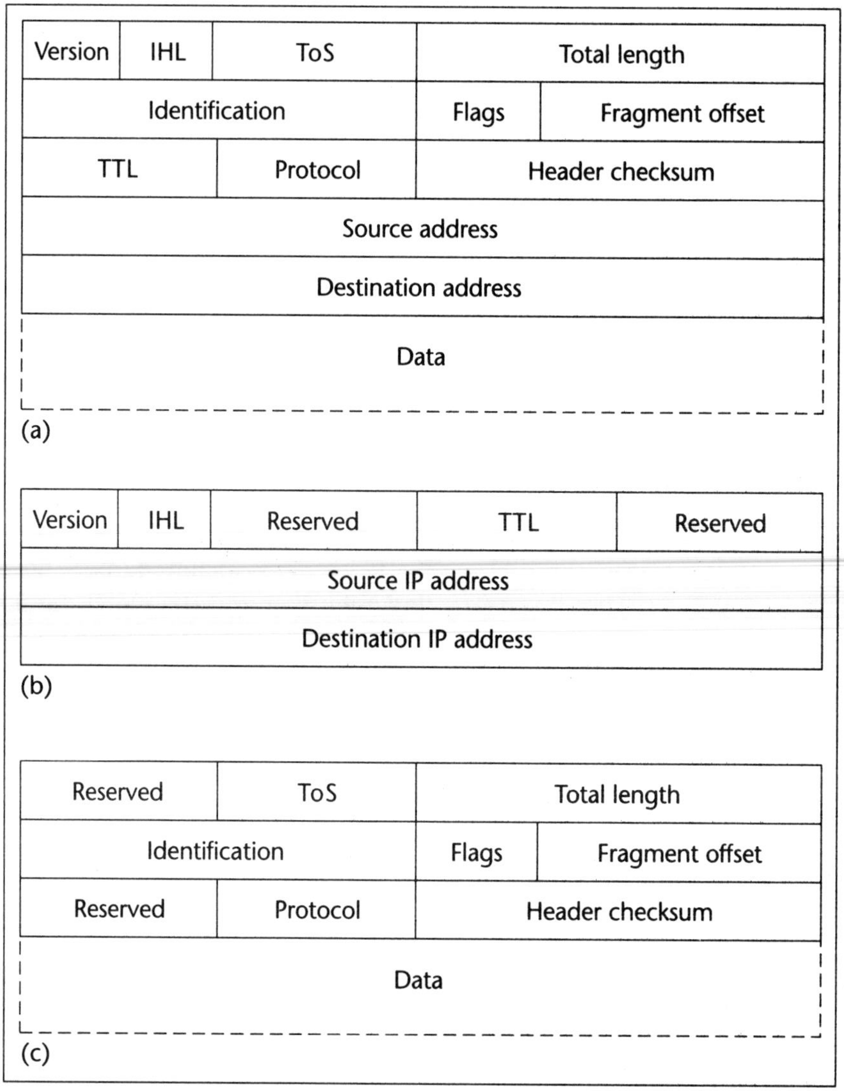

Version	IHL	ToS	Total length		
Identification			Flags	Fragment offset	
TTL		Protocol	Header checksum		
Source address					
Destination address					
Data					

(a)

Version	IHL	Reserved	TTL	Reserved
Source IP address				
Destination IP address				

(b)

Reserved	ToS	Total length		
Identification		Flags	Fragment offset	
Reserved	Protocol	Header checksum		
Data				

(c)

Figure 3.10

IPv4 header compression: IPv4 header (a); IFMP flow Type 2 identifier (b); and flow Type 2 encapsulation (c). The flow identifier and flow encapsulation together contain all the fields of the IP header.

Almost identical mechanisms to those described above are used for flow Type 1. One difference is that now the flow identifier contains the ToS and protocol fields, which means that they don't need to be included in the encapsulation. Also, because the flow identifier includes the source and destination port numbers from the TCP or UDP header, these fields are also removed from the packet before transmission. The reconstruction of the original headers—now including TCP or UDP as well as IP—is performed as before, again relying on the fact that the flow identifier and encapsulated packet together provide everything that is needed to re-create the original packet headers.

There are two fields that require a little extra attention for both flow types. These are the TTL, which needs to be decremented at the end of a label switched path, and the header checksum, which needs to be updated as a result of the change to the TTL. The details of handling these fields are discussed in Section 3.2.5.

Although compression is usually employed to reduce bandwidth utilization, in this case the removal of fields from the packet and reconstruction of those fields at the end of a switched path offers an additional (and perhaps more important) benefit, which is protection against spoofing. We note that the ability to perform compression directly follows from the fine-grained nature of flows. Because many fields in the IP header are the same for all packets in a flow, we can send those fields once—in the flow identifier—rather than sending them in every packet. If flow identifiers were more coarse-grained, representing, say, all traffic to a certain destination prefix, then it would not be possible to remove fields from the IP header.

3.2.4 IFMP and Security

Consider the general label switching paradigm where a label switching router obtains a label and the definition of the corresponding Forwarding Equivalence Class (an FEC, as defined in Chapter 2) from its next hop for that FEC. It is then capable of forwarding traffic belonging to that FEC using the label. At the next hop label switch, only the label is used in deciding how to further forward the traffic. What happens if the upstream node uses the label incorrectly to forward packets that do not belong to the FEC? It may help to rephrase this in the more familiar terms of destination address-based forwarding. If a switch says to a peer "send me traffic for address 171.69.210.139 using label y," then what happens if the peer sends packets addressed to 155.3.21.139 using this label? The simple answer is that they will get sent along the wrong label switched path. What happens beyond that—that is, what the effect of the packets traveling on the wrong path is—is a much harder question to answer. The result may simply be an annoying lack of connectivity. It is also possible that the filtering rules that might have prevented packets from passing through a certain point in the network might be violated. This would certainly be undesirable.

The IP header regeneration operation described in the previous section makes this kind of mistake (or attack), and others like it, more difficult. The IP address fields are under the "control" of the receiving system. Unless the receiving system at the end of the IP Switched path is compromised, it will regenerate a packet addressed to the correct system (for that VC) with a source address that matches the flow ID.

This feature of IP Switching clearly helps mitigate the effects of one form of operational error or deliberate attack. There are undoubtedly many that it will not catch. However, this feature is a capability that none of the other label switching schemes possess. The fact that only IP Switching has this capability reflects both an attention to detail in bringing the product to market, as well as a focus on particular deployment scenarios. For example, this type of attack could not be launched on an Internet service provider using label switching only within its backbone.

3.2.5 IFMP and TTL

Recall from Chapter 2 that time-to-live (TTL) is used to mitigate the effects of loops. The TTL field is part of the IP header and can be processed by a conventional router. In fact, it is a requirement that IP routers process this field, decrementing it by one before they forward a packet and discarding the packet if the TTL becomes zero after the decrement operation. The IP TTL cannot be processed by an ATM switch; as a cell switch it is only capable of operating on fields in the ATM cell header. An IP Switch, which uses an ATM switch to forward label switched IP packets, can therefore not decrement TTL at every hop. However, IP Switching does manage to decrement TTL at the end of a label switched path and to mitigate the effect of loops, using some mechanisms that we now examine.

IP Switching ensures that the TTL field in an IP datagram at the end of an IP Switched path contains the same value it would have had if it had passed through a path of conventional routers with the same number of hops. In simple terms, what happens is that the IP TTL is removed from the IP datagram at the start of an IP Switched path, and a new TTL value is decremented by the number of IP Switch hops the packet has traversed and is inserted at the end of the path. Note the difference between this case and the conventional one: although the TTL is correct at the *end* of the IP Switched path, that "correctness" is achieved by a mechanism that is different from the decrement at each hop required of routers.

If we look again at the flow identifiers in Figures 3.7 and 3.8, we see that they contain a TTL field. The value in this field is copied from the header of an IP datagram that an IP Switch has selected for redirection. A REDIRECT message for the datagram contains both a label and a flow identifier. In Figure 3.11 we see switch B partway through setting up a switched flow. Switch B has already elected to redirect the flow y. It has sent a REDIRECT message to A saying "redirect flow y to me on VPI/VCI 3/57." As part of the flow identifier, B has specified that the TTL for packets eligible to be sent on the redirected circuit is n.

Now suppose that switch C has not yet elected to redirect the flow. Switch B must, therefore, forward the flow y, now arriving on 3/57, on the default VC. To do this B uses the flow label (3/57) to obtain the flow identifier record and from that obtains the IPv4 header information that would normally be in the packets that constitute flow y at this point. The TTL is part of this information. Switch B regenerates the header by combining the flow encapsulation and flow identifier in the manner we discussed previously (see Section 3.2.3 and Figure 3.10). Switch B now performs the normal router forwarding procedures on this packet, including decrementing the TTL. The new TTL is set to $n - 1$, as shown in the figure, and the packet is forwarded on the

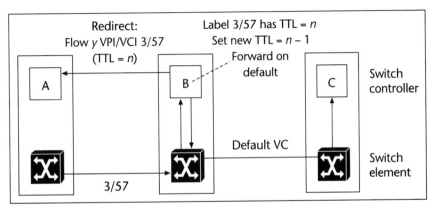

Figure 3.11
TTL handling in switched flow setup.

default VC toward C. Now if C were to select this same flow for redirection, it would include the TTL of $n - 1$ in the flow identifier. Once redirection had taken place, C would insert the value $n - 1$ in the TTL field and process the packet. Thus, it should be clear that, for a label switched path of any length, the TTL placed in the packet at the end will be the correct one, based on the number of hops in the path.

An interesting side effect of the inclusion of TTL in the flow identifier is that all the packets going down a label switched path must have exactly the same TTL. Because the flow identifier already restricts the packets of a flow to be from the same host, and because the host almost certainly puts the same TTL value in every packet it sends (unless it is running some diagnostic tool such as traceroute), this is not really a big restriction. It does mean that if a routing change between the sending host and the start of the label switched path changes the number of hops the packets go through, then the established label switched path will become useless. This is likely to be a rare occurrence in a healthy network. It is also worth noting that, if some new flow type were defined that was less fine-grained than host-to-host flows, some other means of dealing with TTL would be needed.

By decrementing TTL correctly from one end of a label switched path to the other, the mechanism just described ensures that, if a forwarding loop that includes both IP Switches and conventional routers develops, looping packets will be discarded when their TTL reaches zero. If the loop was purely among IP Switches, then the worst that can happen is that a label switched "spiral" would form, ending at the IP Switch that was receiving packets with TTL = 1. This last IP Switch would discard the packets as their TTL expired and thus would never be able to set up a switched path to the next hop. This is illustrated in Figure 3.12. The spiral would of course be resolved when routing reconverged to break the loop. Note that this spiral is the same one that packets would follow if normal IP routing were used, but in the IP Switching case packets get to the end of the spiral without having their TTL decremented by one at every hop. The crucial fact is that packets do not loop *infinitely*, which would be possible in a label switching scheme that did not somehow deal with TTL. (All label switching schemes have some mechanism to prevent infinite loops.) Note that in the taxonomy of Chapter 2, this is a loop mitigation scheme, not a loop prevention scheme.

We mentioned in Section 3.2.3 that header fields were copied from the IPv4 header into the flow encapsulation used on the redirected VC or into the flow identifier. One field, however, is treated in a slightly

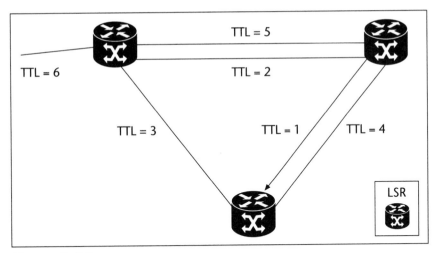

Figure 3.12
IP Switching in the presence of a routing loop. In the worst case, a label switched spiral forms, terminating at the IP Switch that receives packets with TTL = 1.

different way. The IPv4 header checksum is, as its name implies, a checksum over all the data in the IPv4 header. Because the TTL is modified at the downstream end of the label switched path, it follows that the checksum must be as well. It is possible to recalculate it, as all the data needed to do so is present. However, this would mask any corruption of the header that might have happened up to the point of recalculation, either on the label switched path or before it. So instead, at the start of a switched path, the value of the TTL is subtracted from the value of the header checksum and the result is sent in the encapsulation. The switch at the end of the path only has to add the value that it inserts in the TTL field to the value of the header checksum in the encapsulation to regenerate the correct IPv4 checksum. This is the exact checksum that would have been in the packet if it had been transmitted by a sequence of conventional routers.

3.3 General Switch Management Protocol (GSMP)

We provide an introduction to the GSMP here because it was invented as part of the overall IP Switching architecture. However, it is important to realize that, from a technology perspective, IP Switching is essentially independent of GSMP, and vice versa. GSMP is used solely to control an ATM switch and the VC connections made across it. We could make an IP Switch without using GSMP. Also, we can use GSMP to control ATM switches without building an IP Switch. For example, we could build a controller that implemented standard ATM signalling (e.g., Q.2931), or some label switching approach other than IP Switching, and use it to control a switch via GSMP. Because of this wide applicability of GSMP, various efforts to standardize it outside of the confines of MPLS are under way.

It is not technologically necessary to run a protocol between an external controller and a switch—we could just write custom switch control software for each different ATM switch. However, as noted at the start of this chapter, such an approach is not efficient if the goal is to support IP Switching on multiple switch platforms. The same argument does not hold with the Ipsilon Flow Management Protocol (IFMP). Because IP Switching requires cooperation between peers, a standard protocol is needed to transport flow information between them. It makes no sense to consider building an IP Switch without defining the interswitch protocol. Thus, we make a distinction between the two protocols: IFMP is clearly a key architectural component of IP Switching, whereas GSMP is more an implementation optimization.

GSMP is a master/slave protocol where an ATM switch is the slave. The protocol specifies that the master and slave are connected via an ATM link. The master could be any general-purpose computer (and in Ipsilon's products is actually an Intel-based PC). The specification describes the protocol as being one for "general-purpose ATM switch control." The protocol allows the master to

- Establish and release VC connections across the switch
- Add and delete leaves to point-to-multipoint connections
- Perform port management (Up, Down, Reset, Loopback)
- Request data (configuration information, statistics)

In addition, the protocol allows the slave to inform the master if something interesting, such as a link failure, happens on the switch.

As with IFMP, GSMP has an adjacency part and a connection management part, and we will consider each in turn. Before doing that, we will look briefly at the GSMP packet format illustrated in Figure 3.13, because it is common to both parts of the protocol. GSMP packets are LLC/SNAP encapsulated and sent over an ATM link using AAL5. This is a common encapsulation for data sent over ATM links (see RFC 1483).

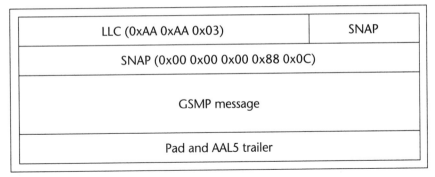

LLC (0xAA 0xAA 0x03)	SNAP
SNAP (0x00 0x00 0x00 0x88 0x0C)	
GSMP message	
Pad and AAL5 trailer	

Figure 3.13
GSMP packet format.

The LLC/SNAP encapsulation allows other packets (from different protocols) to be sent on the link at the same time and be distinguished from the GSMP packets at the receiver. The actual values in the LLC and SNAP fields together identify that the protocol thus encapsulated is GSMP.

Note that GSMP messages, unlike IFMP messages, are not sent as IP packets. They are sent directly inside the LLC/SNAP encapsulation. This reflects the fact that GSMP is used to control a node that is assumed to know nothing about IP—an ATM switch—whereas IFMP is a peer-to-peer protocol between a pair of IP-capable nodes.

3.3.1 GSMP Adjacency Protocol

We have already discussed the general purpose behind adjacency protocols—to provide some initial information to the communicating parties before they begin their "real" work. It is not surprising that the GSMP and IFMP adjacency protocols are quite similar. The GSMP adjacency protocol message format is illustrated in Figure 3.14. The sender and receiver names contain a number that identifies the switches. The field is long enough to accommodate a standard MAC address. This is convenient because most hardware has one of these and MAC addresses are assigned to ensure that they are globally unique; this makes it easier to manage networks of machines than might otherwise be the case.

The port numbers are locally assigned numbers for the link between the sender and the receiver. The instance field is used in the manner that we discussed previously for IFMP and is changed if a loss of

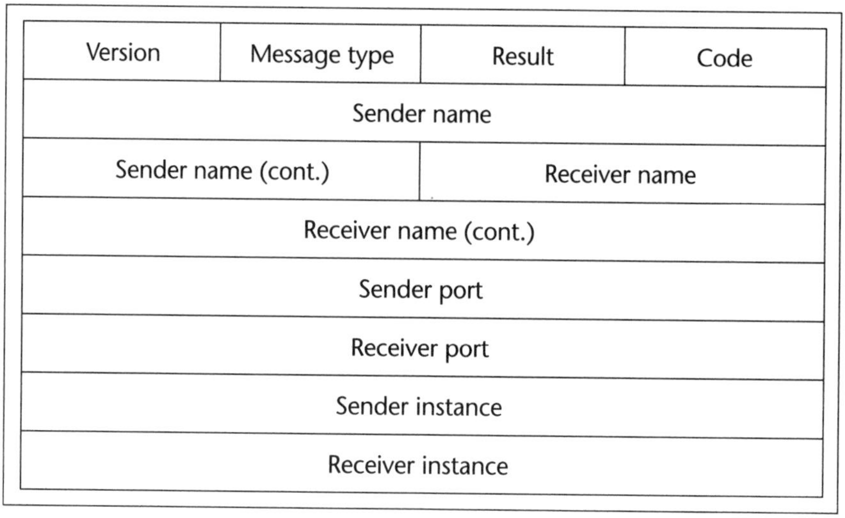

Version	Message type	Result	Code
Sender name			
Sender name (cont.)		Receiver name	
Receiver name (cont.)			
Sender port			
Receiver port			
Sender instance			
Receiver instance			

Figure 3.14
GSMP adjacency protocol message.

synchronization between sender and receiver occurs, so that old messages can be ignored. In fact, all the fields are used in a way semantically equivalent to those in the IFMP adjacency protocol. They are used initially to gain information about the system at the other end of the link and then to monitor the link's status. For example, if sender port or name were to change from one message to another, then clearly some remedial action would be called for (in this case resetting the link).

3.3.2 GSMP Connection Management Protocol

All the connection management messages, with the exception of MOVE BRANCH, have the same format. The master can set a field that indicates to the slave whether it requires a response. Responses are only provided if requested. The format of the connection management messages is shown in Figure 3.15. The names of most of the fields are fairly self-explanatory. There are two fields that are worthy of further comment: port session number and priority.

The port session number is used to ensure consistency between the GSMP master and slave. If a port on a switch goes out of service and is restored, its port session number must change, and the GSMP master

Version	Message type	Result	Code
Transaction identifier			
Port session number			
Input port			
Zero	Input VPI		Input VCI
Output port			
Zero	Output VPI		Output VCI
Number of branches		Reserved	Priority

Figure 3.15
GSMP connection management message format.

will be unable to control that port until it learns the new port session number. This enables the master to reestablish state that may have been lost while the port was out of service.

Note that in this message there is only one "port session number" field, even though a connection involves two ports. This is because GSMP associates connection state with an input port, implying that GSMP does not need to know if an output port has gone down and come back up. In the event that this happens, the switch is required to reestablish any lost connections.

The other field of interest is priority. A great part of the complexity of ATM switch hardware and ATM signalling software is involved with quality of service (QoS). By contrast, the IP Switching approach as originally specified had very little to say about QoS. The simple priority field in GSMP provides a basic capability to use priority-based queuing at an output port.

Simple priority queuing is not the same as the more powerful and complex techniques available from ATM cell switching, but it may be that it is adequate for switching IP flows, given the lack of QoS mechanisms generally available to IP traffic today. It is not specified how these priorities are to be set, but one possible way is to do so based on the contents of the IP Type of Service field.

Some of the research papers produced by Ipsilon and some of their partners suggest ways in which the queuing, scheduling, and traffic management capabilities of ATM hardware could be exploited in combination with RSVP (among other mechanisms) to provide QoS capabilities for IP flows. This is certainly possible but not with GSMP as specified in RFC 1987. However, QoS extensions to GSMP are under way at the time of writing, and some references are provided in the Bibliography. Certainly, the fact that IP Switching allows each application flow to have its own VC, coupled with the fact that many ATM switches can provide sophisticated per-VC queuing capabilities, suggests that significant QoS capabilities may be provided by this approach.

Another interesting feature of the protocol when compared with ATM signalling is that it makes no distinction between unicast and multicast connections. There is, for example, a single ADD BRANCH message. Whether it means "make a unicast connection" or "add this branch to an existing connection" is determined by the slave and depends on the context existing at the time the message is received. If the specified port already has a connection from the specified input VPI/VCI to another output connection, a new branch will be added. If there is no connection, then one will be established.

As mentioned earlier, GSMP also contains some messages for statistics gathering, for example, counts of the number of cells transmitted on a VC, and general port and switch management. These capabilities are not really central to the theme of this book and so we do not deal with them here. The GSMP specification, RFC 1987, describes these details.

3.4 Implementations

IP Switching products became available in 1996. The Ipsilon product family used an Intel Pentium-based PC running a highly modified version of Free BSD (UNIX) as the switch controller. Ipsilon also offered a number of ATM switches that were controlled by the switch controller, which attached to one port of the switch. In addition to ATM-only switches, a number of edge devices that allowed Ethernet and FDDI LANs to be connected to an IP Switching backbone were available. These latter devices provided the edge LSR function, as defined in Chapter 2. Ipsilon also put some effort into providing ATM network interface device drivers to allow hosts to connect directly to an IP Switching backbone.

Ipsilon established partnerships with a considerable number of switch vendors. These partners implemented GSMP, and thus it was possible to buy an IP Switch controller from Ipsilon—a PC with Ipsilon software and an ATM interface—and an ATM switch from an established switch vendor. The result was a fully functional IP Switch.

A variety of factors contributed to a lack of success for IP Switching products in the marketplace. One of these was performance concerns about the data-driven label binding approach that is fundamental to the architecture. Another factor was the large amount of industry momentum behind MPLS, which adopted a control-driven approach. About two years after announcing their first products, Ipsilon was acquired by Nokia, and IP Switching products are no longer readily available.

3.5 **Summary**

IP Switching is a data-driven approach to label switching specified for use over ATM hardware and links. It was invented soon after CSR, to which it bears some similarity, but it had a much larger impact in the marketplace.

The IP Switching approach has made many major contributions to the label switching effort. Although it was not the first approach invented, it was the first that delivered real products and caused the flurry of activity that resulted in the development of Tag Switching and, ultimately, the formation of the MPLS working group in the IETF.

In addition to IFMP, the label binding protocol, IP Switching contributed GSMP, a useful general-purpose technique for controlling ATM switches with third-party software, thus enabling a large number of vendors' switches to easily become IP Switches. GSMP may also be used by any other software that can control an ATM switch, for example, software to support standard ATM signalling. GSMP appears likely to have a future as a standard, general-purpose switch control protocol.

Alone among label switching approaches, IP Switching offers some protection against the dangers of incorrect flows being submitted on a label switched path. It is also unique in enabling label switched paths to extend all the way to hosts, provided they have ATM interfaces and suitable software.

3.6 Further Reading

The three informational RFCs (1953, 1954, 1987) describe the protocols and the transmission of flow labeled IPv4 on ATM datalinks. In addition, some excellent papers that treat IP Switching in more depth are

Lin, S., and N. McKeown. "A Simulation Study of IP Switching." In Proceedings of the ACM SIGCOMM 97, Cannes, France, September 1997.

Newman, P., T. Lyon, and G. Minshall. "Flow Labeled IP: A Connectionless Approach to ATM." In Proceedings of the IEEE Infocom, March 1996.

Newman, P., T. Lyon, and G. Minshall. "IP Switching: ATM under IP." *IEEE/ACM Transactions on Networking* 6, no. 2, April 1998:117–129.

Newman, P., G. Minshall, T. Lyon, and L. Huston. "IP Switching and Gigabit Routers." *IEEE Communications Magazine,* January 1997.

GSMP is undergoing standardization at the IETF at the time of writing; details can be found at the IETF Web site:

www.ietf.org

Tag Switching

I n this chapter we look at Tag Switching. We begin with an overview of the Tag Switching design goals and how it provides a variety of different functions. These include destination-based routing, hierarchy of routing knowledge, multicast, and explicit routes. Following this, we describe possible alternatives for carrying tag information in packets. Unlike IP Switching, Tag Switching is not restricted to running only on ATM hardware. In fact, there are some special procedures required to cover the case of ATM. We conclude this chapter with a brief overview of the main new protocol that Tag Switching requires, the Tag Distribution Protocol (TDP).

Like IP Switching, Tag Switching has its own terminology. A router that supports Tag Switching is called a Tag Switching Router (TSR). Labels are called *tags* (which is why the scheme is called "Tag Switching"). Instead of incoming label we'll use *incoming tag,* and instead of outgoing label we'll use *outgoing tag*. A label switching forwarding table is called a *Tag Forwarding Information Base* (TFIB).

The material in this chapter is largely based on the publicly available documents on Tag Switching. More details are provided in Section 4.8, Further Reading, at the end of this chapter.

4.1 Tag Switching Overview

In Chapter 1 we saw that there were many motivations behind the development of the various label switching approaches, such as additional routing functionality, improved scalability of the routing system, better forwarding performance, and more flexibility of the routing system. However, the one that has been most widely appreciated is the easiest to understand: performance. The idea is simple: provide the functionality of a router (IP forwarding) with the performance (and cost) of an ATM switch.

The design goals of Tag Switching are rather broad. In particular, Tag Switching has focused on adding functionality (such as explicit routes) and improving scalability (e.g., through the use of a hierarchy of routing knowledge), as the following sections will illustrate. Moreover, Tag Switching aims at being link layer independent, thus allowing operation over virtually any media type, not just ATM. High performance is just one among many goals for Tag Switching.

Tag Switching can be implemented in a variety of devices, such as routers or ATM switches. Implementing Tag Switching on routers doesn't require hardware modifications to the routers, although you certainly could provide specialized hardware support for high performance Tag Switching forwarding. Implementing Tag Switching on ATM switches doesn't require any modifications to the hardware used by these switches (although Tag Switching could benefit from certain hardware modifications, as we'll describe below); support for Tag Switching on ATM switches can be achieved purely by upgrading software.

A Tag Switching network consists of Tag Edge Routers and Tag Switching Routers (TSRs). The role of Tag Edge Routers is to turn untagged packets into tagged packets, and vice versa. The role of TSRs is to forward tagged packets. In the terminology of Chapter 2, Tag Edge Routers are the Edge Label Switching Routers (Edge LSRs) and TSRs are equivalent to LSRs.

4.1.1 Support for Destination-Based Routing

In the IP Switching approach, destination-based routing—the ability to deliver a packet to its IP destination using label switching—is really the only capability provided. In Tag Switching (and in MPLS, as we will see later), it is one function of many. It is, however, the fundamental capability that any approach must provide.

Recall that, in the context of destination-based routing, a Forwarding Equivalence Class (FEC) is associated with an address prefix. Using the information provided by unicast routing protocols (e.g., OSPF, RIP, BGP), a conventional router constructs mappings between FECs (address prefixes) and their corresponding next hops and uses this mapping for the actual packet forwarding.

To support destination-based routing, a TSR, just like an ordinary router, participates in unicast routing protocols and uses the information provided by these protocols to construct its mapping between FECs (expressed as address prefixes) and their corresponding next hops. However, in contrast with an ordinary router, a TSR doesn't use this mapping for the actual packet forwarding—this mapping is used by the Tag Switching control component only for the purpose of constructing its Tag Forwarding Information Base (TFIB); the TFIB is used for the actual packet forwarding.

Once a TSR has constructed a mapping between a particular FEC and its next hop, the TSR is ready to construct an entry in its TFIB. The information needed to construct the entry is provided from three sources:

1. A local binding between the FEC and a tag
2. A mapping between the FEC and the next hop for that FEC (provided by the routing protocol(s) running on the TSR)
3. A remote binding between the FEC and a tag that is received from the next hop

To create a local binding for a particular FEC, the TSR takes a tag from its pool of free tags and updates its TFIB as follows. The TSR uses the tag as an index in its TFIB to determine a particular TFIB entry that has to be updated. Once the entry is determined, the incoming tag in that entry is set to the tag that the TSR took from the pool of free tags, the next hop in the entry is set to the address of the next hop associated with the FEC, and the outgoing interface is set to the interface that should be used to reach the next hop. Note that the local binding procedure relies on the information provided by the routing protocols to determine the next hop and the outgoing interface for a particular FEC (address prefix). Therefore, the existence of the FEC to next hop mapping is a prerequisite for creating a local binding.

Once a TSR creates a local binding, it is ready to distribute the information about this binding to other TSRs. The binding information that a TSR distributes to other TSRs consists of a set of tuples <address prefix, tag>, where *address prefix* identifies a particular FEC and *tag* defines the tag value that the TSR uses for its local binding associated with the FEC.

When a TSR has completed its local binding, the only missing information in the TFIB entry is the outgoing tag. The TSR obtains this information from the tag binding information distributed by other TSRs. When a TSR receives tag binding information from another TSR, the TSR proceeds as follows. First, the TSR checks for the presence of its local binding for the FEC carried as part of the received tag binding information. If the local binding is present, the TSR checks whether the information was received from the TSR that is the next hop for the FEC. If it has, then the TSR locates an entry in its TFIB that contains the binding for that FEC and updates the outgoing tag of that entry with the tag from the received binding information. At this point the TFIB entry is completely populated and could be used for packet forwarding.

If the TSR receives tag binding information from another TSR, but the TSR doesn't have a local binding for the FEC carried as part of the received binding information, the TSR has two options. The first one is to keep this information, in case the TSR is able to use it later (if the local binding is created at some later point). The second option is to discard the binding information. Of course, if the TSR decides to use the second option, the TSR should be able to ask the other TSR to resend the tag binding information, which in turn places certain requirements on the mechanism(s) used to distribute tag binding information. The same two options apply when the TSR receives tag binding information from another TSR and the TSR has a local binding for the FEC carried as part of the received binding information, but the next hop contained in the local binding is different from the TSR from which the information was received.

The specific mechanisms for distributing tag binding information depend on the routing protocol that the TSR uses for constructing its FEC to next hop mapping. If the mapping is constructed via link-state routing protocols (e.g., OSPF), the distribution of tag binding information is provided via a separate protocol, called the Tag Distribution Protocol (TDP). The reason for this is that with link-state protocols, routing information is flooded unmodified among a set of (not necessarily adjacent) routers participating in a protocol, whereas the tag binding information is usually distributed only among adjacent routers. This makes link-state routing protocols not well suited for piggybacking tag binding information. Thus, you might imagine that tag bindings could be piggybacked on a distance vector protocol such as RIP. In fact, even if the routing protocol used is RIP or RIP-II, the

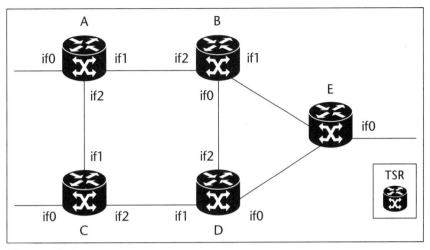

Figure 4.1
Destination-based forwarding with Tag Switching.

distribution of tag binding information is provided via TDP as well. The reason for this is that it would be fairly hard (if not impossible) to modify these protocols in a backward-compatible fashion to allow piggybacking of tag binding information. However, when the mapping is constructed via BGP, the tag binding information could be piggybacked on top of BGP as a separate BGP attribute. This is because BGP distributes information about address prefixes (FECs) and is extensible enough to allow piggybacking in a backward-compatible way.

In order for a TSR to distribute tag binding information, the TSR has to know the set of other TSRs to whom this information must be distributed. The TSR constructs this set by using the information provided by the routing protocol(s) running on the TSR. The TSR includes in this set every TSR with whom the TSR maintains a routing peer relationship. Note that usually this results in a situation where the set includes all the TSRs that share a common subnetwork with at least one of the interfaces of the local TSR. However, as we'll see in the following section, there are some exceptions.

To illustrate how Tag Switching supports destination-based forwarding, consider an example shown in Figure 4.1. Assume that there is a set of destinations (expressed as an address prefix 192.6/16[1]) that are directly connected to TSR E, and further assume that in a steady

---

1. We use the notation *A.B/y* to indicate an address prefix and its length in bits (*y*). Prefixes in an IP version 4 routing table can be of various lengths up to 32 bits.

state (when all the links are operational) both TSR B and TSR D use TSR E as the next hop for the FEC associated with 192.6/16, TSR A uses TSR B as its next hop for this FEC, and TSR C uses TSR D as its next hop for this FEC. Each TSR has three interfaces, labeled if0, if1, and if2. For the purpose of this example, it is irrelevant whether these interfaces correspond to point-to-point or multiaccess (e.g., Ethernet) subnetworks. It also does not matter what routing protocol was used to determine the next hops. In this example we also assume that all the TSRs maintain their TFIBs, as well as their pools of free tags, on a per-TSR (rather than on a per-interface) basis.

First consider how all the TSRs construct their TFIBs. As soon as TSR A determines the next hop (TSR B) for the FEC associated with 192.6/16, TSR A takes a tag from its pool of free tags. Let's assume that the value of this tag is 100. TSR A uses this tag as an index in its TFIB to find an entry that should be updated. Once the entry is found, A sets the incoming tag of this entry to 100, the next hop to B, and the outgoing interface to if1. As soon as B determines the next hop (TSR E) for the FEC associated with 192.6/16, TSR B takes a tag from its pool of free tags. Let's assume that the value of this tag is 6. TSR B uses this tag as an index in its TFIB to find an entry that should be updated. Once the entry is found, A sets the incoming tag of this entry to 6, the next hop to E, and the outgoing interface to if1. TSRs C and D use similar procedures to create their local bindings.

Table 4.1 shows the state of the TFIB entries associated with 192.6/16. Note that each line represents an entry from the TFIB of a different TSR.

Observe that at this point none of the entries have their outgoing tags populated. This is because so far we only covered local bindings,

Table 4.1

Initial TFIB entries.

	Incoming tag	Outgoing tag	Next hop	Outgoing interface
On TSR A	100	?	TSR B	if1
On TSR B	6	?	TSR E	if1
On TSR C	17	?	TSR D	if2
On TSR D	5	?	TSR E	if0
On TSR E	6	?	TSR E	if0

and local binding doesn't provide the information about the outgoing tags.

Now consider what happens once each of these TSRs starts to distribute information about its local binding to other TSRs and how this information is used to populate the outgoing tags. TSR A sends the information about its local binding to B and C. However, when B receives this information, it notices that it didn't come from B's next hop for 192.6/16. So TSR B can't use this information for the purpose of updating the outgoing tag of the TFIB entry associated with 192.6/16. The same applies when C receives this information.

TSR B sends the information about its local binding to A, D, and E. Because neither D nor E uses B as its next hop for 192.6/16, neither of these TSRs can use this information for the purpose of updating the outgoing tag in their TFIB entries for 192.6/16. However, when TSR A receives this information, it notices that this information came from its next hop for 192.6/16. Therefore, TSR A uses this information as a remote binding for 192.6/16 and uses the tag provided by this information (tag 6) to update the outgoing tag in its TFIB entry associated with 192.6/16. At this point A has a fully populated entry in its TFIB.

The local binding information that TSR C sends to A and D is not going to be used by either of them, since neither of them uses C as the next hop for 192.6/ 16.

The local binding information that D sends to B, C, and E is used only by C, since only C uses D as its next hop for 192.6/16. Once TSR C receives this information, it populates the outgoing tag of the TFIB entry associated with 192.6/16 with the tag received as part of this information (tag 5).

The local binding information that TSR E sends to B and D is used by both of these TSRs, as both B and D use E as the next hop for 192.6/ 16. So, as soon as B and D receive this information, they update the outgoing tag in their TFIB entry associated with 192.6/16 with the tag carried as part of this information.

The TFIB entries associated with 192.6/16 at this point are given in Table 4.2.

Note that on TSR E there is still no outgoing tag in the TFIB entry for 192.6/16. Moreover, the next hop in this entry points to itself (TSR E). This is because 192.6/16 is directly connected to E. When E receives a packet that carries tag 6, TSR E acts as an edge TSR and just strips the tag from the packet.

At this point all the TSRs have their entries for 192.6/16 fully populated. Now let's look at the actual packet forwarding. When TSR A receives a packet, and the packet carries tag 100, A uses this tag as an

Table 4.2

TFIB entries after tag distribution.

	Incoming tag	Outgoing tag	Next hop	Outgoing interface
On TSR A	100	6	TSR B	if1
On TSR B	6	6	TSR E	if1
On TSR C	17	5	TSR D	if2
On TSR D	5	6	TSR E	if0
On TSR E	6	?	TSR E	if0

index in its TFIB to locate the entry that A will use for forwarding. Once the entry is found (the incoming tag in the entry is equal to the tag carried in the packet), A replaces (swaps) the tag carried in the packet (tag 100) with the outgoing tag from the found entry (tag 6) and sends it to TSR B over its outgoing interface if1. When TSR B receives this packet, it uses the tag carried in the packet (tag 6) as an index to locate the entry that it will use for forwarding. Once the entry is found (the incoming tag in the entry is equal to the tag carried in the packet), TSR B replaces (swaps) the tag carried in the packet (tag 6) with the outgoing tag from the found entry (tag 6), and sends it to E over its outgoing interface if1. When E receives this packet, it just strips the tag from the packet and delivers it to its destination (which is reachable via if0 on TSR E).

Behavior during Routing Changes

To illustrate how Tag Switching works in the presence of changes in the network topology, let's look at what happens when the link between TSRs D and E goes down. Once D detects that the link is down, it uses the information provided by the unicast routing protocol(s) to change its next hop for 192.6/16 from TSR E to TSR B. As a result, the outgoing tag in TSR D's TFIB entry associated with 192.6/16 is no longer valid. To provide a correct outgoing tag for that entry, D needs to get tag binding information from its new next hop, TSR B. Obtaining this information depends on how B treats tag binding information received from TSRs that are not next hops for the FECs carried as part of this information. If D keeps the tag binding information it received from B, then as soon as D determines its new next hop (TSR

B), it can immediately use this information to populate the outgoing tag. Otherwise, if D doesn't keep this information, it would need to re-request this information from its new next hop, TSR B.

Observe that creation of tag binding is driven by creation of a mapping between a particular FEC and its next hop, which, in turn, is driven by routing updates. Therefore, according to the taxonomy presented in Chapter 2, Tag Switching uses control-driven creation of tag binding. Also observe that whereas the binding between an incoming tag and an FEC is created locally by a TSR (local binding), the binding between an outgoing tag and the FEC is created as a result of receiving the tag binding information (remote binding) from the next hop TSR associated with that FEC. Thus, tag switching uses downstream label binding in our taxonomy. Finally, note that the only prerequisite for a TSR to create its local binding for a particular FEC is the availability of the mapping between this FEC and its next hop; specifically, the TSR doesn't have to wait for the matching remote binding before creating its local binding.

4.1.2 Improving Routing Scalability via a Hierarchy of Routing Knowledge

Recall that one of the design goals of Tag Switching is to improve scaling properties of the routing system. Tag Switching addresses this goal via the notion of a hierarchy of routing knowledge. To help us understand what *hierarchy of routing knowledge* means, we briefly review some aspects of the Internet routing architecture.

The routing architecture used today in the Internet models the Internet as a collection of routing domains, where routing within individual domains is provided by intradomain routing protocols (e.g., OSPF, RIP, EIGRP), whereas routing across multiple domains is provided by interdomain routing protocols (e.g., BGP). One of the advantages of partitioning routing into intra- and interdomain components is the reduction in the volume of routing information that has to be maintained by routers, which is essential to providing scalable routing. However, this partitioning at the level of routing protocols doesn't result in a complete partition of routing information. Specifically, every router within a transit routing domain (a domain that carries traffic that neither originates in the domain nor is destined to a node in the domain) has to maintain in its forwarding tables all the routes provided by the interdomain routing, regardless of whether this is an interior router (a router connected only to the routers within the same routing domain as the router itself) or a border router (a router connected both to routers within the same routing domain and to routers in other routing domains). Maintaining all the routes provided by the interdomain routing at all the routers, including all the interior routers, is necessary in order to forward the transit traffic through the domain.

Note that the interior routers in a transit domain are basically just transferring packets from one border router to another, so it seems somewhat wasteful for them to have to maintain complete routing tables for all routes in the Internet. Tag Switching provides a means by which those routers can store only the routing information they really need—just enough to get packets to the right border router, where full routing information is still maintained. Specifically, the interior routers within a domain would have to maintain routes only to the destinations within the domain, rather than to all the destinations in the Internet. Thus, we can think of this as a further step in the hierarchical partitioning of intra- and interdomain routing.

Avoiding the need for the interior routers to maintain interdomain routing information results in faster routing convergence. One reason for this is that when an interdomain route changes, by using the hierarchy of routing knowledge, only the border routers, but not the internal routers, have to be updated with the change. In contrast, without the hierarchy of routing knowledge, all the routers, both the border and interior, have to be updated with the change. And the more routers that need to be updated, the longer it takes for the system to converge.

Another reason why avoiding the need for interior routers to maintain interdomain routing information results in faster routing convergence is that when an interior router restarts, with the hierarchy of routing knowledge the router needs to establish only routes to other routers within its domain, but doesn't need to establish any of the interdomain routes. In contrast, without the hierarchy of routing knowledge, when an interior router restarts, the router has to establish both intra- and interdomain routes. And the more routes the router has to establish, the longer it will take for the system to converge.

Avoiding the need for the interior routers to maintain interdomain routing information also provides better fault isolation, as interior routers would be totally immune to any problems in the interdomain routing. Faster convergence, and better fault isolation, would result in improved scalability of the routing system.

Construction of TFIBs to support a hierarchy of routing knowledge is based on the procedures used to support the destination-based forwarding with Tag Switching. All the TSRs within a routing domain participate in a common intradomain routing protocol and employ procedures described in Section 4.1.1 to construct entries in their TFIBs for the FECs associated with the destinations within the domain. These entries are sufficient to provide Tag Switching from any TSR within the domain to any destination within the domain, including all the border TSRs of that domain. Because an ingress border router can determine the egress border router to which it wants to send a packet, a packet can be Tag Switched all the way to the egress of the domain by interior TSRs that know only interior routes.

To enable the border TSRs to perform Tag Switching as well, all the border TSRs within a domain and the directly connected border TSRs in different domains may also create and exchange tag binding information for every route (and FEC associated with that route) received via interdomain routing (BGP). Again, the creation and exchange of this tag binding information follows the procedures described in Section 4.1.1, except that the notion of the "next hop" TSR is generalized to include the next border TSR. Specifically, when a border TSR, TSR A, receives tag binding information from another border TSR, TSR B, and TSR A has the local binding for the FEC carried as part of the tag binding information received from TSR B, TSR A checks whether B is the next border TSR for the FEC (the information needed to perform this check is provided by BGP). If that is the case, then TSR A locates an entry in its TFIB that contains the binding for that FEC and updates the outgoing tag of that entry with the tag carried as part of the received binding information.

As a result of the procedures described above, the TFIB of a border TSR contains entries for FECs corresponding to both inter- and intradomain routes, whereas the TFIB of an interior TSR contains entries for FECs corresponding to only the intradomain routes.

To support forwarding in the presence of a hierarchy of routing knowledge, Tag Switching allows a packet to carry not one, but several tags organized as a tag stack. When a packet is forwarded from one routing domain to another, the tag stack carried by the packet contains just one tag. However, when a packet is forwarded through a transit routing domain, the tag stack contains not one, but two tags. For the purpose of finding a TFIB entry that should be used for forwarding, a TSR always uses the tag at the top of the stack. When a packet carries a stack of tags, a TSR, in addition to swapping the tag at the top of the stack, could also push or pop a tag onto/off of the stack. Pushing tags onto and popping tags off of the stack occur at the domain boundaries. At the ingress a tag is pushed onto the tag stack, and at the egress a tag is popped off of the stack.

To illustrate how Tag Switching supports a hierarchy of routing knowledge, consider the example shown in Figure 4.2. Routing domain A consists of two border TSRs, TSR T and TSR W, and two interior TSRs, TSR X and TSR Y. There is a set of destinations (an address prefix) in routing domain C that is reachable through the border TSR of that domain (TSR Z). TSR Z distributes the routing information about these destinations to TSR W, which in turn distributes it to TSR T, which in turn distributes it to TSR V.

Because all the TSRs within A participate in A's intradomain routing, they all have routes to each other. That means that TSR T, TSR X, and TSR Y all have a route to TSR W. Each of these TSRs creates a local binding for that route and distributes information about this binding to other TSRs. Using a combination of local and remote bindings, TSR T, TSR X, and TSR Y construct a TFIB entry associated with TSR W, as shown in Table 4.3.

Note that the next hop in TSR W's TFIB entry points to itself (TSR W). This is used to indicate to TSR W that when it receives a packet with the tag that matches this entry (tag 17), it has to pop off the top tag of the stack carried by the packet. TSR W then performs another

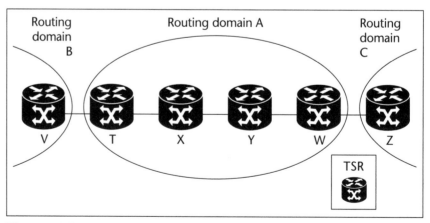

Figure 4.2
Tag Switching with a hierarchy of routing knowledge.

Table 4.3

TFIB entries in routing domain A.

	Incoming tag	Outgoing tag	Next hop
On TSR T	N/A	10	TSR X
On TSR X	10	12	TSR Y
On TSR Y	12	17	TSR W
On TSR W	17	N/A	TSR W

lookup in its TFIB using the tag at the top of the stack (after the stack has been popped) and uses the entry determined by this lookup for the actual packet forwarding.

So far we have described how TSRs within routing domain A populate their TFIBs with entries associated with the intradomain routes (and more specifically with routes to TSR W). Now let's look at how border TSRs (TSR T, TSR W, TSR V, and TSR Z) populate their TFIBs with entries associated with interdomain routes.

Assume that TSR Z creates a local binding for the FEC associated with the set of destinations in C, with 6 as the local tag. Following the procedures described in Section 4.1.1, TSR Z distributes this binding information to TSR W. Further, assume that TSR W creates a local binding for the same FEC with 2 as the local tag. Following the procedures described in Section 4.1.1, TSR W distributes this binding information to TSR T. When TSR W receives tag binding information from its next hop border TSR (TSR Z), TSR W uses the tag carried in this binding (6) as the outgoing tag. Finally, assume that TSR T creates a local binding between the FEC with 5 as the local tag. Following the procedures described in Section 4.1.1, TSR T distributes this binding information to TSR V. When TSR T receives tag binding information from its next hop border TSR (TSR W), TSR T uses the tag carried in this binding (2) as the outgoing tag.

When TSR T receives a tag binding from its next hop border router TSR W, TSR T notices that the next hop associated with the binding (TSR W) is not directly connected to TSR T. Therefore, TSR T looks in its TFIB for the entry that corresponds to the address of the next hop (TSR W). The outgoing tag from the found entry (tag 10) is the tag that TSR T has to push onto the tag stack of a packet whose tag is 5.

Now let's consider packet forwarding and assume that TSR T receives from TSR V a packet with tag 5. TSR T finds that the outgoing tag in its TFIB entry with incoming tag 5 is 2. So TSR T replaces (swaps) the tag carried in the packet with tag 2. In addition, TSR T pushes tag 10 onto the tag stack carried by the packet and then sends the packet to the next hop (TSR X). When TSR X receives the packet, it finds in its TFIB an entry with incoming tag 10. The outgoing tag in the found entry is 12, and the next hop is TSR Y. So TSR X replaces the tag carried in the packet with 12 and sends the packet to the next hop (TSR Y). When TSR Y receives the packet, it replaces the tag carried in the packet with 17 and sends it to TSR W. Finally, when TSR W receives the packet, it finds that the entry in its TFIB whose incoming tag is 17 indicates that the TSR has to pop the label stack. After TSR W pops the stack, the tag at the top of the stack (label 2) will be the tag that was placed there by TSR T. TSR W uses this tag as an index in its TFIB to find an entry whose incoming tag is equal to the tag in the packet. Using the information from the found entry, TSR W replaces the tag carried in the packet with tag 6 and sends the packet to TSR Z.

To summarize, the use of a hierarchy of routing knowledge allows complete isolation of the interior routers within a routing domain from interdomain routing, thus improving the stability, convergence, and scalability of routing.

4.1.3 Multicast

Fundamental to multicast routing is the notion of a *multicast distribution tree*. Such a tree is constructed by multicast routing protocols (e.g., DVMRP, PIM, CBT, MOSPF) and is used by the forwarding component of network layer routing to forward multicast packets. In this section we describe how Tag Switching supports multicast when the multicast distribution trees are constructed by Protocol Independent Multicast (PIM).

To support multicast with Tag Switching, a TSR should be able to select a particular multicast distribution tree based solely on (a) the tag carried in a packet and (b) the interface on which the packet was received. As we mentioned in Chapter 2, this requires a TSR to maintain its TFIB on a per-interface basis and also imposes the following two requirements on the Tag Switching control component:

■ No two TSRs connected to a common subnetwork may bind the same tag on that subnetwork to different multicast distribution trees.

■ TSRs that are connected to a common subnetwork, and are part of a common multicast distribution tree, have to agree among themselves on a common tag that will be used by all these TSRs when sending and receiving packets associated with that tree on the interfaces connected to that subnetwork.

Let's look at how Tag Switching addresses these two requirements.

Note that the first requirement is always satisfied when TSRs are connected on a point-to-point subnetwork. To satisfy the first requirement when TSRs are connected on a multiaccess subnetwork (e.g., Ethernet), Tag Switching defines procedures by which such TSRs partition the set of tags that they use for multicast into disjoint subsets, with each TSR getting its own subset. Each TSR advertises via PIM HELLO messages a range of tags that the TSR wants to use for its local bindings. When a TSR connected to a multiaccess subnetwork boots up, it checks that the range it wants to use is disjoint from the ranges used by other TSRs connected to the same subnetwork by listening to the PIM HELLO message received on its interface connected to the subnetwork. If a TSR receives from some other TSR a PIM HELLO message with a range of tags that overlaps with the range of tags it is advertising in its PIM HELLO messages, one of these TSRs has to get another range of tags. Maintaining TFIBs for multicast on a per-interface (rather than on a per-TSR) basis allows a TSR to perform the above procedures on a per-interface basis. The range of tags that the TSR gets (and uses) on one of its interfaces is completely independent from the range of tags the TSR gets on another interface(s).

To meet the second requirement, Tag Switching defines procedures by which TSRs that are connected to a common subnetwork and are part of a common multicast distribution tree elect among themselves one particular TSR that will be responsible for creating a local binding for the FEC associated with that tree, and defines procedures for distributing this binding information among these TSRs.

To join a particular multicast distribution tree, a TSR, just like a conventional router, needs to send a PIM JOIN message toward the root of that tree. To create a local binding for that tree, the TSR takes a tag from the pool of tags associated with the interface over which the message should be sent and creates an entry in its TFIB with the incoming tag set to the tag taken from the pool of tags. The TSR then includes this tag in the PIM JOIN message and sends the message toward the root of the tree. When a TSR that is a part of a particular multicast distribution tree receives a PIM JOIN message from a downstream (with respect to the root of the tree) TSR, the TSR updates the entry in its TFIB that corresponds to the tree with the tag carried by the message and the interface on which the message was received. Specifically, the TSR uses the tag to populate the outgoing tag in the entry and the interface to populate the outgoing interface in the entry.

The procedure we described in the previous paragraph is sufficient to meet the second requirement when TSRs are connected on a point-to-point subnetwork. Now let's look at how this works when TSRs are connected on a multiaccess subnetwork. Observe that on multiaccess subnetworks PIM JOIN messages are multicasted. Thus, all the TSRs connected to a multiaccess subnetwork receive all the PIM JOIN messages transmitted by any of these TSRs over the interfaces connected to the subnetwork. The first TSR on that subnetwork that decides to join a particular multicast distribution tree is the TSR that creates the binding between a tag and the tree. All other TSRs on the subnetwork receive information about this binding from the PIM JOIN message that the TSR sends toward the root of the tree, as the TSR periodically sends this message, and this message is multicasted to all the TSRs connected to the subnetwork. Thus, any TSR connected to the subnetwork that decides later on to join the multicast distribution tree would know the tag that is bound to the tree on that subnetwork. As that TSR joins the tree, it uses the tag from the received PIM JOIN message as an incoming tag for its TFIB entry associated with the tree. If a TSR connected to a particular subnetwork wants to determine whether a binding for a particular multicast tree among other TSRs connected to that subnetwork already exists, the TSR sends the PIM JOIN message with 0 as the tag. When some other TSR (connected to the same subnetwork) receives this message, and that other TSR already has the binding, that other TSR sends a PIM JOIN message that includes the tag associated with the binding. Because TSRs maintain their TFIBs used for multicast on a per-interface (rather than on a per-TSR) basis, a TSR can apply the procedure described above on a per-interface basis, without requiring coordination among the procedures the TSR applies on each of its interfaces.

To illustrate how Tag Switching supports multicast, consider an example shown in Figure 4.3, where TSR D, TSR E, and TSR F are connected on a multiaccess subnetwork (e.g., Ethernet), while all other connections are on point-to-point subnetworks.

Let's assume that there is a multicast tree rooted at TSR A and that this tree initially includes just TSR A and TSR D. When TSR B wants to join the tree, it has to send a PIM JOIN message toward TSR A, which means that B has to send this message on its interface if0. Before

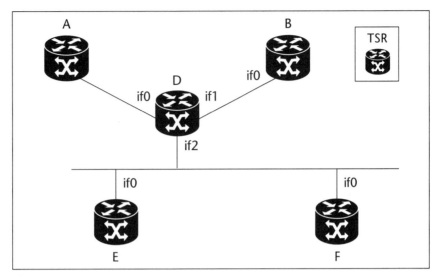

Figure 4.3
Multicast with Tag Switching.

sending this message, B takes a tag from the pool of free tags associated with its interface if0 and creates in its TFIB an entry with this tag as an incoming tag. TSR B then sends the PIM JOIN message that includes this tag to TSR D. When D receives this message, it finds in its TFIB an entry that corresponds to the tree, and then it adds the tag that was received in the message as an outgoing tag for the entry and adds the interface on which the message was received (interface if1) as an outgoing interface. This covers the case where connection from a TSR toward the root of a multicast distribution tree is via a point-to-point subnetwork. Next we'll look at the case where the connection is via a multiaccess subnetwork.

Consider what would happen when TSR E decides to join the tree. To join the tree, E has to send a PIM JOIN message toward TSR A, which means that E has to send this message on its interface if0 to D. Before sending this message, E takes a tag from the pool of free tags associated with the interface on which the message has to be sent (interface if0) and creates in its TFIB an entry with this tag as an incoming tag. TSR E then sends a PIM JOIN message that includes this tag. Note that because this message is multicast, it will be received by all the TSRs connected to the subnetwork, which means that it will be received by TSRs D, E, and F. When TSR D receives this message, it finds in its TFIB an entry that corresponds to the tree, and then it adds the tag that was received in the message as an outgoing tag for the entry and adds the interface on which the message was received (interface if2) as an outgoing interface. Note that at this point the entry in D has two outgoing interfaces (if1 and if2) and, corresponding to them, two outgoing tags.

Now assume that TSR F wants to join the same multicast distribution tree. Note that at the time F decides to join the tree, it should already have the tag that is bound to the tree, as this tag was carried in the PIM JOIN messages that were sent (multicast) by TSR D. So, at this point F finds an entry in its TFIB that corresponds to the tag and sets the incoming tag in the entry to that tag.

For dense-mode multicast groups, PIM doesn't require routers to send JOIN messages. To support dense-mode multicast groups with Tag Switching, the PIM dense-mode procedures are modified to require that a TSR send PIM JOIN messages for dense-mode groups as soon as the TSR creates a multicast route for such a group. This modification allows use of a common mechanism for distributing tag binding information that works both for sparse and for dense groups.

You could argue that supporting multicast with Tag Switching by piggybacking tag binding information on top of PIM prevents the use of Tag Switching in the environments where multicast routing is provided by other protocols (e.g., MOSPF, DVMRP). Although it is certainly true that in the area of multicast the primary focus of Tag Switching is Tag Switching with PIM, Tag Switching also provides a way to distribute tag binding information associated with multicast routes via the Tag Distribution Protocol (TDP). This way, Tag Switching can support multicast with multicast routing protocols other than PIM.

Observe that the creation of tag binding is driven by PIM messages. Therefore, according to the taxonomy presented in Chapter 2, Tag Switching uses control-driven creation of tag binding for multicast. The binding between an outgoing tag and a particular multicast distribution tree is created as a result of receiving tag binding information from a downstream TSR; that is, the downstream mode of binding distribution is used. Finally, observe that to distribute multicast tag binding information Tag Switching piggybacks this information on top of PIM and does not require a separate protocol for distributing this information.

4.1.4 RSVP with Tag Switching

In this section we provide a brief overview of how RSVP—the Resource Reservation Protocol—is supported by Tag Switching. We assume here some basic familiarity with the operation of RSVP. Further details on RSVP and its role in supporting IP quality of service (QoS) appear in Section 6.1.

Tag Switching provides support for RSVP by defining a new RSVP Object—the Tag Object. The Tag Object contains tag binding information for an RSVP flow and is carried in the RSVP RESV message.

Supporting RSVP with Tag Switching doesn't impact handling of RSVP PATH messages; these messages are handled in precisely the same way as they are without Tag Switching. The place where Tag Switching imposes additional procedures is the handling of RSVP RESV messages.

In the case of supporting RSVP unicast flows with Tag Switching, when a TSR wants to send a RESV message for a new RSVP flow, the TSR allocates a tag from its pool of free tags, creates an entry in its TFIB with the incoming tag set to the allocated tag, places the tag in the Tag Object, and then sends out the RESV message with this object. The newly created TFIB entry, in addition to tag information, contains information about local resources (e.g., queues) that packets whose tag matches the incoming tag of the entry will use. The information about the local resources to be used is derived from the resource reservation information carried in RSVP. The TSR populates the outgoing tag component as it receives the RESV message from its next hop TSR. Once an RSVP flow is established, the reservation state needs to be refreshed. In this case, a TSR sends RESV messages associated with the flow and includes in them the same tag that the TSR bound to the flow when it first created the RSVP state for the flow.

Observe that the creation of tag binding is driven by RSVP messages; binding is thus control-driven. Because the binding between an outgoing tag and a particular RSVP flow is created as a result of receiving tag binding information (remote binding) from a downstream TSR, the label distribution is once again downstream. Finally, we note that Tag Switching piggybacks the label binding information on top of RSVP and does not require a separate protocol for distributing this information.

4.1.5 Explicit Routes

The ability to support forwarding paradigms other than destination-based forwarding is one of the important design goals of Tag Switching. In this section we outline how Tag Switching can support *explicit* routes, by which we mean routes that are explicitly chosen to be other than the normal route chosen by the routing protocols. Such a route may, for example, be chosen to manage the load on a particular link (see Section 1.1.4 for an example).

Tag Switching provides support for explicit routes by using the Resource Reservation Protocol (RSVP) and defining a new RSVP Object—the Explicit Route Object. The Explicit Route Object is used to specify a particular explicit route. This object is carried in the RSVP PATH message. The tag binding information for the route is carried in the Tag Object by the RSVP RESV message, as described in the previous section.

The Explicit Route Object itself is composed of a sequence of variable-length subobjects, where each subobject identifies a single hop within an explicit route. Each subobject contains a strict/loose indicator, followed by the type, length, and value fields. The type field allows individual hops to be expressed as either an IPv4 address prefix, an IPv6 address prefix, or an Autonomous System number. Expressing individual hops as IPv4 (or IPv6) addresses is accomplished by specifying the appropriate prefix length (32 for IPv4 addresses, 128 for IPv6 addresses). When an individual hop is expressed as an IP (either IPv4 or IPv6) address prefix, this hop includes any TSR that has an IP address that matches the prefix. When an individual hop is expressed as an autonomous system number, this hop includes any TSR that belongs to the autonomous system identified by that autonomous system number.

The ability to express individual hops not just in terms of individual TSRs within a network topology, but in terms of a group of TSRs, provides the routing system with a significant amount of flexibility, as a TSR that computes (establishes) an explicit route need not have detailed information about the route (e.g., all the TSRs along the route). For example, a TSR can establish an explicit route expressed in terms of autonomous systems (by using autonomous system numbers as subobjects), without knowing detailed network topology within each of these autonomous systems.

The Explicit Route Object allows TSRs in the middle of an explicit route carried in the object to modify the explicit route by inserting a sequence of one or more subobjects in the Explicit Route Object. This features adds to the flexibility that is provided by explicit routes by allowing TSRs in the middle of an explicit route to compensate for the lack of detailed information at the TSR that originated the explicit route.

One of the main motivations for using RSVP to support explicit routes is the assumption that quite often explicit routes will be used in conjunction with reserving resources along such routes. This assumption is based on the expected use of explicit routes in such applications as providing forwarding in support of QoS-based routing. In such cases use of RSVP for supporting explicit routes allows both the establishment of an explicit route and the allocation of resources for the traffic that will be forwarded along the route. This is accomplished just using RSVP, rather than having one protocol for establishing explicit routes and another for making resource reservations along such routes. Note that the use of RSVP for supporting explicit routes doesn't mean that these routes always have to have reserved resources. To the contrary, this mechanism could be used as well to support explicit routes for best-effort traffic (traffic that doesn't require any resource reservations).

Use of RSVP for supporting explicit routes with Tag Switching means that RSVP is originated by a router rather than a host. There is nothing in RSVP that precludes this.

The set of packets that could be forwarded along a particular explicit route is determined solely by the TSR that establishes the route. In other words, the rules for determining the set of packets that would map into a Forwarding Equivalence Class associated with that explicit route are purely local to the TSR that establishes the route. For example, these rules may include such criteria as the interface on the TSR that the packets arrive on or the time of day. Explicit routes provide such flexibility because rules for determining mapping between packets and FECs are purely local to a TSR that establishes an explicit route and require no coordination among TSRs. Different TSRs could establish explicit routes without any coordination of the rules each of them uses for determining the mapping. Because the rules by which a TSR that establishes an explicit route maps packets into FECs are purely local to the TSR, there is no need to standardize them.

The creation of label bindings in support of explicit routes with RSVP is much the same as in the pure RSVP case. Similarly, all of the observations about how Tag Switching with RSVP fits into the taxonomy described in Chapter 2 apply in the case of explicit routes as well.

4.2 Tag Switching over ATM

In this section we describe how Tag Switching operates on ATM switches. We refer to such switches as ATM-TSRs. Because ATM and Tag Switching use precisely the same forwarding paradigm, label swapping, Tag Switching can use ATM forwarding (ATM User Plane) pretty much "as is." This means that Tag Switching can run on unmodified ATM switch hardware. Although it preserves the ATM User Plane, Tag Switching replaces the ATM Control Plane with the Tag Switching control component. Supporting Tag Switching on an ATM switch means that operations of the switch are controlled by the Tag Switching control component rather than by the protocols defined by either the ITU or ATM Forum. Thus, an ATM-TSR controls its operations by running protocols such as OSPF, BGP, PIM, and RSVP, rather than protocols such as UNI and PNNI.

When Tag Switching is used with ATM switches, the forwarding performance of such a device is determined by the capabilities of the ATM switches, whereas its functionality is comparable to a router. This is because, from the forwarding point of view, it is totally irrelevant whether the ATM forwarding table is constructed using the Tag Switching control component or using UNI, PNNI, and so forth. And from the functionality point of view, the functionality is determined largely by the control component, rather than by specifics of how such a device forwards data.

We begin the discussion by describing how tag information can be carried when Tag Switching operates over ATM switches. Then we describe modifications to the procedures used by non–ATM-TSRs in order to support Tag Switching on ATM-TSRs.

4.2.1 Carrying Tag Information

When Tag Switches are built out of ATM-TSRs, tag information is carried in the ATM header. If the tag stack has just one level of tags, then the tag is carried in the VCI field of the header. Because the size of the VCI field is 16 bits, that allows up to 2^{16} tags. Because the forwarding tables of ATM switches are usually organized on a per-interface basis, when tags are carried in the VCI field the total number of tags on an ATM-TSR can be more than 2^{16}. If the tag stack has two levels of tags (as described in Section 4.1.2), then the first level is carried in the VCI field, and the second level can be carried in the VPI field of the header. Note that because the size of the VPI field is 12 bits, a limit is imposed of 4096 tags (2^{12}) that can be carried in the VPI field per interface.

A predefined VPI/VCI is reserved for exchanging tag binding information. Use of a predefined VPI/VCI is necessary to bootstrap the system.

4.2.2 Destination-Based Forwarding

Supporting destination-based forwarding on an ATM-TSR involves some modifications to the procedures Tag Switching uses to support destination-based forwarding on a non–ATM-TSR. In this section we highlight these modifications.

The most important modification is that remote binding is always acquired *on demand*. Acquiring remote binding on demand means two things. First, an ATM-TSR doesn't advertise its local binding to another TSR until that other TSR sends a request for this binding. Second, in order to receive information about the remote binding from some other TSR, the TSR has to explicitly send a request to that other TSR. Acquiring remote binding on demand allows conservation of the use of tags, which may be important because ATM switches normally have some hardware limitations on the number of tags they can support. On-demand binding also deals with the problem of cell interleave, which we will now examine.

To understand the problem of cell interleave, consider an example shown in Figure 4.4(a), and assume that the TFIB associated with both if0 and if1 on ATM-TSR X contains the following entry:

Incoming tag	Outgoing tag	Outgoing interface
7	3	if2

Now consider what would happen when both TSR A and TSR B each send a packet with tag 7. First, these packets are broken into ATM cells by the ATM interfaces on TSR A and TSR B. Then each of these TSRs transmits these cells to ATM-TSR X. Let's assume that the first cell that is received by ATM-TSR X is the cell that was sent by B. X performs normal ATM forwarding procedures, replaces VCI 7 with VCI 3, and sends the cell on interface if2 to the next hop. Assume that the next cell that is received by X is the cell that was sent by TSR A. As it did with the previous cell, X replaces VCI 7 with VCI 3 and sends the cell on interface if2 to the next hop. Now assume that the next cell received by ATM-TSR X is again the cell that was sent by TSR A. X replaces VCI 7 with VCI 3 and sends the cell to the next hop.

Observe that cells that ATM-TSR X sends on its interface if2 form an intermix in the sense that two consecutive cells sent on this

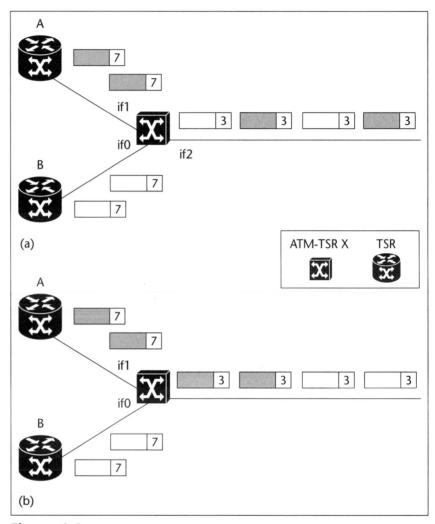

Figure 4.4

Cell interleave example. Frames from different destinations are interleaved by conventional switch (a); VC-merge delays cells of one frame to prevent interleaving with another (b).

interface may belong to different packets. As a result, the next hop (not shown in the figure) wouldn't be able to correctly reassemble these cells into packets. This is the problem of cell interleave: the procedures described above result in a cell stream in which cells from different packets are interleaved.

One way to eliminate cell interleave is to require an ATM-TSR not to intersperse cells from different packets when forwarding these cells. That, in turn, requires the ATM-TSR to buffer cells that are part of a single packet until the last cell of that packet is received. Once the last cell is received, the ATM-TSR sends all the cells that are part of the packet. Moreover, the ATM-TSR sends all these cells without interspersing them with cells from other packets. This approach is known as *VC-merge*.

Using the example shown in Figure 4.4(b), when ATM-TSR X receives a cell with VCI 7 on its interface if0, X checks whether this cell carried the end-of-packet indicator and, if not, places the cell into a buffer associated with the interface if0. Likewise, when X receives a cell with VCI 7 on its interface if1, X checks whether the cell carries the end-of-packet indicator and, if not, places the cell into a buffer associated with the interface if1. As soon as X receives a cell with VCI 7 on an interface if0, and the cell carries the end-of-packet indicator, X sends out all the cells stored in the buffer associated with if0 and then transmits the cell with the end-of-packet indicator as well. X sends these cells without interspersing them with other cells on the same VC.

Using the VC-merge approach requires an ATM-TSR to be able to detect cells with the end-of-packet indicator and to buffer cells based on the packet boundaries. Although neither of these requirements is part of the ATM standards, from a practical point of view both of these requirements are either already supported or likely to be supported by ATM switches. In fact, the first requirement (the ability to detect cells with the end-of-packet indicator) is necessary to perform such algorithms as Early Packet Discard (EPD) and Partial Packet Discard (PPD), and both of these algorithms are necessary to improve handling of frame-based traffic in the presence of congestion within an ATM network.

Note that VC-merge is used in Tag Switching just to support destination-based routing; it isn't used for traffic that requires resource reservations. Therefore, the impact of buffering (the result of VC-merge) on such factors as jitter is not important.

Another way to eliminate cell interleave is to maintain more than one tag associated with a particular route. To understand how that would help to solve the cell interleave problem, observe that one of the necessary conditions for cell interleave is for ATM cells that belong to different packets to have the same VCI field. If cells from different packets had different VCIs, there would be no confusion when these cells needed to be reassembled into packets. In fact, it isn't even necessary for each packet to have its own VCI—all the packets that are forwarded along the same route by a particular TSR at the edge of a network composed just of ATM-TSRs could use the same VCI. This observation suggests the following procedure for creating and distributing tag binding information in support of destination-based forwarding on ATM-TSRs.

When a TSR at the edge of a network composed just of ATM-TSRs creates a local binding, and the next hop of the route associated with the binding is an ATM-TSR, the TSR sends a message (using the Tag Distribution Protocol) to the ATM-TSR, requesting that this ATM-TSR create a binding for the route and return binding information to the TSR. When an ATM-TSR receives the request, the ATM-TSR creates a local binding and returns this binding to the requestor. In addition, the ATM-TSR sends a message (using the Tag Distribution Protocol) to the next hop associated with the route, requesting that this next hop create a binding for the route.

One of the advantages of using multiple tags per route is that it doesn't require any modifications to ATM hardware, and therefore can be used with any ATM switch. With respect to the number of VCs required, this approach scales similarly to the IP over ATM approach described in Section 1.1.3 (which will generally produce a complete mesh of VCs). However, with respect to the amount of routing peering required, this approach scales much better than the IP over ATM approach, as routing peering with Tag Switching is constrained by the physical connectivity. Clearly, with respect to the number of VCs required, this approach scales less well than the approach based on VC-merge.

4.3 Tag Encapsulation on Non-ATM Links

With some link layer technologies (e.g., ATM), the link layer header has adequate semantics to carry tag information. For such technologies, carrying tag information in the link layer header has an advantage of allowing the reuse of existing forwarding functionality (e.g., the ability to use ATM switch hardware). However, there are other link layer technologies (e.g., point-to-point links, Ethernet, FDDI, Token Ring, etc.) whose link layer headers don't have semantics adequate to carry tag information. When Tag Switching is used over subnetworks built out of such technologies, tag information is carried in a small "shim" inserted between the link layer and the network layer headers.

On point-to-point subnetworks, packets that carry tags are identified by the PPP protocol field, with one value used to identify unicast and another to identify multicast. On multiaccess subnetworks, such packets are identified by the ethertype. Like point-to-point subnetworks, multiaccess subnetworks use one ethertype to identify unicast and another to identify multicast.

To support the notion of a tag stack as discussed in Section 4.1.2, the shim layer used by Tag Switching consists of a sequence of tag stack entries, where the top of the tag stack appears in a packet right after the link layer header, and the bottom of the tag stack appears in the packet right before the network layer header. Packet forwarding is determined by the entry at the top of the stack. Each tag stack entry is encoded as shown in Figure 4.5.

The S field is used to indicate an entry that is at the bottom of the tag stack—this entry has the S field set to 1. All other entries have this field set to 0.

The Time-to-Live (TTL) field is similar to the Time-to-Live field carried in the IP header. Note that a TSR processes only the TTL field of the top entry.

The Class of Service (CoS) field is intended to influence the queuing decision by TSRs. When an edge TSR tags a previously untagged packet, the value of the CoS field is determined by the policies local to the edge TSR. When a TSR pushes an additional entry onto the tag stack, the TSR sets the value of the CoS field in the newly pushed entry either to the CoS field from the entry that was at the top of the stack prior to the push or to a value determined by the policies local to the TSR. The CoS field can be used in a way similar to the way the IP Precedence field is used (e.g., to differentiate between different classes of users).

Tag (20 bits)	CoS (3 bits)	S (1 bit)	TTL (8 bits)

Figure 4.5
Tag stack entry format.

The tag field contains the value that a TSR uses as an index in its TFIB. Note that the size of this field (20 bits) allows for up to 1,048,576 tags. Because unicast packets are distinguished from multicast packets by either PPP protocol field (on point-to-point subnetworks) or by ethertype (on multiaccess subnetworks), this allows for up to 1,048,576 tags for multicast and 1,048,576 tags for unicast. In principle, the tag space could be increased by assigning additional PPP protocol fields or ethertypes. In practice, the number of usable tags is more likely to be limited by factors other than the tag space, such as the number of routes that can be supported.

Because inserting the shim layer in a packet increases the length of the packet, and because performing IP fragmentation is undesirable, especially along a Tag Switched path, Tag Switching uses the IP Path MTU Discovery procedures to ensure that even after the shim layer is added to the packet, the resulting packet size doesn't exceed the maximum packet size that could be transmitted without fragmentation.

Use of the shim layer allows TSRs to communicate over LANs that include existing link layer bridges without imposing any additional requirements on such bridges.

4.4 Handling Tag Faults

When a TSR receives a packet with a tag, but either (a) there is no entry in the TFIB maintained by the TSR with the incoming tag equal to the tag carried in the packet or (b) there is such an entry, but the entry doesn't indicate local delivery and the outgoing tag component of the entry is empty, we call this condition a *tag fault*. In this section we describe how Tag Switching handles this problem.

When a TSR encounters a tag fault caused by a packet, one possible option for the TSR is to strip the tag information from the packet and try to forward the packet based on the information carried in the network layer header of the packet. However, this option may not always be feasible. For example, when a packet carries a stack of tags, the TSR may not have sufficient routing information to forward the packet (e.g., TSR X in Figure 4.2 has routing information only about destinations within its own routing domain and thus doesn't know how to forward a packet destined to a host in some other routing domain). When the TSR is an ATM-TSR, requiring the TSR to forward the packet based on the network layer header would require the ATM-TSR to reassemble ATM cells that form the packet into a packet and then process the network layer header of the packet. Clearly, this may be a rather unreasonable requirement.

Because handling tag faults by stripping tag information and forwarding the packet based on the information carried in the network layer header is not always feasible, Tag Switching makes this optional for a TSR. If a TSR can't support this option, then the TSR, when it encounters a tag fault, discards the packet that caused the tag fault. Note that this behavior (discarding a packet) is very similar to the behavior of a conventional router when it receives a packet but doesn't have the routing information needed to forward the packet (which could happen, for example, during routing transients).

4.5 Handling Forwarding Loops during Routing Transients

As we discussed in Section 4.2, because routing protocols used by the control component may produce temporary (transient) forwarding loops, we need mechanism(s) to contain the adverse effects of these loops. In this section we describe the mechanisms used by Tag Switching.

For the cases where tag information is carried in a packet in a shim, Tag Switching uses the time-to-live as the loop mitigation mechanism. The shim header contains the TTL field; each TSR that forwards a packet decrements this field; if a TSR receives a packet with TTL in the shim equal to 0, the TSR discards the packet. The effectiveness of this mechanism is comparable to the TTL-based loop mitigation used in IP. Moreover, use of a common mechanism by both IP and Tag Switching makes coexistence and interoperation between loop mitigation mechanisms used by Tag Switching and IP a nonissue.

For the cases where tag information is carried as part of the link layer header (e.g., ATM, Frame Relay), use of time-to-live–based loop mitigation is not a viable option because there is no TTL field in the ATM or Frame Relay header. For these cases, Tag Switching uses a two-pronged approach. First, all the traffic exchanged by the Tag Switching control component (e.g., routing traffic, Tag Distribution Protocol) is segregated from the rest of the traffic by using a separate tag (e.g., separate VPI/VCI for the case of ATM) and allocating resources (e.g., buffers, link bandwidth) for that tag. This prevents the detrimental effects of transient forwarding loops on control traffic (which includes routing traffic as well). This, in turn, guarantees that such transient

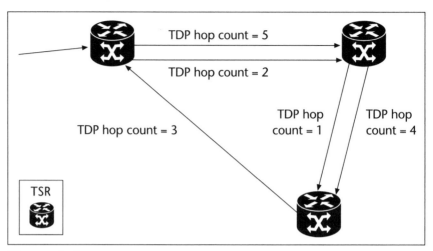

Figure 4.6
Use of hop count in TDP for loop avoidance.

forwarding loops do not affect routing convergence. Furthermore, many ATM-TSRs employ per-VC buffering and queuing. This isolates traffic that follows different routes by constraining the amount of resources that could be consumed by traffic that follows a particular route. As a result, if a route forms a (transient) forwarding loop, the amount of resources that could be consumed by packets forwarded by using this route would be constrained, which, in turn, constrains the negative impact of forwarding loops on traffic that has to be forwarded along nonlooping paths.

The second mechanism to avoid loops when ATM-TSRs are involved uses a hop count in the TDP requests and responses. Because the on-demand binding method forces requests to propagate from the point of a topology change toward the egress of the ATM-TSR cloud, transient loops can be detected and broken (as shown in Figure 4.6). The hop count works like a TTL, but it is carried in the TDP messages. When it reaches 0, the request for label bindings fails, and the spiral path shown here is torn down. When routing stabilizes, a new binding request will be issued and a nonlooping path will be established.

It is important to realize that, in the absence of misconfiguration, loops are a transient phenomenon. They are also a fact of life with IP routing protocols, like IS-IS, OSPF, RIP, and BGP. Tag Switching accepts that they happen and tries to ensure that the consequences are not too severe, just as conventional IP does.

4.6 Tag Distribution Protocol (TDP)

For reasons mentioned in Section 2.3.5, Tag Switching views piggy-backing tag binding information on top of routing protocols as the preferred way of distributing tag binding information. However, because this option may not always be viable, Tag Switching provides its own mechanism to distribute tag binding information: the Tag Distribution Protocol (TDP). In this section we present a short overview of TDP.

A TSR that exchanges routing information with some other TSR also maintains a TDP session with that other TSR in order to exchange tag binding information for the routes that have been constructed from the exchanged routing information.

Information exchanged via TDP consists of a stream of messages, where each message consists of a fixed header, followed by one or more Protocol Information Elements (PIEs). The fixed header consists of the version field, followed by the length field, followed by the TDP identifier field. The version field identifies a specific version of TDP. The length field specifies the total length of a message. The TDP identifier field identifies the TSR that sends the message. Each PIE is encoded as a <type, length, value> structure, where the type field defines the semantics of the value field and the length field defines the length of the value field. All the information carried within a PIE is encoded as <type, length, value> as well. Use of the <type, length, value> encoding provides flexibility and extensibility to the protocols.

TDP defines the following PIEs:

- TDP_PIE_OPEN. This is the first PIE that a TSR sends to another TSR once the TSR opens a TCP connection with the other TSR.
- TDP_PIE_BIND. This PIE is used to convey tag binding information between a pair of TSRs. The binding information consists of a sequence of tag binding entries. For destination-based (unicast) routing, each entry contains a tag and an address prefix. The tag in the entry is the incoming tag associated with the FEC identified by the address prefix on the TSR that sends a TDP_PIE_BIND that contains the entry.
- TDP_PIE_REQUEST_BIND. This PIE allows a TSR to request some other TSR to send the tag binding information to the requestor TSR for a particular FEC (in the case of destination-

based routing the FEC is identified by an address prefix) that is maintained by that TSR. The other TSR will use the `TDP_PIE_BIND PIE` to send this information to the requestor TSR.

- `TDP_PIE_WITHDRAW_BIND`. This PIE is used by a TSR to withdraw a tag binding that the TSR previously advertised to other TSRs.
- `TDP_PIE_RELEASE_BIND`. This PIE allows a TSR that received a tag binding as a consequence of sending `TDP_PIE_REQUEST_BIND` to some other TSR to indicate to that other TSR that the TSR no longer needs the binding. The other TSR, when it receives this PIE, may delete the binding.
- `TDP_PIE_KEEP_ALIVE`. A TSR uses this PIE to verify "liveness" of another TSR with whom the TSR maintains a TDP session.
- `TDP_PIE_NOTIFICATION`. This PIE is used to convey any errors.

Exchange of tag binding information via TDP is based on the technique of incremental updates, where only changes to the tag binding information (e.g., creation of a new binding, deletion of an existing binding) are communicated via the protocol. Use of incremental updates requires reliable, in-order delivery of information. To meet this requirement, TDP uses TCP as a transport to carry all the TDP messages. This design choice is largely based on the positive experience gained with BGP, where routing information is exchanged via incremental updates and TCP is used as a transport to carry the exchange of the routing information. This approach has very low overhead in the presence of stable topology, because there is no need to refresh any information that has not changed.

4.7 Summary

Tag Switching is an approach to label switching that seeks to address many of the problems described in Chapter 1. These include enhancing routing functionality and improving the scalability and stability of routing. In this respect it has a broader set of goals than the other approaches described so far. It also addresses IP/ATM integration and performance issues.

Tag Switching takes advantage of the flexibility provided by the label switching forwarding component by supporting in its control component a wide spectrum of forwarding granularities. At one end of the spectrum, Tag Switching allows FECs to be identified with address prefixes or even whole groups of prefixes, which is essential for providing scalable routing. Tag Switching also allows FECs to be associated with a source/destination address pair. This is essential for supporting multicast with Tag Switching. By associating FECs with a combination of source address, destination address, transport protocol, source port, and destination port, Tag Switching provides support for RSVP and application flows. Finally, Tag Switching allows association with FECs based on purely local rules in order to support explicit routes according to local policy.

Tag Switching allows any number of different FECs to coexist in a single TSR, as long as these FECs provide unambiguous (with respect to that TSR) partitioning of the universe of packets that could be seen by the TSR.

One of the key innovations of Tag Switching is the use of a hierarchy of tags, organized as a tag stack. This enables enhancements to routing scalability by allowing FECs to form a hierarchy that reflects the hierarchy in the underlying routing system.

Notably, Tag Switching has paid more attention to non-ATM links than IP Switching. This is reflected both in the encapsulation for frame-based links and in the attention to issues such as tag partitioning on multiaccess media.

In Tag Switching the creation of tag binding information is driven mostly by control, rather than data, traffic. Tag Switching uses downstream tag binding. Distribution of tag binding information, whenever practical, is accomplished by piggybacking this information on top of routing or signalling protocols. To cover the cases where piggybacking is impractical, Tag Switching provides a separate protocol, TDP, for distributing tag binding information.

4.8 Further Reading

There are three published papers on Tag Switching:

Rekhter, Y., B. Davie, D. Katz, E. Rosen, and G. Swallow. *Cisco Systems' Tag Switching Architecture Overview.* RFC 2105, February 1997.

Rekhter, Y., B. Davie, E. Rosen, G. Swallow, D. Farinacci, and D. Katz. "Tag Switching Architecture Overview." In Proceedings of the IEEE 82, no. 12, December 1997, 1973–1983.

Davie, B., and J. Gibson. "Enabling Explicit Routing in IP Networks." In Proceedings of Globecom '98, Sydney, Australia, November 1998.

It is also possible to find a great deal of Tag Switching information at Cisco's Web site at

www.cisco.com.

For an overview of PIM, we recommend

Deering, S., D. Estrin, D. Farinacci, V. Jacobson, C. Gung Liu, and L. Wei. "An Architecture for Wide-Area Multicast Routing." In Proceedings of ACM SIGCOMM 94, London, September 1994.

CHAPTER

MPLS Core Protocols

W e have considered the fundamental concepts that underlie label switching, and we have looked at two approaches in detail. The IETF's MPLS working group is in the process of defining a standard approach to label switching. At the time of writing, the group has met nine times officially, plus its original Birds of a Feather (BOF) at the 37th IETF in December 1996. In this chapter we examine the core protocols and architectural concepts that have been standardized by this group. The following three chapters expand on some of the more advanced MPLS capabilities, most of which are still in the midst of the standardization process. Before looking at the protocols, however, we begin with a brief survey of the working group's history and examine its charter.

5.1 Working Group Origins and Charter

The MPLS working group was formally chartered by the IETF in the spring of 1997 after the December 1996 BOF established beyond a doubt that there was sufficient interest to form a working group—an estimated 800 people attended the session, perhaps creating a record.

The impetus to form the group had come from Cisco Systems, which had declared its intention to pursue standardization of label switching at the time the first Tag Switching Internet drafts were published. Support was quickly forthcoming from several other companies, notably IBM. The working group was formed with two cochairs representing Cisco and IBM.

The charter of the MPLS working group is available on-line at the IETF Web site. The document contains a problem statement, high level requirements, a charter statement, and a set of objectives, goals, and milestones. The problem statement should look familiar to readers of this book, as it describes the problems examined in the preceding chapters. It mentions scalability and flexibility of network layer routing, increasing forwarding performance, and simplification of the integration of routers with cell switching technologies. As we have seen, these are all areas where solutions based on a label switching paradigm hold some promise.

The high level requirements are that the solution developed by the MPLS working group must work with existing datalink technologies and routing protocols, although it may propose "appropriate optimizations." It must allow a variety of forwarding granularities to be associated with a label, and it must address hierarchical networks and the issues of scalability.

The charter statement itself asserts that the group is responsible for standardizing a base technology for using label forwarding in conjunction with network layer routing over a variety of media. The base technology is expected to include procedures and protocols for label distribution, encapsulation, support of multicast, reservation and QoS mechanisms, and definition of host behaviors.

The working group objectives require the group to specify label maintenance and distribution protocols that support unicast, multicast, a hierarchy of routing knowledge, and explicit paths. An encapsulation specification is also required. ATM technology is called out for special treatment, reflecting its importance to label switching technology. A protocol to allow direct host participation is to be specified. It seems that direct host attachment to label switched networks is of low priority for the members of the working group since no contributions have been made on this subject at the time of writing. As noted previously, host participation in label switching is a little easier in data-driven approaches, and the MPLS group is focused on a control-driven approach. Finally, the working group is required to "discuss" the issue of QoS, which it has indeed done; we return to this topic in the next chapter.

5.2 The MPLS Architecture

The MPLS architecture document is the work of a design team formed after the first working group meeting in April 1997. The team consisted of representatives from Cisco Systems, IBM, and Ascend Communications. Given the composition of the team (which reflected the most active players in the working group at that time), it should come as no surprise that the emerging architecture is close to a union of the Tag Switching and ARIS proposals.

Much of the MPLS architecture specification is devoted to a description of the principles of label switching that we discussed in Chapter 2. It also addresses many of the design decisions that were presented in that chapter. The MPLS architecture uses downstream assignment of labels for unicast traffic. Both downstream-on-demand and unsolicited downstream assignment are allowed. It allows labels to be globally unique, unique per node, or unique per interface. Labels are allowed to have a variety of granularities; the document acknowledges the problems that arise when there is a mismatch of granularity between neighboring LSRs. A last-in-first-out (LIFO) label stack, such as the one specified for Tag Switching, is employed as the mechanism for supporting hierarchical labels. Forwarding decisions are always made on the label at the top of the stack.

Two alternative path selection mechanisms are proposed for the architecture: hop by hop and explicit routing. With the hop by hop mechanism, the next hop is chosen using the results of the normal network layer routing computations. An explicit route is completely specified by the source. All LSRs are required to be able to forward explicitly routed packets, but they do not have to be capable of originating them.

It is perhaps somewhat surprising that control-driven label assignment is not explicitly required by the document (although it has been clear almost from the outset that control-driven assignment is the approach favored by the working group). However, all examples of MPLS applications in the architecture use control-driven label assignment. These examples include the application of MPLS to normally and explicitly routed traffic, to tunneling, to multicast (which is discussed only briefly), and in backbone networks to support tunneling between BGP peers. The majority of these topics are discussed in more detail below; explicit routing is discussed in Chapter 7.

The architecture does not define an encapsulation for labeled data but does allow for two options: using an encapsulation specifically developed for MPLS or using "available locations" in the datalink or network layer encapsulations. (The ATM VPI/VCI fields are the obvious example of this.) Although the generic MPLS encapsulation is not defined here, the necessary components are the label stack, a TTL field, and a Class of Service field. We return to the encapsulation in the next section.

A large section of the architecture document deals with the special case of ATM. The various possible encodings of labels in the VCI and VPI fields are discussed, as are the scaling problems that have led to the notion of VC-merge and VC-merge–capable hardware.

One of the most controversial issues in the MPLS architecture is the matter of looping and the measures that are required either to detect or to prevent the formation of loops. We discuss the alternatives in Section 5.2.2. Another area of controversy was the choice of "ordered" or "independent" control of label switched path (LSP) setup, which we discuss below.

5.2.1 Ordered versus Independent Control

In the description of Tag Switching in Section 4.1.1, we saw an example of independent control of LSP establishment. When label switching is used in support of destination-based routing, each LSR may make an independent decision to assign a label to a Forwarding Equivalence Class (FEC) and to advertise that assignment to its neighbors. In this way, the establishment of an LSP follows the convergence of routing almost immediately.

The alternative to independent LSP control is ordered control. This technique was used in the ARIS approach to label switching. In ordered control, label assignment proceeds in an orderly fashion from one end of an LSP to the other. Under ordered control, LSP setup may be initiated by the head (ingress) or tail (egress) end of an LSP. For example, ARIS required ordered control and egress initiation of LSPs. In such an environment, the only LSRs that can initiate the process of LSP establishment are the egress LSRs, that is, the edge LSRs that are at the tail end of one or more LSPs. An LSR knows that it is an egress for a given FEC if its next hop for that FEC is not an LSR. It would then assign a label to the FEC and advertise the assignment to its neighbor LSRs. Any neighbor that believes the egress LSR is the next hop for that FEC would then proceed to assign a label for that FEC and advertise the assignment to *its* neighbors, and so on. In this way the assignment of labels would proceed in an orderly fashion from egress to ingress. An example of this process is shown in Figure 5.1. In Figure 5.1(a), node E has identified itself as an egress for the address prefix 192.69/16, to which it has a direct route. It allocates a label for this FEC (6) and advertises the binding of that label to the FEC to its only

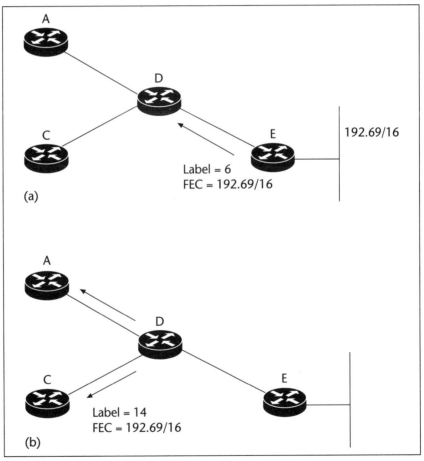

Figure 5.1

Ordered LSP establishment. Label is advertised by egress (a); LSR D assigns label and advertises it to neighbors after receiving advertisement from E (b).

LSR neighbor, D. Upon receiving the advertisement (Figure 5.1(b)), D then allocates a label (8) and advertises the binding to its LSR neighbors, A and C. In this way LSP establishment proceeds in an orderly fashion from egress to ingress.

The questions that arise are, What are the respective merits of independent and local control? and, Are both required? The MPLS architecture eventually settled on allowing both, because each offers its own set of advantages and drawbacks. The ordered approach, as we will see in the next section, helps to provide loop prevention capabilities. A less apparent consequence of the choice between ordered and independent approaches is that it affects the way FECs are selected for label bindings. Clearly, with the independent approach, each LSR makes its own choice about how it will partition the set of possible packets into FECs. For example, it might decide that each prefix in its routing table will represent an FEC. If neighboring LSRs make different decisions about the FECs they will use, then it will not be possible to establish label switched paths for some of those FECs. Normally, the neighboring LSRs are configured so that this does not happen. However, this situation may arise when an LSR aggregates routes at an area boundary.

In the ordered approach, the selection of FECs can be made at the LSR that initiates the LSP. As path setup proceeds along the LSP, all LSRs use the same FEC as was chosen by the initiator—there is no chance of different choices being made by different LSRs. All that is required is that the LSRs are able to determine the next hop for the FEC in question, so that they can determine whether the binding came from the correct next hop.

The ordered approach may also be advantageous in a network that is undergoing a transition from conventional routing to MPLS. In such a network, a network administrator may want to have very tight control over which packets are forwarded via MPLS. With the ordered approach, this control can be obtained by configuring access lists at the edge LSRs that initiate LSP setup. By contrast, to achieve the same control using the independent approach, it would be necessary to configure each LSR in the network.

The downside of the ordered approach is an increase in the amount of time it takes to set up a label switched path. In general, the ordered approach requires that bindings propagate across an entire region of LSRs before a label switched path is established. During the period when this is going on, packets must either be dropped or processed using longest match in the control processor, neither of which is desirable. By contrast, the independent approach allows every LSR to establish and advertise label bindings at any time, without the delay of waiting for messages to propagate in order from one side of the network to the other. Furthermore, the fact that LSRs can remember label bindings from neighbors who were not next hops at the time of advertisement enables almost instantaneous establishment of new label switched paths when routing changes. Thus, the overall effect of independent control is to provide faster convergence times than would occur with ordered control.

Fortunately, it is possible to accommodate both ordered and independent control into the architecture without introducing interoperability problems. However, if a network operator desires the full benefits of ordered control, it is necessary for all LSRs in the network to support ordered control.

5.2.2 Loop Detection and Prevention

As noted in Chapter 2, the issue of transient loops is one that must be addressed in a label switching environment. While IP routing protocols attempt to establish loop-free routes, almost all protocols can lead to looping during transient conditions, for example, during the period immediately following the failure of a link. We observed that there are two basic ways to tackle loops:

- Loop prevention: prevent the formation of a looping path before any packets are sent on it

- Loop mitigation: take steps to minimize the negative effects of loops

Since most IP routing protocols cannot prevent the formation of transient loops, IP forwarding uses the mitigation approach. The time-to-live field (TTL) in a packet is decremented at every IP hop; if it reaches zero, the packet is assumed to be looping and is discarded. By discarding packets that are stuck in loops, the routers in the looping path are not overwhelmed with packets that must be forwarded, and they can devote their resources to updating the routing tables. Once the routing tables are stable, the loop should be broken (unless a configuration error has been made in one of the routers).

In many cases, MPLS can adopt exactly the same approach to loops that IP uses. As discussed in the next section, MPLS labelled packets may carry a TTL field that operates just like the IP TTL to enable packets caught in transient loops to be discarded. However, there are cases where this TTL field is not available, notably on ATM links. Such links are referred to as *non-TTL segments* by the MPLS architecture.

One solution that is described in the architecture (but not mandatory) is to use buffer allocation as a form of loop mitigation. Many ATM switches have the ability to limit the amount of switch buffer space that can be consumed by a single VC, and the application of this capability in an MPLS environment can control the damage done by looping packets. Recall that the goal during transient loops is to allow routing to reconverge, and that the best way to do this is to make sure that routers are not overwhelmed with the task of forwarding packets stuck in loops. In an ATM-LSR, if the packets that are looping can consume only a limited amount of switch buffer space, then the switches should still be able to forward routing update packets, which will ensure that routing eventually converges. Even if the loop is not transient (e.g., due to misconfiguration), an ATM-LSR could still function correctly—processing control packets and forwarding non-looping packets—if the switch resources that are consumed by looping packets are limited.

A second approach to loop control that may be used on non-TTL segments is the hop count approach employed by Tag Switching, as described in Section 4.5. This form of loop control is required for ATM-LSRs, but may not be sufficient to control the adverse effects of transient loops in all cases.

A third alternative adopted by MPLS is an optional loop detection technique that originally had been developed as part of the ARIS architecture, based on an idea called *path vectors*. This feature is optional in the sense that it is not required to be used at all times, but it is required that ATM-LSRs be able to support it if configured to do so. A path vector is a list of LSRs that a LABEL REQUEST or a LABEL MAPPING message has "passed through." For example, a LABEL REQUEST message sent by a non–ATM-LSR toward an ATM-LSR will contain a path vector with just the address of the requesting LSR. The ATM-LSR adds its own address to the vector before issuing a label request for this FEC to its next hop. If a routing loop causes a request (or mapping) message to travel in a loop, eventually an LSR will see its own address in the request (or mapping) and thus detect the loop. In this case, it can take steps to tear down the looping LSP.

Finally, an innovative approach to loop prevention has been developed for MPLS, based on a concept known as *colored threads*. This technique was not found in any of the earlier approaches to label switching, but was developed during the course of the MPLS standardization effort. It is not, at the time of writing, a required part of the architecture. The approach is ideally suited for ATM-LSRs, but could be used on any type of LSR if desired. It requires the use of ordered LSP control.

The basic idea of colored threads is simple. We model the process of establishing an LSP as one of extending a uniquely colored thread from ingress to egress of the LSP. If the thread loops back on itself, a node will see a color that it has already seen once before and conclude that a loop has formed. At this point it interrupts the LSP establishment process until a routing change breaks the loop.

To gain an intuitive feel for the colored thread technique, consider the network in Figure 5.2. The arrows indicate the direction that each LSR believes is the next hop for a certain FEC. Note the loop B → D → E → C → B. Now assume that node A tries to establish an LSP using downstream-on-demand label allocation. In the LABEL REQUEST message, it includes a "color," which is simply a unique number that identifies this "thread." Node A is said to be "extending a thread." To make the color unique, LSR A uses its own IP address followed by a number that is locally unique (i.e., not in use for any other threads created by A). As the LABEL REQUEST message proceeds around the loop, each node stores the color of the incoming thread and passes on the same color in the outgoing label request. Eventually, a label request from C arrives at B. Since this label request contains the same color that was stored at B when the label request from A was received, B can detect that a loop is present. At this point, B stops forwarding

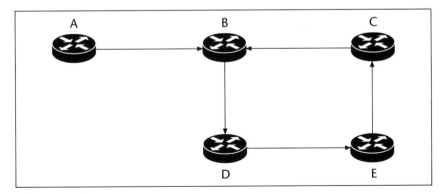

Figure 5.2
Network with a routing loop.

the LABEL REQUEST message. B also provides no response to the label request. Thus, no looping LSP is established.

Now suppose that routing stabilizes and the loop is broken. This might happen, for example, with LSR E deciding that its next hop for this LSP is not C but some other LSR X (not shown in the figure). E will now withdraw the label request it had issued to C and request a label from X. Now suppose that X is the egress of the MPLS domain, that is, its next hop for this FEC is not an LSR. It can now return a label binding to E, which can return a binding to D, and so on back to B, causing a loop-free LSP to be established. This is called *rewinding the thread*.

There are a number of subtleties to the colored thread technique, to improve its efficiency and to deal with the fact that LSPs (and thus threads) may merge. First of all, the technique uses the hop counting method described in Section 4.5 as a last line of defense against looping label request messages (this is called time-to-live in the specification). Next, it uses another form of hop count, which we will call the thread hop count, to enable LSPs to merge. This minimizes the amount of state that needs to be stored for a single LSP and the time taken to graft a new branch onto an LSP.

The thread hop count is carried in LABEL REQUEST messages and is a count of the *largest* number of hops from the ingress end of the LSP to the link on which the label request is sent. This hop count makes it possible for a newly established branch of an LSP to be set up without extending the thread all the way to the egress of the MPLS domain. To

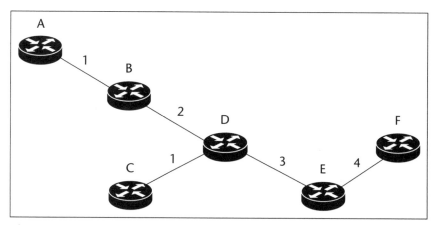

Figure 5.3
Merging threads.

see how this works, consider the example in Figure 5.3. Suppose that an LSP for some FEC has been set up from A to F and it has been found to be loop-free. The hop count on link A–B is 1; for link B–D it is 2, for link D–E it is 3, and so on. Now suppose that LSR C has just learned that the next hop for this FEC is D. C "extends a thread" toward D, with a hop count of 1. When the label request arrives at D, D notices that the hop count of the request (1) is no greater than the hop count of the link from B (2), and so D does not need to extend the thread any further. Instead, D can safely return a label binding to C, and the new branch of the LSP is established. However, the situation would be different if the hop count were greater than that of D's other incoming links. Consider what would happen if a node downstream of D experienced a change of next hop and attempted to form a looping LSP. Such a node must have a larger hop count on its outgoing link than D has on its incoming links. For example, if a link became available between F and D, and F decided that D was the next hop for this FEC, F would need to extend a new thread toward D with a hop count of 5. The specified behavior of a node in this situation is to continue extending the thread downstream, with the new hop count. Thus, D would pass a message to E, E would pass it to F, and F would recognize the color of the thread as being the same as the thread it just created. Therefore, the loop would be detected and the LSP would not be set up.

The colored thread technique is quite complicated to describe—we have only scratched the surface of the algorithm here—but it is not that complicated to implement. It is an optional part of the architecture, since other techniques to mitigate loops exist and may be sufficient in many cases. It is as robust as the path vector method in that it absolutely guarantees that no looping LSP can be set up, but requires much less information to be transmitted and stored at each hop. Note that a path vector may become arbitrarily large as a setup message traverses more hops, whereas the information transmitted and stored in the threads scheme is of constant size.

5.3 Encapsulation

The label encapsulation that was ultimately adopted by the MPLS working group is remarkably similar to that used by Tag Switching, as described in Section 4.3. For those link types that cannot accommodate labels in the link layer header—that is, for all link types except ATM and Frame Relay—MPLS uses a shim header consisting of a stack of 32-bit words. The format of one word is shown in Figure 5.4.

Label (20 bits)	Exp (3 bits)	Stack (1 bit)	TTL (8 bits)

Figure 5.4
Label stack entry format.

The label and TTL fields are reasonably self-explanatory. The stack bit is used, as with Tag Switching, to indicate that the bottom of a stack of labels has been reached. The only field in which we see a difference between this label format and that used by Tag Switching is that the CoS (class of service) field from the Tag header has been renamed "experimental" (Exp). The reason for this change is that the working group was not ready to commit to a definite usage for those 3 bits at the time the header was standardized. As we will see in the next chapter, however, a number of ways to use the bits to support quality of service have since been defined.

The encapsulation specification includes a set of rules for TTL processing. The goal of these rules is to make the behavior of an MPLS network resemble that of a conventional IP network as closely as possible from the perspective of TTL. This means, for example, that an IP packet that crosses an MPLS domain should emerge with a TTL that has been decremented by the number of hops (LSRs) in the MPLS domain. This is achieved by copying the IP TTL into the MPLS header when the packet is first labeled, decrementing the MPLS TTL at each LSR, and copying the TTL from the MPLS header back into the IP TTL field when the label header is removed at the egress of the MPLS domain. Interestingly, an alternative behavior is allowed by the specification, which is to decrement the IP TTL by one when the label is removed. This has the effect of making an LSP look like a single hop to tools such as traceroute. The main advantage of this approach is to allow network operators to conceal details of their network topology from outside observers.

Another topic addressed by the encapsulation specification is fragmentation. It is possible for labeled packets to require fragmentation, just as IP datagrams do; it is also possible that the addition of one or more labels to a packet might cause it to become big enough to require fragmentation even if the unlabeled packet would not have required fragmentation. The rules for handling all the possible cases are spelled out in detail in the specification; we note here only that these rules ensure that fragmentation and related operations, such as path MTU discovery, operate correctly. In particular, it is possible for hosts that implement MTU discovery to determine the correct MTU value for their packets that will ensure they are not fragmented. If labeled packets do need to be fragmented, fragmentation is applied to the enclosed IP datagram; then the appropriate label stack is appended to each fragment.

The encapsulation specification also defines a few reserved label values. These are

- 0. "IPv4 Explicit Null"
- 1. "Router Alert"
- 2. "IPv6 Explicit Null"
- 3. "Implicit Null"

The "Explicit Null" labels are used in cases where a label encapsulation is needed but no valid label is required. This might be done, for example, to retain the Exp fields for QoS purposes on the last hop of an LSP, even though no label is required by the last hop. The reasons for having two different values for IPv4 and IPv6 is that there needs to be some way to distinguish the layer 3 protocol that has been encapsulated. Most layer 2 encapsulations (PPP, Ethernet, etc.) contain a field that indicates the layer 3 protocol, but for MPLS labeled packets that field indicates only that the frame contains an MPLS packet. The layer 3 protocol is therefore determined by looking at the label, and this is true for explicit null just as it is for other (nonreserved) labels. When used, the explicit null label must be the only entry in the label stack.

The "Router Alert" label is used much like the router alert option in an IP packet, to tell a router that it needs to pay more attention to this packet than simply forwarding it. When a packet bearing this label is received, the LSR pops the top label off the stack and forwards the packet using the next label, if forwarding the packet is appropriate. Finally, the "Implicit Null" label is not a value that can appear in the header of a transmitted packet, but is reserved for use in the Label Distribution Protocol.

5.4 Label Distribution

One of the major work items of the MPLS working group has been the definition of mechanisms for distributing label bindings among

LSRs. The Label Distribution Protocol (LDP) is typically the most well known of these mechanisms, being the main new protocol created by the working group. It is also one of the two protocols used to support unicast routing. However, as noted in Section 2.3.5, it is preferable to distribute labels by piggybacking them on other control protocols when possible. Thus, there are a variety of other protocols that are used for label distribution, such as BGP, PIM, and RSVP. We will see how PIM may be used when we examine multicast in Section 5.6; RSVP is discussed in the context of QoS and traffic engineering in the next two chapters. We turn our attention now to the protocols that support unicast routing: LDP and then BGP.

5.4.1 Label Distribution Protocol (LDP)

The LDP specification is the work of a design team representing many vendors, formed after the second MPLS working group meeting. We have seen that the architecture is based on a control-driven model; as a consequence, LDP is based on a union of the (control-driven) TDP and ARIS protocols.

LDP has the following basic characteristics:

- It provides an LSR "discovery" mechanism to enable LSR peers to find each other and establish communication.
- It defines four classes of messages:
  - ❏ DISCOVERY messages
  - ❏ ADJACENCY messages, which deal with initialization, keepalive, and shutdown of sessions between LSRs
  - ❏ LABEL ADVERTISEMENT messages, which deal with label binding advertisements, requests, withdrawal, and release
  - ❏ NOTIFICATION messages, used to provide advisory information and to signal error information
- It runs over TCP to provide reliable delivery of messages (with the exception of DISCOVERY messages).
- It is designed to be easily extensible, using messages specified as collections of TLV (type, length, value) encoded objects.

The TLV encoding means that each object contains a type field to say what sort of object it is (e.g., a label binding), a length field to say how long the object is, and a value field, the meaning of which depends on the type. New capabilities are added with new type definitions. The first two fields are of constant length and are at the start of the object, which makes it easy for an implementation to ignore object types that it doesn't recognize. The value field of an object may itself contain further TLV encoded objects.

LSR Neighbor Discovery

LDP's discovery protocol runs over UDP and works as follows. An LSR periodically multicasts a HELLO message to a well-known UDP port on the "all routers on this subnet" multicast group. All LSRs listen on this UDP port for the HELLO messages. Thus, at some point an LSR will learn about all the other LSRs to which it has direct connections. When an LSR learns the address of another LSR by this mechanism, it establishes a TCP connection to that LSR. At this point an LDP session can be established between the two LSRs. An LDP session is bidirectional, that is, the LSR at each end of the connection can advertise and request bindings to and from the peer at the other end of the connection.

An additional discovery mechanism enables LSRs to discover each other even when they are not directly connected to a common subnet. In this case an LSR periodically unicasts HELLO messages to the well-known UDP port at a specific IP address, which it must have learned by some other means (e.g., configuration). The recipient of this message may respond to the HELLO with another HELLO that is unicast back to the original LSR, and session establishment then proceeds as before. A typical situation in which this discovery mechanism might be useful is when a traffic engineering LSP is configured between two LSRs, and it is desired to send already labeled packets over that LSP. In this case the LSR at the head of the LSP needs to learn what labels to put on the packets that it will send to the LSR at the far end of the LSP.

Reliable Transport

The decision to run LDP over TCP was a somewhat controversial one. The need for reliability is clear: if a label binding or a request for a binding is not successfully delivered, then traffic cannot be label switched and will have to be handled by the control processor or dropped. It is also easy to find examples where the order of message delivery is important: a binding advertisement followed by a withdrawal of that binding, for example, will have a very different effect if the messages are received in the reverse order. The issue, therefore, was whether to use TCP to provide reliable, in-order delivery or to build that functionality into LDP itself.

Building reliability into LDP had some attraction. The idea was to provide exactly the level of functionality needed and no more. For example, TCP provides a congestion avoidance mechanism that may not be strictly necessary for a neighbor-to-neighbor control protocol, and the complete ordering of messages that it provides is more strict than required for label distribution.

The advantages of building reliability into the Label Distribution Protocol, however, were outweighed by the drawbacks. For example, because every label binding message must be acknowledged, a timer would be needed for every unacknowledged message. By contrast, LDP delegates the timer function to TCP, which can use a single timer for the whole session. The overhead of managing large numbers of timers can be significant.

TCP provides a wealth of useful functions that LDP is able to use for free, such as efficient packing of higher layer messages into IP packets, piggybacking of ACKs on data packets, and flow control. Unlike congestion control, flow control (making sure that a sender does not overrun the capacity of a receiver) is necessary for a control protocol.

Transport protocol design is notoriously difficult, and there have been plenty of efforts to "improve" on TCP that have ultimately failed to do so. There are many details to get right and special cases to consider, such as ensuring that old messages from closed sessions are not accepted erroneously by new sessions. This argued in favor of using a well-tested protocol rather than reinventing the wheel.

LDP Messages

As noted above, there are four basic types of LDP messages. The most commonly used messages are

- INITIALIZATION
- KEEPALIVE
- LABEL MAPPING
- LABEL WITHDRAWAL
- LABEL RELEASE
- LABEL REQUEST
- LABEL REQUEST ABORT

We discuss each message type in turn.

INITIALIZATION messages are sent at the beginning of an LDP session to enable two LSRs to agree on various parameters and options for the session. These include the label allocation mode (discussed below), timer values (e.g., for KEEPALIVES), and the range of labels to be used on the link between these two LSRs. Both LSRs may send INITIALIZATION messages, and the receiving LSR responds with a KEEPALIVE if the parameters are acceptable. If any parameters are not acceptable, the LSR responds with an error notification, and session initialization is terminated.

KEEPALIVEs are sent periodically in the absence of any other messages to ensure that each LDP peer knows that the other peer is still functioning correctly. In the absence of a KEEPALIVE or some other LDP message within the appropriate time interval, an LSR concludes that its peer, or the connection to it, has gone down and terminates the session.

LABEL MAPPING messages are at the heart of label distribution. These are the messages that are used to advertise a binding between an FEC (e.g., an address prefix) and a label. The LABEL WITHDRAWAL message reverses the process—it is used to revoke a previously advertised binding. Reasons for withdrawing a binding include the removal of an address prefix from the routing table of the advertising LSR due to a routing change, or a change in configuration of the LSR that causes it to cease label switching packets on that FEC.

A LABEL RELEASE message is used by an LSR that previously received a label mapping and no longer has a need for that mapping. This typically happens when the releasing LSR finds that the next hop for this FEC is not the advertising LSR. An LSR releases bindings in this way when it is operating in conservative label retention mode, which we discuss (along with other modes) in the following section.

Recall that LSRs may operate in unsolicited downstream or downstream-on-demand label assignment modes. In the latter mode, LSRs request label mappings from their downstream neighbors using LABEL REQUEST messages. If a LABEL REQUEST message needs to be revoked before it has been satisfied (e.g., because the next hop for the FEC in question changed), the requesting LSR aborts the request with a LABEL REQUEST ABORT message.

Label Distribution Modes

We have already seen that label distribution and assignment may be performed in a number of different "modes." One such alternative is unsolicited downstream versus downstream-on-demand label assignment, first introduced in Chapter 2. Another is ordered versus independent LSP control, which we discussed in Section 5.2.1. A third choice is between "liberal" and "conservative" label retention. All of these alternative behaviors are negotiated by LSRs during LDP session initialization.

When an LSR operates in conservative label retention mode, it retains only those label-to-FEC mappings that it needs at the current time. Any other mappings are released. By contrast, in liberal mode, an LSR retains all mappings that have been advertised to it, even if some of them were not directly useful at the time of advertisement. The common usage of liberal retention mode is as follows. LSR1 advertises a mapping between some FEC and a label to one of its neighbors, LSR2. LSR2 observes that LSR1 is not currently the next hop for that FEC, so it cannot use the mapping for forwarding purposes at this time, but it stores the mapping anyway. At some later time there is a change in routing, and LSR1 becomes LSR2's next hop for this FEC. LSR2 can now update its label forwarding table accordingly and begin forwarding labeled packets to LSR1 along their new route. This all happens without any new LDP signaling or allocation of labels.

The chief advantage of liberal retention mode is quicker response to changes in routing. Its main drawback is waste of labels. This can be particularly important in devices that store label forwarding information in hardware, notably ATM-LSRs. Thus, it is common to see conservative label retention used on ATM-LSRs.

5.4.2 Label Distribution Using BGP

We saw in Section 4.1.2 that there are situations in which BGP peers might wish to exchange labels as well as the routes (more formally known as Network Layer Reachability Information, or NLRI) that are conventionally exchanged by BGP. We will also see applications of BGP to label distribution when building Virtual Private Networks in Chapter 8. Thus, the MPLS working group has defined a small extension to BGP-4 to enable it to be used as a label distribution mechanism.

BGP-4 is readily extensible, and MPLS makes use of the multiprotocol extensions to BGP. These extensions enable BGP to support different address families, such as IPv4 or IPv6. MPLS simply defines a new address family, where the address includes not only an address prefix but also one or more labels. The encoding of the address prefix and label is shown in Figure 5.5.

The length field is the total length in bits of the label(s) and address prefix. Each label is encoded in 3 bytes, with the low order 20 bits

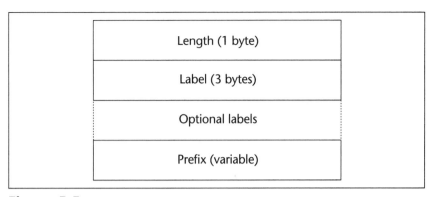

Figure 5.5
Label and address prefix encoding in BGP.

being the label itself, the top bit being a "bottom of stack" bit that performs the same function as the stack bit in the label stack encapsulation described in Section 5.3. The remaining 3 bits in those 3 bytes are zero. Immediately following the label(s) is the address prefix to which the label (or label stack) is bound. The prefix may be any number of bits long (up to 32 for IPv4 addresses), and so it is padded with trailing zero bits to round it up to an even number of bytes.

With this encoding of labels and address prefixes, any BGP speaker that advertises a route may also advertise a label or label stack to be used for packets using that route. All normal BGP procedures, such as withdrawal and redistribution of routes, may be used on these advertisements.

5.5 ATM Issues

In Section 4.2 we observed that Tag Switching requires some special procedures to deal with ATM links and ATM-TSRs. MPLS faces exactly the same set of issues when dealing with ATM and addresses them in similar (but not identical) ways. Recall that the main issues are

- Encapsulation of labeled packets on ATM links
- Looping and TTL adjustment
- Cell interleave and VC-merge

We will now examine how these issues are addressed in MPLS.

Not surprisingly, the encapsulation of MPLS labeled packets on ATM links is just like the encapsulation of Tag Switched packets: the label is carried in the VPI/VCI field. One aspect of the encapsulation that may be slightly surprising is that the label stack header defined in Section 5.3 is always attached to the network layer packet before segmenting that packet into cells. This is illustrated in Figure 5.6. Here we see the network layer packet (e.g., an IP datagram) with a label stack attached in front and an AAL5 trailer at the end. The resulting AAL5 PDU is then segmented into ATM cells, each of which carries the label in the VPI/VCI field of its header.

Why carry the label both in the ATM header *and* inside the AAL5 PDU? The main reason is to allow a label stack of arbitrary depth, just as on non-ATM links. The top label of the stack is carried in the VPI/VCI field of the ATM cell header, as it must be so that ATM-LSRs can read the label and use it to make forwarding decisions. The complete label stack is carried along with the network layer packet in the AAL5 PDU, and the top label in the stack is ignored. You might imagine that it would make more sense to omit the top label altogether in this case,

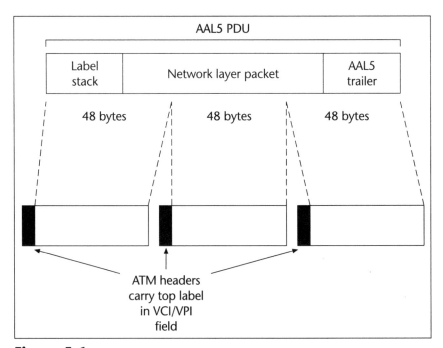

Figure 5.6
Encapsulation of labeled packet on ATM link.

but this presents a problem: packets with only one label would have no label stack header, whereas packets with two or more labels would have a stack header, and there would be no way to tell whether the label stack was present or not.

Another function of the label stack is that it carries the TTL and the Exp bits. Both of these fields may be needed if the packet is to be label switched further by a non–ATM-LSR after reassembly.

One subtle distinction that is introduced by the MPLS ATM specification is between a "label switching controlled" ATM (LC-ATM) interface and a "conventional" ATM interface. An LC-ATM interface is one on which labels assigned by MPLS control procedures are carried in the VPI/VCI field of ATM cells. On a conventional ATM interface, the VPI/VCI fields would contain values assigned by ATM control procedures. Note that when an ATM switch operates as an LSR, all of its interfaces are LC-ATM interfaces. The encapsulation we just described applies to LC-ATM interfaces. It is possible for a non–ATM-LSR to have conventional ATM interfaces, on which conventional ATM virtual circuits could be established. Such VCs are treated just like PPP links, in the sense that MPLS labeled packets using the encapsulation of Section 5.3 can be sent over them.

The topic of looping was addressed in Section 5.2.2. This handles the most important problem arising from the lack of a TTL on ATM links, but there are other TTL issues to consider. The first is that the TTL of a packet should be adjusted correctly, that is, decremented by the number of ATM-LSRs it has passed through. Since the ATM-LSRs cannot perform this adjustment, it is performed by the non–ATM-LSR that transmits the packet onto an LC-ATM link. This LSR learns the appropriate amount by which the TTL should be adjusted using the hop count field in label mappings. If the adjustment would cause the TTL to become zero or negative, the packet is not sent as a labeled packet across the region of ATM-LSRs. Either it is dropped and an ICMP message is sent back to the sender or it is sent hop by hop as an unlabeled packet across the cloud, with the TTL being decremented by one at each hop. This will cause the TTL to reach zero at the appropriate LSR, which is important to the correct functioning of diagnostic tools such as traceroute.

The final issue is cell interleave, which was introduced in the Tag Switching context in Section 4.2.2. The solutions specified for MPLS are essentially the same as those described in that section: downstream-on-demand label assignment and using multiple labels per FEC, or VC-merge. One additional solution has been proposed for

MPLS, known as *VP-merge*. This solution was first published as part of IBM's ARIS proposal.

In the VP-merge approach, the label is carried only in the VPI field of the ATM cells. The VCI field is then used as an identifier to distinguish frames that come from different sources but are being sent on the same link with the same label in the VPI field. This is illustrated in Figure 5.7, where the VPI is shown to the left of the VCI in each cell. The ATM-LSR forwards based on the VPI and rewrites the VPI value, just like a conventional ATM VP switch. However, because the two incoming streams of cells have different VCI values, which are not modified by the ATM-LSR, there is no confusion between cells from different frames on the outgoing link.

This approach does have its drawbacks. First, it limits the number of labels to the size of the VPI space, which is at most 12 bits. Second, it requires a unique 16-bit identifier to be assigned to each ingress LSR, which requires some degree of extra administration and configuration. Third, the majority of existing switch hardware cannot perform Early or Partial Packet Discard (EPD or PPD) when switching on the VPI only. These features aim to discard whole frames (or the tail end of a frame in the case of PPD) once it is necessary to drop a single cell from the frame, since the rest of the frame is rendered useless by the single cell loss. They are valuable in reducing congestion and improving overall network throughput. Finally, we note that no full specification of how to perform VP-merge has been provided to the MPLS working group at the time of writing.

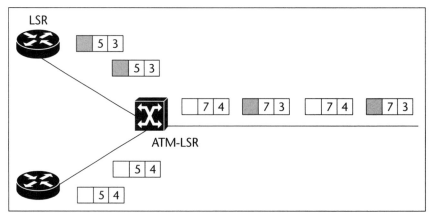

Figure 5.7
VP-merge example.

5.6 Multicast

The support of multicast in MPLS networks remains an open issue for the working group at the time of writing. The working group has produced a multicast framework document, which provides an overview of the issues and outlines possible solution approaches. We will examine some of the major issues in the following paragraphs. We have already looked at one possible approach to supporting multicast in MPLS: an approach based on Protocol Independent Multicast (PIM) and using Tag Switching was described in Section 4.1.3. This solution is one of the candidate solutions for MPLS.

One question to ask before looking in detail at multicast issues is, What are the potential benefits of MPLS to multicast routing? One possible answer to this is performance. Whereas the performance benefits of MPLS for unicast appear quite modest, the higher complexity of multicast forwarding (relative to unicast) might lead to a more significant performance advantage when label switching is used for multicast. A second benefit of MPLS for multicast would be the ability to perform IP multicast on ATM-LSRs, thus removing the need for complex mappings from IP to ATM multicast, as discussed in Chapter 1.

The one part of MPLS multicast that is well defined is the encapsulation. Multicast packets use the same encapsulation as unicast packets, with one exception. When using the label stack encoding of Section 5.3, the link layer protocol (e.g., Ethernet or PPP) uses a layer 3 protocol identifier (e.g., ethertype or PPP protocol ID) to indicate that MPLS labeled packets are carried inside the L2 frame. However, different L3 protocol identifiers are used for unicast and multicast. This has several advantages. First, it makes multicast packets easy to recognize without first examining the label. Second, it enables multicast packets and unicast packets to use different label spaces. This in turn enables the multicast Label Forwarding Information Base (LFIB) to be defined on a per-interface basis (which it generally must be) even if the unicast LFIB is defined on a per-LSR basis.

Looping is a particularly important issue for multicast because packets that are stuck in loops may be replicated by multicast forwarding, leading to large amounts of unwanted traffic (some of which will probably be sent outside the loop) until the loop is broken. The TTL field in the MPLS encapsulation addresses this problem as well as it is addressed in IP, so the main area of concern is "non-TTL segments" such as LC-ATM links. Loop prevention methods would be desirable in this case but have not been developed at the time of writing.

MPLS support for multicast is complicated by the fact that there are many different multicast routing protocols. Furthermore, whereas any unicast routing protocol produces a routing table that can then be used in a consistent way to drive label distribution, different multicast routing protocols produce different sorts of forwarding state that need to be handled differently when establishing LSPs.

Some multicast routing protocols, such as PIM sparse mode (PIM-SM), create two types of forwarding state, known as *shared trees* and *source-specific trees*. A shared tree delivers packets from any sender toward the receivers, whereas a source-specific tree delivers packets only from one sender to the receivers. Receivers must be on the shared tree to receive packets from previously unheard-of senders, and may join source-specific trees to create a more optimal path from specific senders. This can create difficulties in an MPLS environment when a multicast LSP is established for both a shared tree and a source-specific tree. A sender's packets need to be sent on both the shared tree (to be sure of reaching all receivers) and to any source-specific trees created for this sender. As a result, a receiver on the source-specific tree will receive duplicate copies of all packets sent by this sender. One possible solution to this problem is to use MPLS only on the source-specific trees, which are typically created in response to high traffic flows, and to use conventional IP forwarding (which can suppress the duplication of packets) for the shared tree.

In multicast, the issue of whether to piggyback label distribution on the control protocol or to use a separate protocol such as LDP arises once again. As discussed in Section 4.1.3, there may be some advantages to piggybacking, at least in the case of PIM. However, some protocols such as DVMRP are not well suited to piggybacking and thus would probably benefit from multicast label bindings in LDP.

Many other trade-offs that were discussed in Chapter 2 and in earlier sections of this chapter, such as ordered versus independent control, need to be evaluated again in the context of multicast, and there is no guarantee that the same choices as were made for unicast will prevail. Even the choice of control-driven versus data-driven label binding could be reexamined.

It should be apparent by now that the complexity of multicast support for MPLS may prevent the rapid development of a complete solution. At the time of writing, the most complete approach—albeit one that is limited to PIM as its only routing protocol—is that described for Tag Switching in Section 4.1.3.

5.7 Summary

At this point we have seen the major components that lie at the heart of MPLS. The most basic function of MPLS is to support the forwarding of label switched packets along paths selected by destination-based routing. This function is supported by the Label Distribution Protocol, LDP, which is a descendent of TDP and the ARIS protocol. LDP runs over TCP for reliability and supports a variety of label distribution modes: downstream or downstream-on-demand assignment, independent or ordered LSP control, and liberal or conservative label retention. LDP may use a variety of loop detection and prevention mechanisms or may rely on TTL to mitigate the consequences of looping LSPs.

Several mechanisms other than LDP may be used to distribute label bindings. In this chapter we described the use of BGP to distribute labels associated with routes; in the following chapters we will see other mechanisms for traffic engineering and QoS applications.

As with all label switching approaches, MPLS aims to effectively support ATM-LSRs. The issues that need to be addressed include TTL processing, looping, encapsulation, and LSP merging.

Finally, we examined multicast support in MPLS networks. While a partial solution has been proposed using PIM sparse mode as both the routing protocol and label distribution mechanism, there remain a number of open issues before full multicast support can be provided.

5.8 Further Reading

The MPLS working group charter can be found on the IETF's Web site at

www.ietf.org/html.charters/mpls-charter.html

While only one RFC has been published at the time of writing (on traffic engineering, discussed in Chapter 7), several have been approved for publication as standards track documents. RFCs can be found at

www.rfc-editor.org

The various working group drafts that have not yet progressed to RFC status can also be found on the MPLS page listed above or in the usual Internet draft directories:

www.ietf.org/ID.html

One draft of particular interest is the multicast framework, which describes in great detail the difficulties of supporting multicast in MPLS.

Quality of Service

To many people, quality of service (QoS) is the driving factor behind MPLS. This is actually something of a misconception. Compared to other factors, such as traffic engineering and Virtual Private Network support, QoS is not a very strong reason to deploy MPLS. As we will see in this chapter, most of the work that has been done in the realm of MPLS QoS has focused on supporting the features of IP QoS in a network that happens to be using MPLS. In other words, the goal has been to establish parity between the QoS features of IP and MPLS, not to make MPLS QoS somehow superior to IP QoS.

One of the main reasons that MPLS supports, rather than extends, the IP QoS model is that MPLS, unlike IP, is not an end-to-end protocol. MPLS does not currently run in hosts, and for the foreseeable future, many IP networks that do not run MPLS will exist. QoS, on the other hand, usually is an end-to-end characteristic of the communication between peers. For example, if one link of an end-to-end path has high delay, high loss, or low bandwidth, that limits the QoS that can be provided along that end-to-end path. Another way to think of this is that MPLS does not fundamentally change the IP service model. Service providers do not sell MPLS service; they sell IP service (or Frame Relay service or a variety of other services), and thus, if they offer any QoS at all, they must offer IP QoS (or Frame Relay QoS, etc.).

This is not to say that MPLS has no role in IP QoS (which would cause this to be a very short chapter). First, MPLS may help providers to offer IP QoS services more efficiently or on a wider range of platforms (such as ATM-LSRs). Second, there are some novel QoS capabilities that can be supported across a provider network using MPLS that, while not being truly end-to-end, nevertheless may prove very useful. One of these, guaranteed bandwidth LSPs, is discussed in Section 7.5.2.

Because of the close relationship between IP QoS and MPLS QoS, this chapter is structured around the major components of IP QoS. IP provides two different models of QoS: Integrated Services (which uses and is often considered synonymous with RSVP) and Differentiated Services. In the next two sections we will give an overview of each model, followed by a description of how MPLS supports it and in some cases enhances it. We then turn to explicit congestion notification (ECN), another IP capability that is supported by MPLS.

6.1 Integrated Services and RSVP

The full description of Integrated Services and RSVP would take at least an entire book chapter. Readers unfamiliar with these topics may wish to consult Section 6.5, Further Reading, at the end of this chapter. We aim here only to provide enough background to enable a clear description of the role of MPLS in Integrated Services.

6.1.1 Integrated Services Overview

The term *Integrated Services* refers to an overall QoS architecture that was produced by the IETF in the mid-1990s. The Integrated Services (or int-serv) working group developed this architecture with the goal of enabling end-to-end QoS guarantees for those applications that need them. Such guarantees would ensure that an application that needed some minimum amount of bandwidth or some bound on end-to-end delay could have its needs met.

Part of the working group's output was the specification of a number of *service classes* designed to meet the needs of a wide variety of application types. It also defined how the Resource Reservation Protocol, RSVP, could be used to make requests for QoS using these service classes. RSVP itself was produced in a separate working group, and considerable effort was made to provide a clean separation between

Integrated Services and RSVP. Specifically, Integrated Services can accommodate a variety of signalling protocols, of which RSVP is just one,[1] and RSVP can signal various types of information, not just int-serv requests. In spite of this separation, many people incorrectly use the term *RSVP* to refer to the entire Integrated Services QoS architecture. In this book we use RSVP to refer only to the signalling protocol and Integrated Services to refer to the QoS architecture defined by the working group of that name.

The int-serv architecture includes a number of components in addition to a signalling protocol. As we will see below, it also includes some service class definitions. Another aspect of the architecture is the notion that an application can specify the traffic that it will inject into the network and the level of QoS it would like to receive from the network. The traffic specification is known as a *TSpec,* and the request for a certain QoS level, which may be thought of as a request for some amount of network resources, is known as an *RSpec.* Int-serv also requires network elements such as routers and switches to perform a variety of functions, such as

- Policing: verifying that traffic conforms to its TSpec and taking action such as dropping packets if it does not

- Admission control: checking to see if there are enough resources to meet a request for QoS and denying the request if not

- Classification: recognizing those packets that need particular levels of QoS

- Queuing and scheduling: making decisions about when packets are transmitted and which packets are dropped that are consistent with the QoS requests that have been granted

Service Classes

After considering many candidates, the int-serv working group defined two service classes. These service classes are known as *guaranteed service* and *controlled load.* Applications can choose to request either of these services depending on which one meets their needs.

Guaranteed service is intended to serve the needs of applications that require a hard guarantee of bandwidth and delay. To obtain this hard bound, the application provides a TSpec that precisely bounds

---

1. Other possible signalling protocols include ST-II and SNMP, but in practice RSVP is the only deployed signalling protocol for Integrated Services.

the traffic it will inject, including such parameters as a peak rate, a maximum packet size, a burst size, and a "token bucket rate." The burst size and token bucket rate together comprise a token bucket specification, which is the standard way to represent the bandwidth characteristics of an application that generates data at a variable rate. A traffic flow is characterized by a token bucket of rate r and burst size b if, for any time interval T, it sends no more than $rT + b$ bytes. A more intuitive way to think of this is that such a flow may send data at rate r bytes per second on average, but may occasionally send at a rate greater than r if the bursts sent at the higher rate contain no more than b bytes.

The most important parameter in a guaranteed service RSpec is the service rate, which describes the amount of bandwidth to be allocated to this flow. It has been shown that by knowing this parameter, plus those in the TSpec, plus a number of other parameters not discussed here, the maximum delay that could possibly be experienced by a packet can be calculated. Furthermore, an application can control its delay bound by increasing the service rate in its RSpec.

Guaranteed service comes at some cost. It requires every flow using the service to be queued separately, and it often results in rather low network utilization. Controlled load overcomes these drawbacks by giving up on hard, mathematically provable delay bounds. Instead, controlled load simply tries to make sure that an application receives service comparable to what it would receive if it were running on an unloaded network of adequate capacity for just that application. To achieve this, an application using controlled load provides a TSpec much like the one used for guaranteed service, and the network elements ensure that

- There are enough resources to provide the specified QoS to the controlled load flows (admission control)
- The controlled load flows are queued and scheduled in a way that prevents other flows from degrading with their performance.

RSVP

Now that we have seen the main components of the int-serv architecture, we focus on the primary signalling protocol, RSVP. This is the component where MPLS has a major role to play. Simply stated, RSVP is the protocol that allows applications to signal QoS requirements to the network, and the network responds with notifications of success or failure. It follows from the preceding discussion that RSVP must carry the following information:

■ Classification information, so that flows with particular QoS requirements can be recognized within the network. This information typically includes sender and receiver IP addresses and UDP port numbers.

■ Traffic specification and QoS requirements, in the form of TSpecs and RSpecs, including the desired service (guaranteed or controlled load).

It should also be clear that RSVP needs to carry this information from hosts to every switch or router along the path from sender(s) to receiver(s), since all these network elements must participate in meeting the QoS needs of the application.

RSVP carries its information using two basic message types: PATH and RESV (reservation) messages. PATH messages travel from a sender to one or more receivers and include TSpecs and classification information provided by the sender. The reason that we allow for multiple receivers is that RSVP is explicitly designed to support multicast. A PATH message is always sent to an address that is the *session* address; this may be a unicast or multicast address. We often think of a session as representing a single application, since it is identified by the destination address and (usually) the destination port number that is used by the application for which we wish to make reservations. As we will see, however, there is no reason to view a session in such a restricted way.

When a receiver gets a PATH message, it can send a RESV message back toward the sender. The RESV message identifies the session for which the reservation is to be made and includes an RSpec indicating the level of QoS required by this receiver. It may also include some information regarding which senders are allowed to use the resources being allocated. Figure 6.1 shows the flow of messages between a sender and a receiver. Note that the reservation is unidirectional. If a bidirectional reservation were required (e.g., for a normal telephone conversation), there would be an additional set of messages flowing in the opposite direction. Also note that the messages are intercepted and forwarded by every router along the path, so that resource allocation can take place at all the necessary hops.

Once a reservation is established, the routers between the sender and the receiver recognize packets that belong to a reservation by

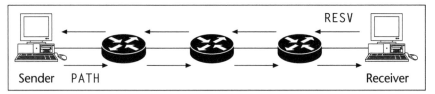

Figure 6.1
PATH *messages flow from sender to receiver and* RESV *messages follow the reverse path.*

inspecting up to five fields in the IP and transport protocol headers: the destination address and destination port number, the protocol number (e.g., UDP), and the source address and port. We refer to a set of packets that are recognized in this way as a *reserved flow*. Packets in a reserved flow are usually policed (to ensure that the flow is not generating more traffic than advertised in the TSpec) and receive appropriate queuing and scheduling to meet the desired QoS. For example, one way to implement guaranteed service is to use a weighted fair queuing (WFQ) scheduler, where each distinct reservation is treated as one flow by the scheduler, and the weight assigned to each flow is proportional to the service rate requested in its RSpec.

When operating on unicast flows, RSVP is reasonably simple. It becomes more complex in a multicast environment, because there may be many receivers making reservations for a single session and different receivers may request different levels of QoS. Since MPLS has, at the time of writing, mostly focused on unicast applications of RSVP, we will not dwell on the multicast aspects of RSVP here.

One last point to note about RSVP is that it is a "soft state" protocol. As we discussed in Section 3.2, the distinguishing feature of such a protocol is that any state will automatically expire after some time unless it is refreshed periodically. In the case of RSVP, this means that PATH and RESV messages must be sent periodically to refresh a reservation. If they are not sent for some interval (the time-out period), then the reservation is automatically torn down. This has a number of consequences, both positive and negative, that we examine in Section 6.1.3.

6.1.2 MPLS Support of RSVP

We have already seen a brief description of how RSVP can be supported in a Tag Switching network, in Section 4.1.4. The support of RSVP in MPLS is directly derived from the approach used by Tag

Switching. Now that we have a fuller understanding of RSVP, we examine in detail how it is supported in an MPLS network. In this section we focus only on the role of RSVP in supporting QoS; its role in traffic engineering is discussed in Section 7.2.3.

The first goal in adding RSVP support to MPLS is to enable LSRs—which classify packets by examining labels, not IP headers—to recognize packets that belong to flows for which reservations have been made. In other words, we need to create and distribute bindings between flows and labels, for those flows that have RSVP reservations. We can think of the set of packets for which an RSVP reservation has been made as just another instance of an FEC.

It turns out to be rather easy to bind labels to reserved flows in RSVP, at least in the unicast case. A new RSVP object is defined—the LABEL object—and is carried inside an RSVP RESV message. When an LSR wants to send a RESV message for a new RSVP flow, the LSR allocates a label from its pool of free labels, creates an entry in its LFIB with the incoming label set to the allocated label, and sends out the RESV message containing this label in the LABEL object. Note that, since RESV messages flow from receiver to sender, this is a form of downstream label allocation.

Upon receipt of a RESV that contains a LABEL object, an LSR populates its LFIB with this label as the outgoing label. It then allocates a new label to use as the incoming label and inserts that in the RESV message before sending it upstream. It should be clear that, as RESV messages propagate upstream, an LSP is established all along the path. Also note that, since the labels are provided in the RESV messages, each LSR can easily associate the appropriate QoS resources with the LSP.

Figure 6.2 illustrates the process. In this case we assume that the hosts do not participate in label distribution (although there is nothing to prevent them from doing so). LSR R3 allocates a label (5) for this reservation and advertises it upstream to its neighbor R2. R2 allocates

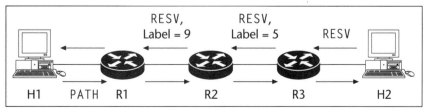

Figure 6.2
Labels distributed in RESV *messages.*

a label (9) for the same reservation and advertises it to R1. There is now an LSP for this reserved flow from R1 to R3. When packets matching this reservation (i.e., packets sent from H1 to H2 with the appropriate source and destination port numbers and transport protocol number) arrive at R1, R1 classifies them using the IP and transport layer header information and performs the appropriate QoS actions for this reservation, such as policing and scheduling the packets in the output queue. In other words, it does all the normal functions of an Integrated Services router running RSVP. In addition, R1 prepends a label header to the packets and inserts the value 9 as the outgoing label before forwarding the packets to R2.

When R2 receives packets bearing the label 9, it is able to look up that label in its LFIB and find all the QoS related state that tells it how to police the flow, queue the packet, and so on. It does not of course need to examine the IP or transport layer headers. It then replaces the label on the packet with the outgoing entry from its LFIB—5—and forwards the packet.

Observe that, since the creation of label bindings is driven by RSVP messages, binding is control-driven, just as in other MPLS environments. Also note that this is another example of piggybacking the label binding information on top of an existing protocol, and it does not require a separate protocol such as LDP.

One interesting consequence of setting up an LSP for a flow with an RSVP reservation is that only the first router in the LSP—R1 in the example above—needs to be concerned with which packets belong to the reserved flow. This enables RSVP to be applied in MPLS environments in a way that is not possible in conventional IP networks. Conventionally, RSVP reservations could be made only for individual "microflows," that is, flows identified by the five header fields described above. However, it is quite possible to configure R1 to select packets based on a wide range of criteria. For example, R1 could take all packets destined for a particular prefix and put them on the LSP. Thus, rather than having one LSP for each microflow, a single LSP can provide a QoS guarantee for a large aggregate of traffic. An obvious application of this capability would be to provide a guaranteed bandwidth "pipe" from one site of a large company to another site, emulating a leased line between those sites. As we will see in the next chapter, this capability is also useful for traffic engineering purposes, where large aggregates of traffic need to be sent along LSPs with sufficient bandwidth to carry the traffic.

In order to support some of these enhanced uses of RSVP, MPLS defines a new RSVP object that may be carried in a PATH message: the

LABEL_REQUEST object. This object performs two functions. First, it is used to tell an LSR at the tail end of an LSP to send back a RESV to establish the LSP. This is useful for setting up site-to-site LSPs as discussed above. Second, since an LSP may be established for any collection of packets, not just a single microflow, the object contains a field to identify the higher layer protocol that will use the LSP. This field is used much like an ethertype or similar demultiplexing key to identify the higher layer protocol (IPv4, IPX, etc.), since there is no demultiplexing field in the MPLS header. Thus, one LSP would need to be established for each higher layer protocol that is to be carried, but there is no limit on the protocols that can be supported. In particular, there is no requirement that the packets carried over an LSP established using RSVP must be IP packets.

6.1.3 RSVP and Scalability

One of the most widely held beliefs about RSVP is that it suffers from certain scalability problems. In fact, this characterization is not strictly accurate. RSVP was originally designed to support resource reservations for individual application flows—microflows—and this is a task with inherent scalability challenges. Any protocol that attempted to make reservations at this level of granularity would face similar issues.

What exactly is meant by scalability? In general, the term is used to indicate how quickly some measure of resource usage increases as a network gets larger. For example, in a large IP network such as an Internet service provider backbone, we are likely to be concerned with how large the routing tables are, since they consume memory in routers, processor power (to update), and perhaps link bandwidth (when update information is transmitted). Thus, it is desirable for routing tables to grow more slowly than the number of users attached to the network, for example.

Making reservations for individual microflows is clearly a bad idea for scalability. We might reasonably expect that each user will make reservations at some average rate, so the number of reservations that might be made across a large network is likely to grow about as fast as the number of users of the network. This will have a large cost if each router has to store some state and process some messages for each microflow reservation.

To summarize, it is much more accurate to say that microflow reservations scale badly than to say the same for RSVP. This distinction is particularly important when we consider that RSVP is not required to make reservations only for individual microflows, but can also make reservations for highly aggregated traffic, as discussed in the preceding section.

RSVP Refresh Reduction

Another aspect of RSVP that has an impact on scalability is the fact that it uses soft state. This means that periodic refresh messages must be sent to keep an RSVP reservation in place. If a single router is maintaining a large number of RSVP reservations, then the volume of refresh traffic and the cost of processing it could start to become significant. This situation is exacerbated by the fact that RSVP provides no reliability mechanism for the delivery of messages. If a message is dropped, it is assumed that a later refresh will provide the lost information. So, if timely delivery of information is important, we would tend to choose a short refresh interval, leading to a higher rate of refresh traffic.

This problem is not unique to MPLS, but MPLS has focused attention on it partly because of the desire to use RSVP to set up very large numbers of LSPs. We now describe the solution that was developed in the MPLS and RSVP working groups of the IETF.

Given the relationship between reliable delivery and refresh overhead, one step to reduce the amount of refresh processing would be to add a reliable delivery mechanism to RSVP. This has been done by defining a pair of RSVP objects, the MESSAGE_ID and MESSAGE_ID_ACK objects. The use of these objects to provide reliable delivery of messages is as follows. Suppose node A has an RSVP message representing a new piece of state (e.g., a new PATH message) that it needs to send to a neighboring node B. Node A creates a locally unique identifier for this state, puts that identifier in a MESSAGE_ID object, and adds it to the RSVP message. It also sets an "acknowledgement required" flag in the object. Node B then acknowledges receipt of the message by sending a message to A containing a MESSAGE_ID_ACK object with the same identifier. If B already has a message to send to A, it just includes the MESSAGE_ID_ACK object; otherwise, it will need to send a specially created message. For this reason a new ACK message has been created.

This simple mechanism can be used to address the refresh overhead issue in the following way. An RSVP node can use a very short refresh timer for messages it sends that cause new state to be installed. Then, upon receiving an acknowledgement from its neighbor that the new state has been installed, it can switch to a very long refresh timer. Thus, the refresh overhead is reduced without sacrificing the timeliness of reservation establishment.

Note that this mechanism stops short of "hard" state, in that refreshes must still be sent periodically to ensure that neighbors remain in sync. Thus, the "self-healing" properties of soft state, including graceful handling of crashes, are retained. The mechanism is also entirely backward compatible, in that it does not introduce any problems if some nodes implement it and some do not.

A further reduction in refresh overhead is achieved by a mechanism called *summary refresh*. The basic idea is that once a message identifier has been associated with an RSVP message, there is no need to keep sending that entire message again to refresh the state, as is normally done. Instead, a node can just send the message identifier itself. Furthermore, it is possible to pack quite a lot of message identifiers into a single message, so that one RSVP message can refresh a large amount of state. This is helpful since there is often a significant processing cost just to receive a message into the processor of a router, independent of how big it is or how much work must then be done with its contents.

Summary refresh requires a new RSVP message type, called SREFRESH. In the unicast case, this message contains just a list of previously sent message identifiers. A node receiving such a message behaves as if it had received a set of refresh messages, each of which was identical to the message that originally carried the MESSAGE_ID object. That is, it resets the timer for that piece of state and retains the state awaiting the next refresh.

One possible problem would be the receipt of a MESSAGE_ID that was unrecognized. This might happen if the next hop for some route changed but the change was not noticed by the sending node. To recover from this situation, a node may send a MESSAGE_ID_NAK (negative acknowledgement) if it does not recognize the message identifier. The sending node takes this as a signal that it should send the entire RSVP message to which the MESSAGE_ID referred.

As a result of these enhancements, the scaling concerns for RSVP when it is used for MPLS have been addressed. Large numbers of reservations and LSPs can be maintained with a small amount of refresh traffic.

6.2 Differentiated Services

Following the IETF's work on Integrated Services and RSVP, it was recognized that a more "coarse-grained" model of QoS would be valuable, as it would avoid the need to maintain per-flow reservation state inside large IP networks. The model that was eventually developed is known as the Differentiated Services, or diff-serv, model. Because both MPLS and diff-serv are expected to be deployed in ISP networks, it is important that the two technologies work together. This section provides a brief overview of the diff-serv architecture and then examines how diff-serv can be supported in a network using MPLS.

6.2.1 Differentiated Services Overview

Whereas resources are allocated to individual application flows in the int-serv architecture, the diff-serv model divides traffic into a small number of classes and allocates resources on a per-class basis. This can be viewed as an incremental approach to building QoS into the IP service model. We start with the conventional best-effort model, in which all packets are treated equally from a QoS perspective, and then add a small number of classes that receive treatment that is better than best effort in some way. For example, a simple diff-serv network might have just two classes of packets: best-effort packets and "premium" packets. These premium packets might be treated in such a way that they receive an assurance of low loss and low delay in the network.

Because diff-serv has only a few different classes of traffic, a packet's "class" can be marked directly in the packet. This contrasts with the int-serv model, in which a signalling protocol was required to tell the routers which flows of packets require special QoS treatment. The mark in the packet is called a *Differentiated Services Code Point,* or DSCP. The DSCP is carried in the 6-bit Differentiated Services field of the IP header, which was formerly part of the Type of Service (ToS) byte. In theory, therefore, we could have 64 different classes of packets, but in practice the number of DSCPs used in a single network is likely to be much smaller. The simple two-class network mentioned above might in fact be a very reasonable initial deployment of diff-serv.

There are several questions we might ask about the DSCP:

1. How does it get set to the right value, that is, how do we decide which packets get "better" treatment than others?
2. Which network elements get to set the DSCP?
3. What does a router do when it receives a packet marked with a certain DSCP?

Let's look at the last question first. The DSCP tells the router something about how the packet should be treated from a QoS perspective. Formally, the DSCP identifies a "per-hop behavior" or PHB. There are some standard PHBs, and it is also possible to define local PHBs within a network. The standard PHBs include

- Default. No special treatment, equivalent to best effort.

- Expedited forwarding (EF). Packets marked EF should be forwarded with minimal delay and experience low loss. This could be realized by putting all such packets in a dedicated EF queue and ensuring that the arrival rate of packets to the queue is less than the service rate.

- Assured forwarding (AF). A set of AF PHBs is defined in the following way. Each PHB in the set is AFxy for a range of values of x and y. The value of x is referred to as the *AF class* and typically selects a queue for the packet, while the value of y determines the *drop preference* for the packet. Thus, for example, packets marked AF11, AF12, and AF13 would all go into the same queue, but the AF13 packets would have a greater chance of being dropped due to congestion than the AF11 packets. AF2y packets, by contrast, belong to a different AF class and would go into a different queue than the AF1y packets.[2] The recommended number of AF PHBs is 12, representing four AF classes with three drop preference levels in each.

There is one aspect of AF that we want to stress because it has a significant impact on MPLS support of diff-serv. Note that the only difference between, say, AF11, AF12, and AF13 is the drop preference. The AF specification requires that packets belonging to a single microflow (e.g., packets from a single application) must not be misordered if they differ only in drop preference. Typically, this means that all packets of the same AF class (i.e., packets marked AFx1, AFx2, and AFx3, where x is a constant) go into a common queue (the AFx queue).

Note that each of the standard PHBs has a recommended DSCP value but that network operators are free to choose different DSCPs. We may think of each router as having a table that maps the DSCP found in a packet to the PHB that will determine how that packet is treated. The DSCPs are simply numbers carried in packets, whereas PHBs are well-specified behaviors to apply to packets.

---

2. RFC 2587, which defines assured forwarding, does not use the word *queue*, but requires AF1y packets to be "independently forwarded" with respect to AF2y. This is intended to avoid overly constraining implementors, but makes for a less clear understanding of the basic idea.

Returning to the first two questions, how and where do we set DSCPs, one answer would be to let hosts do it, based on knowledge of application requirements. For example, a host might set the DSCP in packets from a telephony application to a value indicating EF. Alternatively, a router could apply some locally configured policy to set the DSCP, such as the following: all packets arriving on interface *x* get set to AF11 up to a maximum of 1 Mb/sec, and all packets about that rate get set to AF12. We could imagine arbitrarily complex policies. In general, it is typical to apply such policies on packets as they cross a trust boundary, for example, the edge of an administrative domain. Obviously, a network operator does not want an untrusted entity to inject unlimited amounts of traffic that is consuming a limited resource, and the resources that can be used to provide high QoS (link bandwidth, buffer space, etc.) are clearly limited. Note that the policy can be applied at a single hop, resulting in a DSCP value being placed in the packet, and that the packet might be forwarded through many hops and receive queuing treatment based solely on the DSCP, with no further application of policies. Figure 6.3 illustrates the setting of DSCPs and subsequent forwarding of packets in an example network. This property of DSCPs—that they can be set at one hop and then used to determine QoS treatment at many subsequent hops—proves useful when supporting diff-serv in an MPLS network.

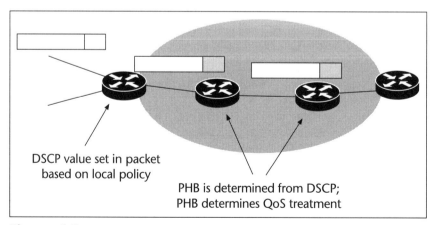

DSCP value set in packet based on local policy

PHB is determined from DSCP; PHB determines QoS treatment

Figure 6.3

DSCP is set on arriving packets at trust boundary; PHB, and thus the QoS treatment, is determined at subsequent hops by examining the DSCP.

6.2.2 MPLS Support of Diff-Serv

The first issue in supporting diff-serv over an MPLS network is to provide some way to ensure that packets marked with various DSCPs receive the appropriate QoS treatment at each LSR in the network. However, the DSCP is carried in the IP header, and LSRs do not examine that header when forwarding packets; clearly, there needs to be some way to determine the appropriate PHB from the label header. There are two ways to achieve this, with some slight variations depending on exactly how the label header is encoded. (Recall that labels may be encoded in a "shim" header or, in some cases, in a link layer header such as an ATM cell header.)

Recall from Section 5.3 that the shim header for MPLS has a 3-bit field defined "for experimental use," the Exp field. The original intent of this field was to support marking of packets for Differentiated Services. However, there is an obvious problem with this field, which is that it is only 3 bits long, whereas the Differentiated Services field is 6 bits. The historical reason for this difference is that the Exp field was defined prior to the formation of the diff-serv working group, at a time when many routers used only 3 bits of the IP header (the old IP Precedence field) to mark the QoS class of packets. Furthermore, there was a strong desire to keep the MPLS shim header as small as possible, and it seemed that eight classes of traffic would be enough for most practical purposes. (Note that one class in a network—best effort—is the norm today, and it is widely believed that providing two or three classes would represent a significant step forward in capabilities and operational complexity.) Nevertheless, the diff-serv standards allow for up to 64 DSCPs, and the MPLS shim header can only carry eight different values in the Exp field.

One observation we can make is that, in a network that supports fewer than eight PHBs, the Exp field is sufficient for our purposes. Just as a conventional diff-serv router maintains a mapping from the possible values of DSCP to the PHBs it supports, an LSR can maintain a mapping from Exp values to PHBs. As long as no more than eight PHBs are required, the diff-serv functionality of an LSR is almost identical to that provided by a conventional IP router. Just as it is necessary to configure a diff-serv router so that it correctly maps DSCPs to the appropriate PHBs, it will be necessary to configure an LSR to map the Exp values to different PHBs. For example, in the simple case of a network supporting only two classes of packets (best effort and premium), we could use the Exp value 000 (binary) to mark the best-effort packets and 001 for the premium packets. LSRs would then be configured to provide default behavior to the 000 packets and to put packets marked 001 into the queue that implements the EF PHB. Note that no additional signalling is required. Any of the label distribution mechanisms described in Chapter 5 (e.g., LDP, BGP, etc.) can be used without modification to assign labels. The label tells an LSR where to forward a packet, and the Exp bits tell it what PHB to treat the packet with. An LSP that is set up under these conditions is referred to as an *E-LSP:* E stands for Exp, meaning that the PHB is inferred from the Exp bits.

What if we want to provide more than eight PHBs? In this case the Exp field alone is not sufficient to indicate the PHB. The obvious choice is to use the label in some way to convey the PHB. In this case we will have L-LSPs: L stands for label, since in this case the PHB is inferred from the label. We will look at the details of how this is done below.

A related problem arises when we consider links that do not use the shim header for forwarding, such as ATM. In this case we have no Exp field at all, so an alternative way of marking packets is clearly required. Again, the label field will have to be used.

It should be clear that if we want to convey information about PHBs inside labels, we need to enhance the label distribution mechanisms. To date, we have seen a variety of label distribution mechanisms that advertise bindings between labels and FECs such as address prefixes. What we need here is a way that a label can be bound to both an FEC and a PHB (or, perhaps, a set of PHBs, for reasons that will shortly become clear).

Before going into details of label distribution, we recall a detail from the AF specification. It requires that packets belonging to a single microflow must not be misordered if they differ only in drop preference. As a result, packets of the same AF class typically go into a common queue. Now some LSRs implement a queue per LSP, and in some cases two LSPs to a common destination could take different paths to that destination. Thus, in order to meet the ordering constraints for AF traffic, it will typically be necessary to send packets of the same AF class (e.g., AF11, AF12, and AF13 packets) on a common LSP.

While AF is currently the only instance of a PHB group that imposes ordering constraints on packets with different PHBs, in principle there might be other such PHBs in the future. For this reason, some new terminology was introduced: a *PHB scheduling class* is defined as a group of PHBs that requires that packets with different PHBs in the group not be misordered. In the MPLS context, packets of a common PHB scheduling class must travel on the same LSP.

Once we have decided to put packets with different PHBs on a common LSP, it follows that, if we want to know the full PHB of a packet, we need to look somewhere other than the label. Fortunately, we have the Exp bits (when the shim header is used) or the CLP (cell loss priority) bit on ATM links. Thus, when the shim header is in use, we carry the AF drop preference in the Exp bits. On ATM links, the drop preference is encoded in the CLP bit, which limits the number of drop preferences to two.

The effect of all this on label distribution is fairly simple. Any existing Label Distribution Protocol can be extended to specify which PHB (or PHB scheduling class) is to be bound to the advertised label. To take the example of LDP, the messages that request and advertise bindings of prefixes to labels are now extended to include a PHB or PHB scheduling class. This allows labels to be bound to <prefix, PHB> pairs. In most cases an LSP established in this way will carry packets of a single PHB, in which case the Exp bits or CLP bit are unused. For AF traffic, an LSP will carry packets of the same AF class but of a different drop preference, with the Exp bits or CLP bit indicating the drop preference.

The two different approaches to conveying diff-serv information are depicted in Figure 6.4. In Figure 6.4(a), a single E-LSP is in use and may carry packets requiring up to eight different PHBs. The PHB to be applied to any packet is determined by examining the Exp bits. In Figure 6.4(b), two L-LSPs have been established. The first one carries only default packets. LSRs R2 and R3 know (since they were told at LSP establishment time) that packets that arrive on the lower LSP must be default packets and should be queued accordingly. The upper LSP carries packets that may be AF11, AF12, or AF13. LSRs R2 and R3 use the label to determine that the packets are AF1y packets, and they examine the Exp bits to find the drop preference, that is, the value of y.

In these examples, we assume that LSR R1 is the label edge router, that is, it is the router at the start of the LSPs. Thus, the job of getting packets onto the correct LSP, and of setting the Exp bits correctly, falls to R1. How does R1 know exactly what to do? As would be the case in a conventional diff-serv network, we assume that R1 has undergone some configuration. First, it may be the case that R1 is responsible for applying the local policy that establishes which packets receive which PHB, just like the router at the entrance to the cloud in Figure 6.3. Or

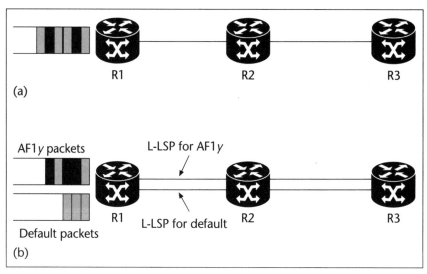

Figure 6.4

A single E-LSP is used to carry packets with up to eight distinct PHBs (a); lower L-LSP carries default packets, and upper L-LSP carries AF1 packets (b).

R1 may receive IP packets whose DSCP has already been set at some prior hop. In either case it can be assumed that, before putting a packet onto an LSP, R1 knows the PHB of the packet. It must also be configured to support some set of PHBs and to use E-LSPs, L-LSPs, or perhaps both to carry packets with those PHBs. Recall that an LSR should always (except in transient conditions) have an LSP to any destination to which it might need to forward a packet; R1 will have an appropriate LSP to any destination *for any PHB* that it is configured to support. R1 uses one or more label distribution protocols to ensure that it has the correct set of LSPs established. Thus, it knows which LSP to put any packet onto, as long as R1 supports the PHB required for that packet.

The details of setting the Exp bits depend on whether a packet is to travel on an E-LSP or an L-LSP. If it is an E-LSP, R1 must have a configured mapping of PHBs to Exp values, which must be consistent with the reverse mapping (Exp to PHB) in R2 and R3. For an L-LSP, the Exp bits are only relevant for AF PHBs, and the mapping is statically defined: the drop preference is carried in the low order bits of Exp.

Table 6.1 summarizes the differences between E-LSPs and L-LSPs. One point we need to stress is that it is possible to use both types of LSPs in a single network, even on a single link, provided that the link uses the shim header and thus has Exp bits to support E-LSPs. Because

Table 6.1

Comparison of E-LSPs and L-LSPs.

E-LSPs	L-LSPs
PHB is determined from Exp bits	PHB is determined from label or from label plus Exp/CLP bits
No additional signalling is required	PHB or PHB scheduling group is signalled at LSP setup (in LDP, RSVP, etc.)
Exp → PHB mapping is configured	Label → PHB mapping is signalled. Exp/CLP → PHB mapping is well known (used only for AF)
Shim header is required; E-LSPs are therefore not possible on ATM links	Shim or link layer header may be used; therefore, L-LSPs are suitable for ATM links
Up to eight PHBs per LSP	One PHB per LSP except for AF; one PHB scheduling group (2–3 PHBs) per LSP for AF

L-LSPs require the signalling of a PHB at LSP setup, any LSP that is set up without explicit signalling of a PHB is assumed to be an E-LSP by default.

One question to ask is, Which sort of LSP is appropriate under various circumstances? Clearly, L-LSPs are the only choice on link types such as ATM where the shim header is not used. On those link types where both types of LSPs may be used, E-LSPs offer several advantages over L-LSPs. First, because more PHBs can be supported on a single E-LSP, E-LSPs reduce the total number of LSPs, which may be helpful if label space is a limited resource. Second, the E-LSP model is most similar to the standard diff-serv model: an LSR just looks at bits in the header to decide what PHB to apply to a packet. However, L-LSPs also offer advantages, including the ability to support an arbitrarily large number of PHBs, not just eight. In addition, because L-LSPs provide one LSP for each PHB or PHB scheduling class, they provide the possibility of engineering different paths for different PHBs. For example, an LSP that carries only EF traffic could be routed over low delay links, while an LSP carrying AF traffic might be routed over links with more delay but high bandwidth. In short, the choice of E-LSPs or L-LSPs, or a mixture of both, requires close examination of the trade-offs of a specific network.

6.3   Explicit Congestion Notification

Having seen how the two main IP QoS models can be supported in an MPLS environment, one QoS issue—explicit congestion notification (ECN)—remains. Like int-serv and diff-serv, ECN is a fairly recent addition to the IP service model, and it is important that MPLS be able to support it. ECN is classified as an "experimental" protocol by the IETF, which means that it has been specified but may not progress to full standardization until some experience is gained with it. In this section we examine ECN and the steps needed to support it in MPLS networks.

6.3.1   ECN Overview

The dominant forms of congestion control in today's IP networks are the congestion avoidance mechanisms of TCP, invented primarily by Van Jacobson in the late 1980s. These mechanisms depend on the generally correct assumption that packet losses in the network are an indication of congestion. Using loss as a congestion indication, TCP senders reduce their sending rates when they experience packet loss and slowly increase their rates during periods when no packets have been lost.

Using loss as the sole indication of congestion works well for many TCP-based applications, but it has several drawbacks. For some applications, the lost packet will need to be transmitted and thus will arrive much later at its destination than it would have done had it not been lost. This can cause degradation of the response time of interactive applications such as telnet. For other applications, such as conferencing, it is out of the question to retransmit a lost packet because the retransmitted data will be useless by the time it arrives, so packet loss causes a degradation in application quality. A third issue is that a lost packet consumes some resources as it traverses the network up to the point where it is lost. It would be preferable not to send the packet at all if it is just going to be thrown away, so that those resources can be more profitably used by other packets that will be delivered successfully.

Given the problems of using loss as an implicit indication of congestion, ECN introduces a way to explicitly signal congestion without dropping a packet. The basic idea is for a router to set a bit in a packet header when it detects congestion, and then to forward the packet rather than dropping it. This requires the router to have some form of queue management such as *random early detection* (RED)—that is, it must actively monitor congestion rather than just dropping packets when the queue becomes full.[3] When a packet with the "congestion experienced" (CE) bit arrives at its destination, the receiver must send a signal back to the sender that will cause the sender to reduce its sending rate. Exactly how this information is conveyed, and how the sender responds to it, is dependent on the end-to-end protocol in use. In the case of TCP, the receiver of a packet with the CE bit set conveys this fact to the sender by setting an "ECN-echo" bit in the TCP header of the next packet destined for the sender (e.g., an ACK packet). When the sender sees the ECN-echo bit set, it responds exactly as if a packet had been dropped in congestion control terms: it reduces the size of its sending window by a factor of two. Of course, it does not retransmit a packet, since no packet was lost.

One of the challenges of deploying new capabilities in the Internet is the fact that deployment is guaranteed to be incremental. Thus, while there might be some routers that support ECN, some will not, and there will be a similar mix of ECN-capable and non–ECN-capable endpoints attached to the network. For those end systems that understand packet loss only as a congestion indication, it won't do much good to set a bit in their packet headers and have them ignore it. The result would be that non–ECN-capable senders would never react to congestion, overwhelming the ECN-capable senders and potentially causing a congestion collapse of the network.

To deal with this significant deployment issue, ECN defines two new bits to be carried in the IP header. (Fortunately, two bits of the old ToS byte were not used by diff-serv.) The first is the congestion experienced (CE) bit described above; the second is the "ECN-capable transport" (ECT) bit. When a sender and receiver agree (as a result of suitable negotiation) that they can support ECN in the way described above, the sender sets the ECT bit in the packets it sends. Routers then set the CE bit if they are experiencing congestion and the ECT bit is set. If the ECT bit is not set, they have no choice but to drop packets when experiencing congestion.

---

3. RED is the most widely deployed active queue management mechanism in IP networks. It monitors average queue length over relatively long time scales—on the order of tens to hundreds of milliseconds—and begins to take action to reduce congestion when this average crosses a threshold. It takes action on only a small percentage of arriving packets, increasing the percentage as congestion worsens. The action may be to drop those packets or to set a bit in their headers if ECN is available.

6.3.2 MPLS Support of ECN

ECN could be trivially supported on MPLS networks by defining a pair of bits in the MPLS header that duplicate the function of the ECT and CE bits in the IP header. Unfortunately, two spare bits are generally not available in the MPLS shim header or link layer headers such as ATM. However, there are situations where *one* MPLS header bit might be available for ECN. When the shim header is used, the three Exp bits may not all be used for diff-serv support; at most, two are needed for L-LSPs, and E-LSPs could support up to four PHBs on an LSP using two of the Exp bits. Similarly, the CLP bit may not always be required for diff-serv support on ATM-LSRs.

Assuming that one bit could be used for ECN, would this be sufficient? Surprisingly enough, the answer is yes. First, note that the two bits used in IP only encode three valid states, not four. Those states are

- Not ECN capable
- ECN capable AND not CE
- ECN capable AND CE

It is not meaningful to have a state in which the CE bit is set for a non–ECN-capable packet—such a packet would be dropped. Now suppose we use our one bit in the manner shown in Table 6.2. What we have given up in going from two bits to one, and from three states to two, is the ability to distinguish between a packet that was sent by a non–ECN-capable end system and a packet that was ECN capable but experienced congestion at some earlier hop. What this means is that if a single packet from an ECN-capable end system is unlucky enough to pass through two congested nodes and to be selected as one of the packets that needs to be marked or dropped on both occasions, it will get dropped the second time. This should be a rare occurrence, compared to the frequency with which the scheme will work exactly as it would with two bits.[4]

There are a few details to fill in for this to work in an MPLS network. First, we need to be clear on the rules for setting the ECN bit in the MPLS header when we add the header to an IP packet. As Table 6.2 shows, we will set the MPLS ECN bit if the ECT bit on the arriving IP packet is clear or the CE bit is set; if ECT is set and CE is not, then we leave the MPLS ECN bit clear. When a packet reaches the end of an LSP

---

4. You might wonder why two bits rather than one were deemed necessary for support of ECN in the IP header, given that one can be made to work. The answer seems to be that, since the extra bit was available, there was no reason not to use it.

Table 6.2
Representation of ECN states in one bit.

Bit value	Meaning
0	ECN capable AND not CE
1	Not ECN capable OR CE

Table 6.3
Updating the IP CE bit on label removal.

IP ECT bit on input	MPLS ECN bit value	IP ECN bits on output
Not ECN capable (ECT = 0)	Must be 1	ECT = 0, CE = 0
ECN capable (ECT = 1)	0	ECT = 1, CE = 0
ECN capable (ECT = 1)	1	ECT = 1, CE = 1

and the label is to be removed, the rules for updating the two ECN bits in the IP header are as shown in Table 6.3. The only situation in which the IP header needs to be modified is when a packet from an ECN-capable sender (ECT = 1) arrives at the end of an LSP with the MPLS ECN bit set. This means that congestion was experienced either on the LSP or before the packet arrived on the LSP, and thus the CE bit must be set to 1 if it is not already set.

Finally, there needs to be a way to ensure that the LSRs along an LSP agree on the usage of one of the Exp bits or the CLP bit for ECN purposes. This could possibly be done by configuration, as is the case when obtaining consistent usage of the Exp bits for E-LSPs. Alternatively, it could be signalled, analogous to L-LSPs. This detail of ECN deployment for MPLS is under investigation at the time of writing.

6.4 Summary

The relationship between MPLS and QoS is a close one, but MPLS does not radically alter the QoS landscape. Rather, MPLS is primarily able to support the QoS models developed for IP and already used in non-MPLS networks. The two main models are Integrated Services (int-serv) and Differentiated Services (diff-serv). Int-serv is designed to provide end-to-end QoS guarantees to individual application flows, while diff-serv enables a large IP network to offer a small number of distinct classes of service. MPLS is also able to support the experimental standard for explicit congestion notification (ECN).

Supporting the IP service models in an MPLS network is essential to the deployment of MPLS, since there should be no loss of IP functionality when adding MPLS. In addition, the support of IP QoS by MPLS devices offers some advantages. Because LSRs may be implemented on ATM switching hardware, MPLS provides an easy mechanism to support IP QoS over ATM networks, a problem that has proven quite challenging in the past. In addition, MPLS enables reservations to be made for highly aggregated traffic. This is accomplished by binding a label to an int-serv reservation and using local criteria at the entrance of the LSP to send an aggregated traffic flow down the LSP. Thus, MPLS helps to address the scaling concerns of int-serv deployment.

6.5 Further Reading

The most important RFCs for Integrated Services, RSVP, and Differentiated Services are

Braden, B., S. Shenker, and D. Clark. *Integrated Services in the Internet Architecture: An Overview.* RFC 1633, June 1994.

Braden, B., et al. *Resource ReSerVation Protocol (RSVP)—Version 1 Functional Specification.* RFC 2205, September 1997.

Blake, S., et al. *An Architecture for Differentiated Services.* RFC 2475, December 1998.

Further information on Integrated Services and diff-serv PHBs can also be found in RFCs. Like all RFCs, they can be found at

www.rfc-editor.org

TCP congestion control is presented in a paper by Jacobson, and explicit congestion notification is described in yet another RFC:

Jacobson, V. "Congestion Avoidance and Control." In Proceedings of ACM SIGCOMM 88, pp. 314–329, September 1988.

Ramakrishnan, K., and S. Floyd. *A Proposal to Add Explicit Congestion Notification (ECN) to IP.* RFC 2481, January 1999.

The MPLS support of these QoS features is, at the time of writing, described in Internet drafts, although most will be published shortly as RFCs.

CHAPTER

Constraint-Based Routing

n this chapter we describe how MPLS can be used to support constraint-based routing. We begin by defining what constraint-based routing is. Following this, we describe the components of constraint-based routing. We then look at several possible applications of MPLS constraint-based routing: traffic engineering, fast reroute, and support for QoS.

7.1 What Is Constraint-Based Routing?

To understand the concept of constraint-based routing, we first look at the routing system that is conventionally used in IP networks, such as the Internet. A network is modeled as a collection of Autonomous Systems (ASs), where routes within an AS are determined by intradomain routing and routes that span multiple ASs are determined by interdomain routing. Examples of intradomain routing protocols are RIP, OSPF, and IS-IS. The interdomain routing protocol that is used today in IP networks is BGP. For the rest of this chapter we focus on intradomain routing.

Path computation for any of the intradomain routing protocols we mentioned above is based on an algorithm that optimizes (minimizes) a particular scalar metric. In the case of RIP, this metric is the number of hops. That is, given the choice of multiple paths to a given destination, RIP uses the Bellman-Ford algorithm to compute a path with the minimum number of hops. In the case of OSPF or IS-IS, this metric is the administrative metric of a path. That is, with OSPF (or IS-IS), a network administrator assigns to each link in the network an administrative metric.[1] Given the choice of multiple paths to a given destination, OSPF (or IS-IS) uses the Dijkstra shortest path first (SPF) algorithm to compute a path that minimizes the administrative metric of the path, where the administrative metric of a path is defined as a sum of the administrative metrics on all the links along the path.

Formally, we can define constraint-based routing as follows. Consider a network that is represented by a graph (V, E), where V is the set of nodes and E is the set of links that interconnect these nodes. Associated with each link is a collection of attributes. For each pair of nodes in the graph, there is a set of constraints that have to be satisfied by the path from the first node in the pair to the second one. This set of constraints is expressed in terms of the attributes of the links and is usually known only by the node at the head end of the path (the first node in the pair). The goal of constraint-based routing is to compute a path from one given node to another, such that the path doesn't violate the constraints and is optimal with respect to some scalar metric. Once the path is computed, constraint-based routing is responsible for establishing and maintaining forwarding state along such a path.

The main difference between conventional IP routing (as described at the start of this section) and constraint-based routing is as follows. Plain IP routing algorithms aim to find a path that optimizes a certain scalar metric (e.g., minimizes the number of hops), while constraint-based routing algorithms set out to find a path that optimizes a certain scalar metric and at the same time does not violate a set of constraints. It is precisely the ability to find a path that doesn't violate a set of constraints that distinguishes constraint-based routing from plain IP routing.

So far we've been talking about finding a path that doesn't violate a set of constraints, but we've said very little about what kind of constraints we have in mind. Now let's look at some of these.

One type of constraint would be the ability to find a path that has certain performance characteristics. For example, you may want to

---

1. There are no strict rules on how to decide what administrative metric should be assigned to a particular link—it is left up to a network administrator to make such a decision. One possibility would be to assign a metric that reflects the propagation delay on a link (so longer links will get a higher metric).

find a path with certain minimum available bandwidth. In this case the constraint imposed on the routing algorithm is that the path computed by the algorithm must have at least that amount of available bandwidth on all the links along the path, and the link attribute we use is the link available bandwidth. Note that different paths within a given network may have different bandwidth constraints associated with them. That is, for one pair of nodes the path from the first node in the pair to the second one may require one value of the minimum available bandwidth, while for another pair of nodes the path from the first node in the pair to the second one may require a different value of the minimum available bandwidth.

Another type of constraint would be administrative. For example, a network administrator may want to exclude certain traffic from traversing certain links in a network, where such links would be identified by a particular link attribute. In this case the constraint imposed on the routing algorithm is that the path for that traffic must not traverse through any of the links that have to be excluded. Or the network administrator may want to require certain traffic to traverse only certain links in a network, where again the links would be identified by a particular link attribute. In this case the constraint imposed on the routing algorithm is that the path for that traffic must traverse only these certain links. Note that just like with performance constraints, with administrative constraints different paths may have different administrative constraints associated with them. For example, for one pair of nodes the path from the first node in the pair to the second one may have one set of links to be excluded, while for another pair of nodes the path from the first node in the pair to the second one may require a different set of links to be excluded.

Constraint-based routing may also include a combination of performance and administrative constraints, not just one or the other. For example, constraint-based routing should be able to find a path that has certain available bandwidth and at the same time excludes certain links.

Can constraint-based routing, where constraints include either performance constraints or administrative constraints (or a combination of both) be supported by plain IP routing? The answer is no. There are several interrelated reasons for this answer. The main reason is that constraint-based routing requires route (path) calculation at the source. This is because different sources may have different constraints for a path to the same destination, and the constraints associated with a particular source router are known only to that router, but not to any other router in a network. In contrast, with plain IP routing, a route (path) is computed in a distributed fashion by every router in a network, and this computation does not take into account constraints of different sources. In fact, plain IP routing can't take into account constraints of different sources, as these constraints are local to the individual sources and are not distributed throughout a network.

Another reason why plain IP routing can't support constraint-based routing is that when a path is determined by the source, forwarding along such a path can't be provided using the destination-based forwarding paradigm, which is the paradigm that plain IP routing uses. Some sort of "explicit" (or "source") routing capabilities are required, because different sources may compute different paths to the same destination; therefore, the destination by itself is insufficient to determine how to forward packets.

Finally, since the path computation at the source needs to take into account the information about attributes associated with the individual links in a network, there should be some way of distributing such information throughout the network. Clearly, plain IP routing doesn't provide this; conventional IP Link-State Routing Protocols (e.g., OSPF, IS-IS) distribute only the information about the state (up/down) of individual links and the administrative metric assigned to each link, and Distance Vector Routing Protocols (e.g., RIP) distribute only the address of the next hop and the distance.

While constraint-based routing can't be supported by plain IP routing, it doesn't mean that the plain IP routing can't be augmented with additional capabilities to support such functionality; in fact it can. Moreover, by augmenting plain IP routing, we can build a single routing system where it is possible to "mix and match" plain IP routing with constraint-based routing. For example, with such a system some traffic could be routed via plain IP routing, while some other traffic could be routed via constraint-based routing.

The most important property of a routing system that combines both plain IP routing and constraint-based routing is that such a system must provide diversity of routing for applications that need it, while at the same time providing good scaling via routing/forwarding information aggregation/abstraction whenever possible.

7.2 Constraint-Based Routing Components

To understand what kind of additional capabilities we need to add to plain IP routing in order to support constraint-based routing, let's look again at the key mechanisms needed to support constraint-based routing.

The first mechanism we need is the ability to compute a path at the source, and to compute it in such a way that the computation can take into account not just some scalar metric that is used as an optimization criteria but also a set of constraints that should not be violated. That, in turn, requires the source to have all the information needed to compute such a path.

The information that a source uses to compute a path can be partitioned into the information available locally at the source and the information that the source has to obtain from other routers in a network. The information available at the source is the information about the constraints of various paths originated by the source. The information that the source has to obtain from other routers in a network includes the information about the network topology, as well as the information about various attributes associated with the links in a network. And since potentially any node in a network may originate traffic that has to be routed via constraint-based routing, this information has to be available to every node in a network. So the second mechanism we need is the ability to distribute the information about network topology and attributes associated with links throughout the network.

Once we compute the path, we also need a way to support forwarding along such a path. So the third mechanism we need is one that supports explicit routing.

Finally, establishing a route for a particular set of traffic may require reservation of resources along the route and therefore may alter the value of the attributes associated with individual links in a network. For example, if available bandwidth is one of the link constraints that we are trying to satisfy for some set of traffic, establishing a route for that traffic requires bandwidth reservation along the route, which, in turn, changes the amount of available bandwidth on the links along the route. So the fourth mechanism we need is one by which network resources can be reserved and link attributes can be modified as the result of certain traffic taking certain routes.

7.2.1 Constrained Shortest Path First (CSPF)

As we mentioned above, constraint-based routing requires the ability to compute a path, such that the path

- Is optimal with respect to some scalar metric (e.g., minimizes administrative metric, hop count)
- Does not violate a set of constraints

One way to accomplish these objectives is to use the shortest path first (SPF) algorithm. Recall that the plain SPF algorithm computes a path that is optimal with respect to some scalar metric (e.g., administrative distance). So, to compute a path that doesn't violate constraints, all we need to do is to modify the algorithm in such a way that it will be able to take into account the constraints. We'll refer to such an algorithm as *constrained shortest path first* (CSPF).

To understand how SPF should be modified to take constraints into account, let's first review the operation of plain SPF. The plain SPF algorithm works by starting at a node, called the root, and then building a shortest path tree rooted at that node. At each iteration of the algorithm, there is a list of "candidate" nodes (initially, this list contains just the root). In general, paths from the root to the candidate nodes are not necessarily the shortest ones. However, for the candidate node that is closest to the root (with respect to the distance used by SPF), the path to that node is guaranteed to be shortest. So at each iteration the algorithm picks from the candidate list the node with the shortest distance to the root. This node is then added to the shortest path tree and removed from the list of candidate nodes. Once this node is added to the shortest path tree, the nodes that are not in the shortest path tree, but are adjacent to that node, are examined for possible addition to/ modification of the candidate list. The algorithm then iterates again. For the case when you want to find the shortest path from the root to all other nodes, the algorithm terminates when the candidate list becomes empty. For the case when you want to find the shortest path from the root to one other specific node, the algorithm terminates when this other node is added to the shortest path tree.

More formally, the plain SPF that computes the shortest path from a given node S to some other node D can be described as follows:

- Step 1 (initialization): Set the set of candidate nodes to empty. Set the shortest path tree to only the root, S. For each node adjacent to the root, set its path metric to the metric of the link between the root and the node. For all other nodes, set this metric to infinity.
- Step 2: Denote the node just added to the shortest path tree as V. For each link attached to that node, examine the node at the other end of the link. Denote this other node as W.

❏ Step 2a: If W is already in the shortest path tree, examine the next link attached to V.

❏ Step 2b: Otherwise (W is not in the shortest path tree), compute the metric of the path from the root to W (this metric is the sum of the metric of the path from the root to V plus the metric of the link from V to W). If W is not on the candidate list, then add W to the candidate list and set the metric of the path from the root to W to that distance. If W is on the candidate list, and its current path metric is greater than the newly computed metric, set the path metric for W to the newly computed metric.

■ Step 3: Among all the nodes in the candidate list, find the one with the smallest path metric. Add this node to the shortest path tree, and remove this node from the candidate list. If this node is D, we are done. Otherwise, go back to Step 2.

Given the operations of the plain SPF, it is quite easy to see the modification we need to make to turn it into CSPF. All we need to do is modify the step that handles addition/modifications of the candidate list. Specifically, in Step 2 as we examine links attached to V, for each such link we first check whether the link satisfies the constraints. If and only if it does, then we examine the node W at the other end of the link. More formally, if we want to find a path from S to D, subject to a certain set of constraints, C1, C2, . . . , Cn, then in Step 2 as we examine each link attached to V, for each such link we first check whether the link satisfies C1, C2, . . . , Cn. Only if the link satisfies all the constraints do we examine the node W at the other end of the link.

In general, the procedures by which we check whether a link satisfies a particular constraint are specific to the nature of the constraint. For example, when the constraint we want to satisfy is the available bandwidth, then the check is whether the available bandwidth on the link is greater than or equal to the bandwidth specified by the constraint; only if it is do we then examine the node W at the other end of the link.

Also observe that checking whether a link satisfies a particular constraint assumes that there is constraint-related information associated with the link. The nature of this information is constraint-related. For example, when the constraint we want to satisfy is the available bandwidth, the information we need to have is the available bandwidth on a link.

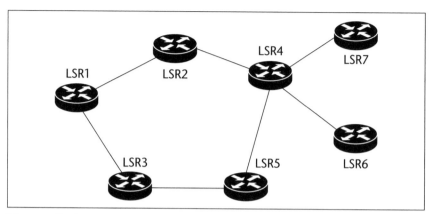

Figure 7.1
Constrained SPF—example.

Note that the algorithm we use for path computation, CSPF, requires the router that performs path computation to have information about all the links in a network. That, in turn, imposes a restriction on the type of routing protocols that we can use to support constraint-based routing—we have to use Link-State Routing Protocols (IS-IS, OSPF), as Distance Vector Routing Protocols (e.g., RIP) are not capable of meeting the requirement.

To illustrate CSPF, consider an example shown in Figure 7.1. Assume that all the links have the same administrative distance and that this distance is equal to 1. Also assume that all the links, except for the link (LSR2, LSR4), have available bandwidth of 150 Mb/sec, while the link (LSR2, LSR4) has available bandwidth of 45 Mb/sec. Our goal is to find a path from LSR1 to LSR6 that has minimum administrative distance and at least 100 Mb/sec available bandwidth. That is, the constraint we need to satisfy is the constraint on available bandwidth.

At initialization the shortest path tree (rooted at LSR1) consists of LSR1 only. Examining two neighbors of LSR1, LSR2 and LSR3, we notice that the available bandwidth on links (LSR1, LSR2) and (LSR1, LSR3) is greater than the bandwidth requirements of the path (100 Mb/sec). Therefore, we conclude that neither of these links violates the constraints, so we add LSR2 and LSR3 to the candidate list. Following this, we find the node in the candidate list with the shortest distance from LSR1. This node is LSR2,[2] and so we add it, along with the

---

2. At this point there are two nodes on the candidate list, LSR2 and LSR3, each with the same distance from LSR1. For the sake of the example, we randomly selected LSR2

(LSR1, LSR2) link, to the shortest path tree (and remove LSR2 from the candidate list). That completes the first iteration of the algorithm.

At the second iteration of the algorithm, we examine LSR2's neighbor—LSR4. With this neighbor we notice that the available bandwidth on the (LSR2, LSR4) link is less than the bandwidth requirements of the path. Therefore, this link violates the constraint. So, at this point, we don't add LSR4 to the candidate list. We still have LSR3 on the candidate list, so we add it to the shortest path tree, along with the (LSR1, LSR3) link (and remove LSR3 from the candidate list). That completes the second iteration of the algorithm.

At the third iteration of the algorithm, we examine LSR3's neighbor—LSR5. With this neighbor we notice that the available bandwidth on the (LSR3, LSR5) link is greater than the bandwidth required by the path. Therefore, we conclude that this link doesn't violate the constraint, so we add LSR5 to the candidate list. Following this, we find that the node in the candidate list with the shortest distance from LSR1 is LSR5. So we add LSR5, together with the (LSR3, LSR5) link, to the shortest path tree (and remove LSR5 from the candidate list). That completes the third iteration of the algorithm.

At the fourth iteration of the algorithm, we examine LSR5's neighbor—LSR4. Notice that we examined LSR4 before—in the second iteration. But at that time we didn't add LSR4 to the candidate list due to the constraint violation on the (LSR2, LSR4) link. Now we can add LSR4 to the candidate list, as the (LSR5, LSR4) link has available bandwidth greater than the one required by the path and therefore doesn't violate the constraint. Following this, we find that the node in the candidate list with the shortest distance from LSR1 is LSR4. So we add LSR4, together with the (LSR5, LSR4) link, to the shortest path tree (and remove LSR4 from the candidate list). That completes the fourth iteration of the algorithm.

At the fifth iteration of the algorithm, we examine LSR4's neighbors—LSR6 and LSR7. Since the available bandwidth on both the (LSR4, LSR6) and (LSR4, LSR7) links is greater than the bandwidth required by the constraint on the path, we add both LSR4 and LSR6 to the candidate list. Following this, we find that a node in the candidate list with the shortest distance from LSR1 is LSR6. So we add LSR6, together with the (LSR4, LSR6) link, to the shortest path tree and remove LSR6 from the candidate list. At this point we notice that our shortest path tree includes LSR6, which is the destination node of the path we

from the candidate list. The results of the algorithm would not change if we selected LSR3 instead.

need to find. Therefore, we terminate the algorithm. The resulting constrained shortest path from LSR1 to LSR6 is (LSR1, LSR3, LSR5, LSR4, LSR6). Notice that this path is different from the path that would be computed by plain SPF, which would be (LSR1, LSR2, LSR4, LSR6).

7.2.2 MPLS as the Forwarding Mechanism

As we mentioned in Section 7.1, support for constraint-based routing requires (among other things) explicit routing (or source routing) capability. To provide this capability, we use MPLS explicit routing capability.

The reasons for using MPLS are twofold. First of all, MPLS allows decoupling of the information used for forwarding (a label) from the information carried in the IP header. Second, mapping between an FEC and an LSP is completely confined to the LSR at the head end of the LSP. In other words, the decision as to which IP packets will take a particular explicit route is completely confined to the LSR that computes the route. And, as we discussed before, it is precisely these capabilities that we need in order to support constraint-based routing.

Just as with any other MPLS capability, support for explicit routing with MPLS may be decomposed into two components: control and forwarding. It is the control component that is responsible for establishing the forwarding (label) state along an explicit route. We'll describe two possible alternatives for the control component in the following two sections. The forwarding component uses the forwarding state established by the control component, as well as some information carried in packets to forward the packets along the explicit routes.

7.2.3 RSVP Extensions

Once we have computed a path with CSPF, the next thing we need to do is to establish the forwarding state along the path, as well as possibly to reserve resources along the path. There are two possible mechanisms to accomplish this: RSVP and CR-LDP (constraint-based routing LDP). In this section we describe how this can be accomplished with RSVP, using techniques similar to those described for Tag Switching in Sections 4.1.4 and 4.1.5, and extending the use of RSVP described in Section 6.1.2. In the following section we describe how CR-LDP—a set of extensions to the LDP described in Chapter 5—could be used.

Since we use MPLS for forwarding, the forwarding state we need to establish is the set of labels on the LSRs along the path. We already know how to establish label forwarding state with RSVP by using the RSVP Label Object—we covered this in Section 6.1.2. What we still miss is the ability to establish this state along an explicit route.

Plain RSVP, augmented by the Label Object, can establish MPLS forwarding state (an LSP) only along the path computed by plain IP routing. This is because with plain RSVP the path taken by the RSVP PATH message is controlled by the destination-based forwarding paradigm, and the path taken by the PATH message determines the path taken by the LSP. When a router has to forward the PATH message, the router uses a combination of its forwarding table constructed by such protocols as IS-IS, OSPF, RIP, or BGP and the destination address in the IP packet that carries the message to determine the next hop router. What is missing is the ability to "steer" the PATH message along a particular explicit route.

To accomplish this RSVP is augmented by a new object, the Explicit Route Object (ERO). This object is carried in the PATH message and contains the explicit route that the message has to take. Forwarding of such a message by a router is determined not by the destination address in the IP header of the packet that carries the message, but rather by the content of the ERO carried in the message.

The ERO consists of an ordered sequence of "hops," where the sequence specifies an explicit route. Each hop is represented by an "abstract node." Each abstract node identifies a group of one or more routers, whose internal topology is opaque to the router that computes the explicit route. One example of an abstract node would be a collection of routers that belong to a particular autonomous system. Another example of an abstract node would be a collection of routers whose addresses fall within a particular address prefix. Associated with each abstract node is a "strict/loose" indicator, which allows an explicit route to be specified as a mixture of strict and loose hops. One possible use of loose hops is when the router that computes an explicit route doesn't have sufficient topology information to compute the path in terms of strict hops, for example, when the route has to cross multiple OSPF or IS-IS areas.

From the encoding point of view, the ERO is a sequence of <type, length, value> triples, where each triple depicts a particular abstract node. At the time of this writing, there are three different types of abstract nodes defined: IPv4 address prefix, IPv6 address prefix, and Autonomous System Number. Note that since an IP address is just one special case of an IP address prefix (e.g., an IPv4 address is an IPv4 prefix with length of 32 bits), you could specify an explicit route as a sequence of routers (each abstract node would correspond to a router).

To illustrate how RSVP is used to establish MPLS forwarding state along an explicit route, let's take a look at an example, shown in Figure 7.2. Assume that LSR1 wants to establish MPLS forwarding state along the explicit route (LSR2, LSR6, LSR7, LSR4). In order to accomplish this, LSR1 constructs an ERO that contains a sequence of four abstract nodes, LSR2, LSR6, LSR7, and LSR4. Each abstract node is represented by an IP address prefix of length 32 (which is nothing but a plain IP address). Note that such an address could depict either one particular interface on an LSR (and in this case it is the IP address associated with that interface) or the whole LSR (in this case, the IP address associated with the loopback address of the LSR). LSR1 then constructs an RSVP PATH message and includes in this message the ERO as well as the LABEL_REQUEST object. Once the message is constructed, LSR1 examines the first abstract node in the ERO, LSR2, finds the link that connects LSR1 to LSR2, and sends the PATH message over that link. When LSR2 receives the PATH message, LSR2 finds itself as the first abstract node in the ERO carried by the message. LSR2 then looks at the next abstract node, LSR6, and finds the link that connects it to LSR6. LSR2 then modifies the ERO by removing the abstract node associated

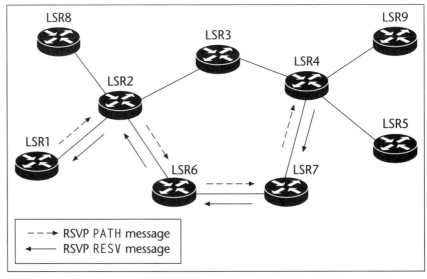

Figure 7.2
Establishing LSP with RSVP.

with LSR2 from the ERO and sends the PATH message that contains the modified ERO and the LABEL_REQUEST object to LSR6. (The modified ERO at this point contains just LSR6, LSR7, and LSR4.) Handling of the PATH message (including handling of the ERO and the LABEL_REQUEST object) by LSR6 is similar to how the message is handled by LSR2. The ERO in the PATH message that LSR6 sends to LSR7 contains just LSR7 and LSR4. Likewise, handling of the PATH message (including handling of the ERO and the LABEL_REQUEST objects) by LSR7 is similar to how the message is handled by LSR6. The ERO in the PATH message that LSR7 sends to LSR4 contains just LSR4.

When the PATH message arrives at LSR4, LSR4 finds, by examining the ERO, that it is the last abstract node in the ERO. Given that, LSR4 creates a RESV message and sends this message to LSR7. This message includes, among other things, the LABEL object. LSR7, when it receives the message, uses the label carried in the LABEL object to populate its label forwarding table. Following this, LSR7 sends a RESV message to LSR6. Again, this message includes the LABEL object. Handling of this message by LSR6 is similar to the way the message is handled by LSR7. LSR6 sends the RESV message to LSR2. Again, this message includes the LABEL object. Handling of this message by LSR2 is similar to the way the message is handled by LSR7. Finally, the message is received by LSR1. At this point the LSP for the explicit route is established.

Note that the procedures described above for handling the ERO are in addition to, not instead of, the procedures for handling RSVP without MPLS. That is, when RSVP is used to establish an LSP, handling of RSVP on the LSRs along the LSP is defined by a combination of plain RSVP procedures and MPLS-specific procedures. So, for example, establishing an LSP along an explicit route may involve reserving resources (e.g., bandwidth) along the route, which is handled by standard RSVP procedures, as described in Section 6.1. Note that in this case the full set of QoS parameters defined for Integrated Services may be used; these were described in Section 6.1.1 and include peak bandwidth and a token bucket, which is defined by a sustained rate and a burst size. LSP setup may also involve adjusting the amount of available resources (e.g., available bandwidth) on all the links along the route. Again, this is handled by standard RSVP procedures.

7.2.4 CR-LDP

We have just seen how RSVP can be used as a mechanism to establish MPLS forwarding state along an explicit route. In this section we look at another alternative for doing this—CR-LDP.

We already know how to establish label forwarding state between adjacent LSRs with LDP. What is missing in LDP is (a) the ability to establish label forwarding state on all the LSRs along an explicit route and (b) the ability to reserve resources along the route. CR-LDP contains a set of extensions to LDP that provides these missing pieces.

To establish label forwarding state along an explicit route, CR-LDP introduces a new object, called Explicit Route (ER). The structure of this object, as well as its handling by LSRs, is almost identical to the ERO we described in the previous section. This ER object is carried as a <type, length, value> triple in the LDP LABEL REQUEST message. Label binding for explicit routes is established by using the downstream-on-demand label advertisement, which, in turn, uses the LDP LABEL REQUEST message. To support explicit routing, this message also includes the ER object.

To illustrate how CR-LDP is used to establish MPLS forwarding state along an explicit route, let's look at the example shown in Figure 7.3. Assume that LSR1 wants to establish MPLS forwarding state along the explicit route (LSR2, LSR3, LSR4). To accomplish this, LSR1 constructs the ER object that contains a sequence of three abstract nodes, LSR2, LSR3, and LSR4. Each node is represented by an IP address prefix of length 32 (a plain IP address). Note that such an address could depict

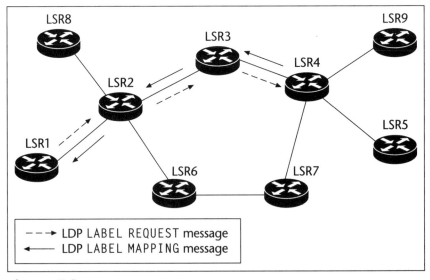

Figure 7.3
Establishing LSP with CR-LDP.

either one particular interface on an LSR (in this case, the IP address associated with that interface) or the whole LSR (the IP address associated with the loopback address of the LSR). LSR1 then constructs an LDP LABEL REQUEST message and includes in this message the ER object. Once the message is constructed, LSR1 examines the first abstract node in the ER object, LSR2, finds the link that connects it to LSR2, and sends the LABEL REQUEST message over that link. When LSR2 receives the LABEL REQUEST message, LSR2 finds itself as the first abstract node in the ER object carried by the message. LSR2 then looks at the next abstract node, LSR3, and finds the link that connects it to LSR3. LSR2 then modifies the ER object by removing the abstract node associated with LSR2 from it and sends the LABEL REQUEST message that contains the modified ER object to LSR3. (At this point the ER object contains just LSR3 and LSR4.) Handling of the LABEL REQUEST message (including handling of the ER object) by LSR3 is similar to how the message is handled by LSR2.

When the message arrives at LSR4, LSR4 finds that it is the last abstract node in the ER object. Therefore, LSR4 creates a LABEL MAPPING message and sends it to LSR3. This message includes, among other things, the label object. When it receives the message, LSR3 uses the label carried in the message to populate its label forwarding table. Then LSR3 sends a LABEL MAPPING message to LSR2. Again, this message includes the label object. Handling of this message by LSR2 is similar to the way the message is handled by LSR3. Finally, the message is received by LSR1, and the LSP for the explicit route is established.

To carry information about resources that need to be reserved along a route, CR-LDP uses the Traffic Parameter object. At the time of this writing, the CR-LDP specifications define seven traffic parameters. These are

- Peak data rate (PDR)
- Peak burst size (PBS)
- Committed data rate (CDR)
- Committed burst size (CBS)
- Excess burst size (EBS)
- Frequency
- Weight

Peak data rate and burst size together define a token bucket, which characterizes the maximum rate of traffic that is expected to be sent down this LSP. (See Section 6.1.1 for a description of token buckets.) Similarly, committed data rate and burst size define a token bucket characterizing the average rate at which traffic is expected to be sent on this LSP. Excess burst size defines another token bucket that can be used to characterize the amount by which bursts may exceed the committed burst size. It is expected that all of these parameters might be used at LSRs along an LSP to determine how to allocate resources to an LSP as it is established. They may also be used to perform policing actions at the entrance to an LSP; for example, packets that do not conform to the token bucket defined by PDR and PBS might be dropped at that point. The CR-LDP specification allows considerable freedom in exactly how these parameters are to be used.

Frequency is a very rough indication of the time interval over which an LSP is expected to provide available bandwidth of CDR or greater. Weight is used to determine how extra bandwidth above the total CDR of all LSPs should be divided among LSPs that share a common bottleneck link.

7.2.5 OSPF and IS-IS Extensions

CSPF assumes that a node that performs CSPF has information not just about the state (up/down) of all the links in a network but also about various link attributes, like available bandwidth, which allow the node to determine whether a particular link violates the constraints associated with a particular path that the node has to compute. And since each node in a network could, at least in principle, perform CSPF, we need to have a way to provide each node in a network with such information.

One way to do this is to utilize flooding mechanisms used by link-state protocols such as OSPF or IS-IS. These flooding mechanisms distribute information about the state of a particular link (link up/down state) to every node in a network (to be more precise, to every node within a single OSPF/IS-IS area). To accomplish such a distribution, we can just piggyback the information on top of the link-state information.

Details of how the link attribute information is piggybacked are protocol-specific. With OSPF this information is carried in the Opaque Link-State Advertisement (Opaque LSA). With IS-IS this information is carried by Link-State Packets (LSPs). In both cases the information is encoded as a collection of type-length-value objects, where each object carries information related to a particular attribute.

As mentioned above, establishing a route for a particular set of traffic may require resource reservation along the route and therefore may alter attributes of the links along that route. When the attribute information of a link changes, it is important to inform all the nodes in a network about such a change. To accomplish this, when the attribute information of a given link changes, the node to which the link is connected floods this information (using the IGP flooding mechanism) throughout the network.

If every change in the attribute information of a link resulted in flooding this information throughout the network, it could result in an excessive amount of routing updates to carry the information, which in turn could overload the control component of the routers involved in flooding. To avoid this, a set of thresholds may be used. So, for example, when the attribute is the available bandwidth, then a change in the available bandwidth of a link would trigger flooding of this information only if the available bandwidth crosses a certain threshold. Also note that both IS-IS and OSPF already have built-in mechanisms that impose an upper bound on how frequently a router can originate flooding of the information associated with one of the router's links. These mechanisms apply as well when flooding is triggered by changes in the link attribute information.

7.2.6 Comparison of CR-LDP and RSVP

As noted above, there are two possible protocols for the path setup component of constraint-based routing—CR-LDP and RSVP. There has been spirited debate in the networking community, to put it mildly, about the relative merits of these two protocols. While much of this debate has centered on issues of standards group politics, we focus here only on the technical differences between the protocols.

First of all, we observe that there are many similarities between the two protocols. The Explicit Route Objects that they use in particular are extremely similar. Both protocols use ordered LSP setup proceeding from the head to the tail along the explicit route, returning to the head as the labels are assigned. Both protocols include some QoS information in the signalling messages to enable resource allocation and LSP establishment to take place atomically.

We can also observe that both protocols are extensions of previously defined protocols. RSVP has been extended for traffic engineering by adding label assignment and explicit route specification to a Resource Reservation Protocol. CR-LDP extends LDP by adding explicit route specification and resource allocation. It is hard to make meaningful claims as to which set of extensions are more reasonable (although that has not prevented proponents on both sides from claiming that their extensions are much simpler than the other approach).

We can divide the technical differences between the two protocols into two broad categories: signalling mechanisms and QoS models. We discuss each in turn. Before doing so, we must first address the issue of scalability, which is often raised as an important differentiating factor between the protocols.

Scalability

When RSVP was first proposed as a standard for QoS signalling, there were concerns about its scalability for deployment in large networks. These concerns centered on the fact that RSVP makes reservations (and installs some state) for individual "microflows," that is, for streams of data corresponding, typically, to a single application running on a pair of hosts (or a group of hosts using multicast). The number of microflows passing through a single router in a large IP network could easily be in the millions, and there could be serious consequences in terms of memory and performance if a single router had to hold millions of pieces of reservation state.

Unfortunately, these scalability concerns are often summarized by the simplistic statement "RSVP doesn't scale." To say that something doesn't scale is to say that it cannot reasonably be deployed in large networks such as ISP backbones. In fact, the aspect of RSVP that does not scale well is the making of reservations for individual application microflows. When RSVP is used for explicit LSP setup, no such reservations are made. The dominant factor in the scalability of an LSP setup protocol is the number of LSPs established, which is clearly independent of the protocol. Thus, the scalability argument really has no place in a comparison of RSVP and CR-LDP.

The one legitimate scaling concern that may need to be examined in the context of constraint-based routing and LSP setup is the effect of soft state on scalability. We consider this factor in the following paragraphs.

Signalling Mechanisms

We noted in Chapter 6 that RSVP, as originally defined, uses a "soft state" approach to signalling. Such an approach displays robustness in the face of failures because unrefreshed state simply times out. However, RSVP's soft state also has two drawbacks:

■ It requires refreshing in the steady state, which consumes bandwidth and processing resources.

■ It lacks a reliable delivery mechanism, depending on refreshes for reliability.

These drawbacks have been addressed by the refresh reduction techniques described in Section 6.1.3. It is also worth noting that the overhead of signalling in the steady state is typically much less of a concern than the overhead during large-scale transients (e.g., after a link or node failure) and that soft state refresh has no effect under such conditions.

CR-LDP, by contrast, runs on top of TCP, since it is an extension to LDP. Thus, it has no refresh overhead and obtains reliability from TCP. Running on top of TCP does present some drawbacks, however:

■ TCP's congestion avoidance may throttle back the transfer of information between LSRs.

■ When there is only one TCP connection between two LSRs, TCP forces FIFO delivery of messages. Thus, there is no opportunity for a critical message to be delivered ahead of a less critical one that was sent first. In addition, when a packet is dropped, all messages sent behind that packet are delayed until the lost packet is successfully retransmitted.

■ There is a moderate amount of overhead involved in establishing an adjacency between two LSRs. They must go through TCP's three-way handshake before initiating an LDP session.

This last point results in an advantage for RSVP, which does not require connection establishment before label distribution can occur. We can say that RSVP has "lightweight adjacencies," which enable new neighbor relationships to be established quickly as needed. An application of this capability is in the area of fast reroute, a subject we discuss in Section 7.4.

QoS Models

The area where the protocols differ most substantially is in their QoS models. RSVP uses the int-serv QoS model, as described in Section 6.1.1. CR-LDP defines a new QoS model, which we discussed in Section 7.2.4. The int-serv model was developed over several years, with the goal of facilitating resource allocation in the heterogeneous network environment typical of IP networks. The service models and QoS parameters defined for int-serv are intended to be supportable on all link layers, and considerable work has been done on mapping int-serv services to specific link layers (in the ISSLL working group of the IETF).

The CR-LDP QoS model defines a relatively large number of parameters that are most similar to those used on ATM and Frame Relay networks. At the time of writing, there is not a full specification of exactly how all these parameters are to be used. Nor is it clear how to support this QoS model on arbitrary link layers. Thus, there does seem to be an advantage to the RSVP QoS model. It is designed for heterogeneous IP networks and, while not deployed in backbone networks, it has been tested and deployed in networks of moderate size.

One Protocol or Two?

A final point of comparison between RSVP and CR-LDP is the fact that CR-LDP can be viewed as an extension to LDP, whereas RSVP is a separate protocol. Clearly, then, you have to run more protocols when using RSVP, assuming it would not be running for any other reason. These facts are obvious, but it is not at all obvious whether it is better to have more or fewer protocols. For example, IP, ICMP, and ARP are three separate protocols that are required to send IP packets over a network; it seems unlikely that networks would run better or be easier to administer if these three protocols were somehow integrated into one. Thus, we can say no more about this argument than to point out that it has been made and that it is not an important distinction between the two approaches.

7.3 Application to Traffic Engineering

In this section we describe how MPLS constraint-based routing could be used as a solution to the problem of traffic engineering.

7.3.1 Problem Description

It has been observed that the efficiency and cost structure of the service provider business is affected by how efficiently a service provider utilizes its infrastructure and, specifically, the available bandwidth. More efficient use of bandwidth resources means that the provider should be able to avoid a situation in which some parts of its network are congested while other parts are underutilized.

A cost savings that results in more efficient use of bandwidth resources helps to reduce the overall cost of operations. This, in turn, helps service providers to gain advantage over their competitors. And this advantage becomes increasingly important as the service provider market gets more and more competitive.

One way to solve the traffic engineering problem is by using routing, as routing determines the paths taken by the traffic that a provider has to carry and thus controls how much traffic traverses through each link in a network. Specifically, a service provider should be able to construct routes in such a way as to avoid causing some parts of the provider's network to be overutilized while other parts are underutilized.

7.3.2 Solving Traffic Engineering with ATM or Frame Relay

In this section we look at one specific solution to the traffic engineering problem that uses routing, known as the "overlay" solution. With the overlay solution a service provider relies on the routing capabilities of a virtual circuit–based network, such as ATM or Frame Relay, to construct routes that avoid the overutilization/underutilization problem described above.

Figure 7.4 illustrates the overlay solution. On the left side of the figure is a collection of ATM (or Frame Relay) switches, indicated by cube-shaped icons, that are surrounded by a collection of routers, indicated by disc-shaped icons. From the IP routing point of view, all routers seem to be directly interconnected with each other, as illustrated on the right side of the figure. So, from the IP routing point of view, routing is trivial, as all the routers are just one IP hop away from each other. With the overlay solution, the traffic engineering problem is solved by using ATM switches and, specifically, by using the routing capabilities provided by the ATM switches.

To illustrate how ATM routing capabilities are used to solve the traffic engineering problem, consider an example shown in Figure 7.5, where R1 through R3 are routers and ATM1 through ATM5 are ATM switches. Assume that all the links have 150-Mb/sec capacity. Further assume that the traffic from R1 to R3 is 100 Mb/sec and that the traffic from R2 to R3 is 100 Mb/sec. To carry this traffic over the network, there is one ATM Permanent Virtual Circuit (PVC) that connects router R1 with R3 and another PVC that connects router R2 with

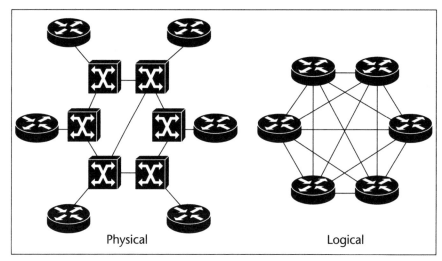

Figure 7.4
The "overlay" model.

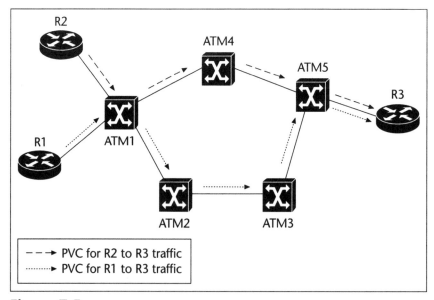

Figure 7.5
Solving traffic engineering with ATM.

R3.[3] Using the ATM switches' routing capabilities, the first PVC is routed via the path (ATM1, ATM4, ATM5), and the second PVC is routed via the path (ATM1, ATM2, ATM3, ATM5). This way traffic from R2 to R3 traverses the path (ATM1, ATM4, ATM5), while traffic from R1 to R3 traverses the path (ATM1, ATM2, ATM3). As a result, traffic between the routers on the left side and the router on the right side can be evenly distributed over the network.

What are the problems with this solution? To begin with, it requires extra devices—ATM switches—introducing extra cost. More important, there is more complex network management because, in effect, we have not one, but two separate networks without integrated network management. So you have to have additional training, technical support, and so on to support not one, but two networks. In addition, as we noted in Chapter 1, existing IP routing protocols and, most noticeably, link-state protocols don't scale well when you have a complete mesh of routers. Finally, ATM consumes additional bandwidth, known as the "cell tax" because of the inefficiency of packing variable-length IP datagrams into fixed-length ATM cells and because of the addition of ATM cell headers. These arguments suggest that an alternative to the overlay solution would be desirable.

7.3.3 Why Plain IP Routing Is Not Enough

If the overlay solution has all these problems, then you could certainly ask, Why not get rid of the overlay solution and solve the problem of traffic engineering at layer 3, using capabilities provided by IP routing? To answer this question, we need to look at what is possible with plain IP routing and compare it with what is possible with the overlay solution.

To understand what could be accomplished with plain IP routing, it is important to keep in mind that IP routing takes into account only the destinations of packets and, moreover, that the only way to change routing is to modify the metrics used by routing protocols. In other words, IP routing could be concisely characterized as destination-based, least-cost routing.

To illustrate why in the area of traffic engineering plain IP routing can't match the capabilities provided by ATM routing, we reuse the example from the previous section (Figure 7.5), but replace ATM

---

3. For the purpose of this illustration, we didn't show the PVC that connects R1 and R2; such a PVC would be needed to create a complete mesh of PVCs among the routers.

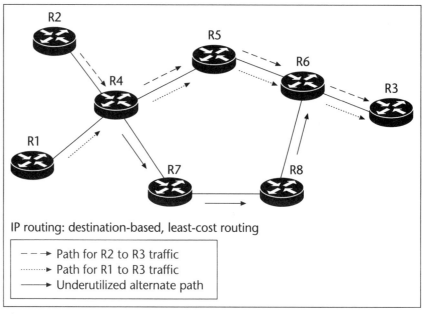

IP routing: destination-based, least-cost routing

    - - - ▸ Path for R2 to R3 traffic
    ·········▸ Path for R1 to R3 traffic
    ————▸ Underutilized alternate path

Figure 7.6
Why plain IP routing isn't enough.

switches with routers, as shown in Figure 7.6. With IP routing, one choice would be to use minimum hop routing. In this case all the traffic, both from R1 to R3 and from R2 to R3, is routed along the path (R4, R5, R6). Links along this path are going to be congested, as the bandwidth of each link is 150 Mb/sec, while the traffic along those links is 200 Mb/sec (the sum of R1 to R3 and R2 to R3 traffic). At the same time links along the path (R4, R7, R8, R6) carry no traffic. An alternative would be to use routing that minimizes administrative distance (such as provided by OSPF or IS-IS) and to set link metrics in such a way as to force the traffic from both R1 to R3 and R2 to R3 to be routed along the path (R4, R7, R8, R6), as shown in Figure 7.7. That changes the set of links that are going to be congested, but it doesn't solve the problem, as we still have a situation where some links are congested while other links carry no traffic.

You could argue that the problem could be solved by using equal-cost, multipath capabilities provided by such protocols as OSPF or IS-IS. To illustrate why this wouldn't solve the problem either, consider the example we used before (Figure 7.7), and assume that all the links, except (R6, R3) and (R8, R6), have 620-Mb/sec capacity. The (R6, R3)

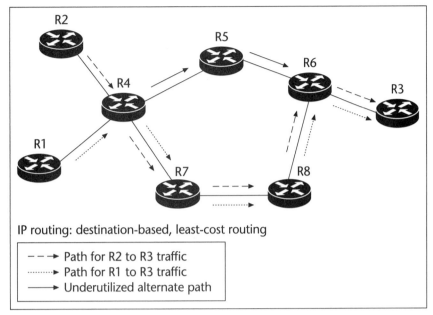

IP routing: destination-based, least-cost routing

- – – → Path for R2 to R3 traffic
- ·········► Path for R1 to R3 traffic
- ———► Underutilized alternate path

Figure 7.7
Why plain IP routing isn't enough (again).

link has 2 Gb/sec, and the (R8, R6) link has 150 Mb/sec capacity. Further assume that the traffic from R1 to R3 is 550 Mb/sec, while the traffic from R2 to R3 is 100 Mb/sec. With OSPF or IS-IS you could certainly set up link metrics in such a way that R4 would have not one, but two (equal-cost) paths to R2 and two (equal-cost) paths to R3. Thus, R4 would equally split the R1 to R3 traffic among these two paths and likewise with the R2 to R3 traffic. As a result, the amount of traffic carried over (R4, R5, R6) would be 325 Mb/sec ((550+100)/2), and the amount of traffic that will be carried over (R4, R7, R8, R6) will be 325 Mb/sec. With this distribution of traffic load, the link (R8, R6) is going to be congested, whereas the links along the path (R4, R5, R6) will be underutilized.

As you can see, no matter how hard we try, we still can't get around a situation where some parts of a network are going to be underutilized while other parts are going to be congested. Also note that the examples we considered above are highly simplistic, which suggests that if we can't even solve the traffic engineering problem with these examples, there is virtually no chance we'll be able to solve it using plain IP routing in more realistic scenarios.

The main reason why plain IP routing fails to solve the traffic engineering problem is that any solution to this problem has to establish routes that are not just optimal with respect to a certain scalar metric (e.g., administrative distance), but that also take into account the available bandwidth on individual links. Plain IP routing provides the former but not the latter.

7.3.4 Solving Traffic Engineering with MPLS Constraint-Based Routing

As we indicated above, any solution to the traffic engineering problem must do two things: (1) establish routes that are optimal with respect to a certain scalar metric and (2) take into account the available bandwidth on individual links. These are precisely the capabilities that can be provided by MPLS constraint-based routing, where the constraint used is available bandwidth.

In order to help us understand how MPLS constraint-based routing solves the traffic engineering problem, we introduce the concept of a "traffic trunk." A traffic trunk is defined as a collection of individual TCP, or UDP, flows, known as "microflows," that share two common properties. The first one is that all microflows are forwarded along the same common path. The second is that they all share the same Class of Service. It is important to keep in mind that the common path shared by the flows of a traffic trunk is just a path within a single service provider, not an end-to-end path.

The reason that we introduce the concept of a traffic trunk is that, for the purpose of traffic engineering, we use MPLS constraint-based routing to route traffic trunks, not individual microflows, within a single service provider. By routing at the granularity of traffic trunks, rather than individual microflows, we decouple the amount of forwarding state and the control traffic needed to establish and maintain this state from the volume of traffic that a service provider has to carry. This is because the number of traffic trunks within a service provider is determined by the provider's topology, independent of the volume of traffic the provider has to carry. So as the traffic increases, the amount of traffic per individual trunk increases; but that doesn't result in an increase of the number of trunks, which means there is no increase in the forwarding state or the control traffic needed to establish and maintain this state. In contrast, if we were to apply constraint-based routing at the granularity of individual microflows, then the amount of forwarding state, as well as the control traffic needed to establish and maintain this state, would grow with the growth of the traffic that a provider has to carry. To summarize, routing at the granularity of traffic trunks has better scaling properties (with respect to the amount of forwarding state and the volume of control traffic) than routing at the granularity of individual microflows.

Using the concept of traffic trunks, the traffic engineering problem reduces to two subproblems. First, there is the problem of representing the traffic that has to be carried by a service provider as a collection of traffic trunks with specific bandwidth requirements. Then there is the problem of using MPLS constraint-based routing to route these trunks within a service provider.

There are multiple ways of determining the bandwidth associated with individual traffic trunks. One such way is for a service provider first to specify that a trunk requires zero bandwidth, then to use constraint-based routing to route that trunk via a particular LSP, and finally to use the amount of traffic carried by that LSP to determine (and adjust) the bandwidth requirements of the trunk.

The primary constraint that needs to be satisfied is the bandwidth constraint. Specifically, the bandwidth constraint requires that the total bandwidth of all the trunks that are routed over a particular link should not be greater than the bandwidth of that link. For the purpose of traffic engineering, it may be useful to support not just bandwidth but administrative constraints as well. More precisely, in addition to the bandwidth constraints, it may be useful to allow a service provider to restrict the set of links that could be used to route a particular traffic trunk. A way to implement this type of constraint is by associating with each link one or more "colors." Colors may be represented as a bit vector, where each bit in the vector signifies a particular color. This information is carried as part of the attribute information of each link. We then define for each trunk the set of colors that the trunk has to avoid,[4] and we use this additional set of constraints (along with bandwidth constraints) for the CSPF calculation.

Rerouting upon Failure

When a link goes down, it is important to reroute all the trunks that were routed over the link. Since the path taken by a trunk is determined by the LSR at the head end of the trunk, rerouting has to be performed by the head end of the trunk as well.[5]

---

4. There are two ways to define this set. The first is by listing the link colors that have to be avoided. The second is by listing the link colors that could be used, which implies that any other color has to be avoided.

5. Later in this chapter we describe how MPLS constraint-based routing can be used to "locally" repair a failed link, without involving the head ends of all the LSPs traversing that link in rerouting those LSPs.

To perform rerouting, the head-end LSR could rely either on the information provided by IGP or on the information provided by either RSVP or CR-LDP. One advantage of using the IGP information is that it is available, regardless of traffic engineering, so each LSR has it anyway. Another advantage of using the IGP information is that the volume of control traffic needed to distribute it is likely to be less than the volume of control traffic that would be generated by either RSVP or CR-LDP. This is because the volume of the IGP information is independent of the number of traffic trunks that were routed over the failed link. In contrast, the volume of RSVP or CR-LDP information is proportional to the number of traffic trunks that were routed over the failed link, and thus is likely to be higher than the volume of the IGP information.

When a link that previously went down comes back, it is important to check if this link could be used to improve routing. Thus, an LSR, either periodically or when it receives the IGP information that a link came back, should determine if use of this link would produce better routes for any of the trunks originated by the LSR, and if so, then reroute these trunks along the better routes.

Forwarding Packets onto an LSP

One important aspect of traffic engineering is the ability to force a group of packets that form a particular traffic trunk to be forwarded along the LSP computed and established for that trunk by MPLS constraint-based routing. To understand how this works, first observe that MPLS allows the mapping between an FEC and an LSP to be local to the LSR at the head end of the LSP. Also observe that packets within a traffic trunk form an FEC, at least with respect to the path taken by this trunk within a service provider. As a result, the ability to force a group of packets to be forwarded along a particular LSP could be provided by mechanisms purely local to the LSR at the head end of the LSP.

One such mechanism is based on a slightly modified version of SPF. With plain SPF, a router computes the shortest path tree routed at the router. This shortest path tree is used to determine the outgoing interface, as well as the next hop, that the router has to use when forwarding packets. The modification we make is that when the SPF algorithm adds a new node to its shortest path tree, the algorithm checks whether the newly added node is a tail end of an LSP whose head end is the router, and if so the algorithm uses the LSP as a "logical" outgoing interface. One important property of this procedure is that it allows routing determined by MPLS constraint-based routing to be intermixed with routing determined by plain IP. This is important, as a service provider may decide to apply traffic engineering to only a portion of the traffic the provider has to carry.

To illustrate how modified SPF works, consider the example shown in Figure 7.8, and assume that constraint-based routing establishes two LSPs, LSP1 and LSP2, each with its own "logical" interface. As LSR1 starts to build its shortest path tree, it follows the standard SPF procedures until it adds LSR4 to the tree. At this point LSR1 notices that there is an LSP, LSP1, that starts on LSR1 and ends on LSR4. Therefore, the outgoing (logical) interface for destinations reachable via LSR4 would be LSP1. As SPF continues, it adds LSR8 to its shortest path tree. Since LSR8 is reachable via LSR4, and since the outgoing interface for LSR4 is LSP1, the outgoing interface for all the destinations reachable via LSR8 is LSP1. Finally, SPF adds LSR5 to its shortest path tree. At this point LSR1 notices that there is an LSP, LSP2, that starts at LSR1 and ends at LSR5. Therefore, the outgoing (logical) interface for the destinations reachable via LSR5 would be LSP2. The resulting forwarding topology is shown in Figure 7.9.

To summarize, all the traffic with destinations reachable via LSR5 and beyond will be forwarded along the path taken by LSP2. All the

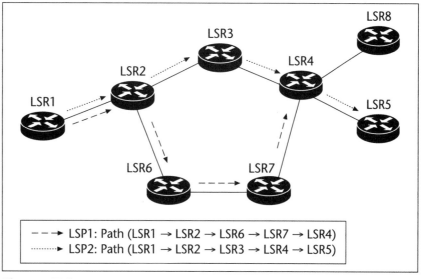

Figure 7.8

Mapping packets into LSPs—example.

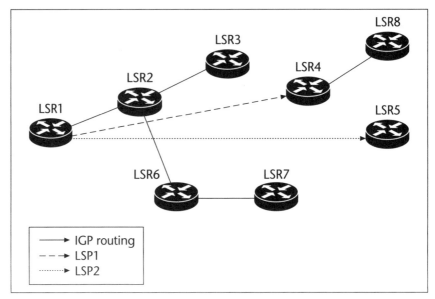

Figure 7.9
Forwarding topology with LSPs.

traffic with destinations reachable via LSR4 and beyond will be forwarded along the path taken by LSR1. For example, all the traffic with destinations reachable via LSR8 will be forwarded along the path taken by LSR1. The rest of the traffic will be forwarded via the paths computed by normal IGP procedures.

7.4 Application to Fast Rerouting

In this section we describe how MPLS constraint-based routing can be used to significantly reduce packet losses during routing transients.

7.4.1 Routing Convergence with Plain IP Routing

As we mentioned in Chapter 2, we use the term *routing transient* to refer to episodes in a network where routing information across a network is changing. These episodes most commonly occur as a result of failures of links or routers or both. At such times, the routing information stored at different routers may be temporarily inconsistent, which may result in formation of temporary (transient) forwarding loops. With conventional IP routing, traffic is allowed to enter the loop, but the amount of resources that can be consumed by such traffic is constrained via loop mitigation.[6]

One undesirable, yet necessary, side effect of loop mitigation is that, during routing transients, a network, rather than delivering packets to their ultimate destinations, may discard the packets. The longer the routing transient lasts, the more packets are likely to be discarded.

With plain IP routing the duration of routing transients due to a link or node failure, and thus the amount of packet loss, depends on two factors. The first is the time it takes for a router adjacent to the failed link (or node) to detect the failure. The second is the time it takes to distribute this information among all the routers and, in turn, for the routers to recompute their forwarding tables based on this information. It is the sum of the time to detect the failure, to distribute the information about failure, and to recompute the forwarding tables on all the routers that determines the duration of packet losses. To reduce the packet losses caused by link or node failure, we need to reduce both the time it takes to detect a failure and the time it takes to distribute the information about the failure and recompute the forwarding tables on all the routers.

To reduce the time it takes to detect link failure, we can use link layer–specific mechanisms. For example, with SONET it is possible to detect link failure (using SONET-specific mechanisms, such as LOF, LRDI, etc.) in less than 10 ms. However, with respect to the time it takes to distribute the information about the failure and recompute the forwarding tables, the distributed nature of route computation used by plain IP routing and, specifically, the need for all the routers to converge to consistent routing information places fundamental limitations on how much this time could be reduced. In practice the time to converge within a single OSPF or IS-IS routing domain is on the order of seconds, which means that within a network composed of such a domain, a link or a node failure, even if detected instantaneously, may cause packet losses that could last on the order of seconds.

---

6. Recall that loop mitigation is achieved via the time-to-live mechanism, where the network layer header contains a field called Time-to-Live (TTL). A router that forwards a packet decrements this field by 1. If a router receives a packet whose TTL value is 0, the router discards the packet. This way, even if a packet enters a forwarding loop, the number of times the packet would be able to circle the loop is bounded—eventually, the TTL field in the packet reaches 0, and the packet is discarded.

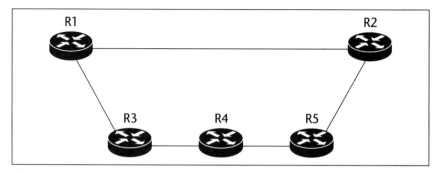

Figure 7.10
Using an alternative path for reroute.

To reduce packet losses during routing transients, you might attempt to reroute the traffic around the failed link or node along some alternative path. Unfortunately, this approach doesn't always work. To illustrate this, consider the example shown in Figure 7.10, and assume that we do minimum hop routing. When the link between R1 and R2 fails, if R1 somehow knows that there is an alternative path to R2 via R3, R4, and R5 with R3 as the next hop, then as soon as R1 detects the link failure, R1 could immediately start forwarding all the traffic destined for R2 to R3, with the hope that this traffic would be delivered to R2. With link-state protocols (e.g., OSPF, IS-IS), R1 could certainly find out that there is an alternative path via R3, R4, and R5. However, when R1 starts to forward the traffic to R3, until R3 receives the information about the link failure and updates its forwarding table, R3 would forward this traffic back to R1, thinking that R1 is only one hop from R2. Thus, for some period of time, there would be a (transient) forwarding loop, which would result in packet losses. This illustrates that, with plain IP routing, forwarding along an alternative path doesn't eliminate the need for routing convergence among the routers and thus doesn't help to reduce packet losses due to link or node failures.

To summarize, the fundamental limitation on how much we could reduce packet losses during routing transients is imposed by the need to distribute the information about a link or node failure among a set of routers that then must process this information and converge to a new set of routes. This limitation, in turn, is caused by the fundamental nature of plain IP routing—independent, hop-by-hop, destination-based forwarding.

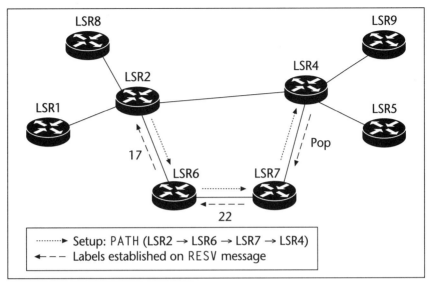

Figure 7.11
Protection LSP.

7.4.2 Fast Reroute with Constraint-Based Routing

Since the difficulty of reducing packet losses during routing transients derives directly from the hop-by-hop, destination-based forwarding paradigm of plain IP, we turn to MPLS constraint-based routing, which relies on explicit routing rather than hop-by-hop, destination-based forwarding. This section explains how MPLS constraint-based routing addresses the issue of fast reroute during routing transients.

To handle link failures, we use MPLS constraint-based routing to construct a "protection" LSP around a link. When the link fails, the LSR attached to the failed link uses the label stacking capability of MPLS to "nest" all the LSPs that used to go over the failed link into the protection LSP.

To illustrate this, consider the example shown in Figure 7.11. To handle failure of the link between LSR2 and LSR4, we construct a protection LSP around that link.[7] This LSP starts and ends at the LSRs

---

7. In this example we construct just one protection LSP, from LSR2 to LSR4. In practice we would also need to construct another protection LSP, from LSR4 to LSR2. This protection LSP would be used to protect such LSPs as an LSP from LSR5 to LSR1. The protection LSPs are unidirectional, just like any other LSP.

connected to the link and is routed along an explicit route (LSR2, LSR6, LSR7, LSR4). So, to forward a packet along that LSP, LSR2 has to place label 17 on the packet and send the packet on the interface that connects LSR2 to LSR6.

Assume that there is an LSP from LSR1 to LSR9 that is routed over LSR2 and LSR4, as shown in Figure 7.12. At LSR2 the label forwarding table entry for that LSP has 37 as the incoming label, 14 as the outgoing label, and the interface that connects LSR2 to LSR4 as the outgoing interface. Thus, when LSR2 receives a packet routed along that LSP (the packet arrives at LSR2 with label 37), LSR2 replaces label 37 with label 14 and sends the packet over the interface that connects LSR2 to LSR4.

When LSR2 detects that the link (LSR2, LSR4) has gone down, LSR2 changes the label forwarding table entry associated with the LSP as follows. In addition to swapping label 37 with label 14, the entry now indicates that label 17 has to be pushed onto the label stack, and the outgoing interface is changed from the interface that connects LSR2 to LSR4 to the one that connects LSR2 to LSR6. Thus, when LSR2 receives a packet with label 37, LSR2 replaces label 37 with label 14 (just as it did before the link failure), pushes one more label, label 17, onto the label stack carried by the packet, and sends the packet over the

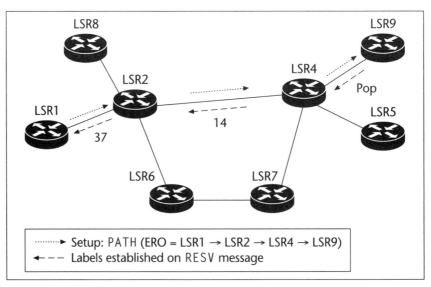

Figure 7.12
Steady state path.

interface that connects LSR2 to LSR6 (rather than sending the packet over the interface that connects LSR2 to LSR4). The label that LSR2 pushes onto the label stack is the label associated with the protection LSP, the LSP from LSR2 to LSR4. Note that when the packet arrives at LSR4, it carries exactly the same label, label 14, that it carried when the link (LSR2, LSR4) was up. From that point on, the fact that the link went down has no impact on the forwarding of the packet to the rest of the LSP. Figure 7.13 illustrates the example.

Note that use of the mechanism we described above may result in suboptimal forwarding. However, this potentially suboptimal forwarding is of short duration. When a link between LSR2 and LSR4 failed, the information about this failure will be distributed (via OSPF or IS-IS) to all the LSRs, including LSR1. Once LSR1 gets this information, it can use constraint-based routing to compute a new route and then establish label forwarding state along the newly computed route. Alternatively, LSR1 may have a precomputed alternative route (e.g., LSR1, LSR2, LSR6, LSR7, LSR4, LSR9), so when LSR1 receives the information about the link failure, LSR1 may just start sending traffic over the alternative route.

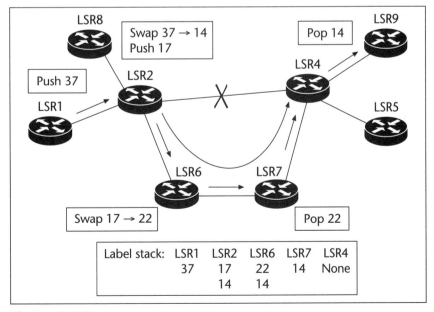

Figure 7.13

Forwarding over the protection LSP.

Note that a single protection LSP could be used to fast-reroute not one, but multiple LSPs. In the example above, if we assume that there is also an LSP from LSR8 to LSR5 that is (in a steady state) routed over LSR2 and LSR4, then the same protection LSP could be used to fast-reroute both the LSP from LSR1 to LSR9 and the LSP from LSR8 to LSR5. The reason why a single protection LSP could be used to fast-reroute multiple LSPs is because MPLS provides the ability to nest LSPs via the label stacking mechanism. The ability to use a single protection LSP to fast-reroute multiple LSPs makes this approach scalable, as the number of protection LSPs (and therefore resources needed to establish and maintain them) is independent of the number of LSPs that require fast reroute capabilities, but depends solely on the number of links you want to protect.

Note that the scheme we just described bears certain similarities to the idea of using an alternative path for rerouting, outlined in Section 7.4.1. However, the use of an alternative path for rerouting as described there doesn't work. So what are the essential differences between that approach and the approach we outlined in this section such that the former doesn't work, while the latter does? The two fundamental reasons why fast rerouting based on MPLS constraint-based routing works are

- Path computation is not distributed.
- Forwarding is not destination-based.

Using the example above, with MPLS constraint-based routing, the protection path for the link (LSR2, LSR4) is determined (and controlled) solely by LSR2. In contrast, with plain IP routing, forwarding along the alternate path is controlled not just by LSR2 but by all other LSRs along that path.

The example we discussed illustrates how you could use MPLS constraint-based routing to provide fast rerouting in the presence of link failure. However, you could generalize this example to cover not just link, but router failure as well. The first essential difference between providing fast reroute in the presence of link failure and in the presence of router failure is that in the former the protection LSP starts/ends at the LSRs of a given link that are one hop away from each other, while in the latter the protection LSP starts/ends at the LSRs that are two hops away from each other. The second essential difference is that in the former case existing link layer mechanism(s) can be used to detect link failure, while in the latter case we need to develop a new mechanism (such as a hello protocol) to detect router failure.

7.5 Application to QoS

As a final application of constraint-based routing, we consider how the techniques described in this chapter might be combined with those of Chapter 6. First, we discuss the role of routing in the provision of QoS. We then consider how the QoS techniques of the previous chapter can be used to provide QoS guarantees along LSPs selected by constraint-based routing.

7.5.1 Relationship between QoS and Routing

QoS is often viewed as being decoupled from routing, especially in the IP networking community. The design philosophy of RSVP, for example, was based on the idea that RSVP would make resource allocation requests along whatever paths routing picked as the "best." A similar philosophy prevails in the current definition of Differentiated Services, where resource allocation decisions are made independently of routing.

While it is tempting to adopt a "divide and conquer" approach by treating routing and QoS separately, in reality there is a close relationship between the two problems, and something is lost when we ignore this relationship. A simple example illustrates this point. Suppose there are two alternative paths from node A to node B and that routing decides one of these paths is the best. Now suppose we start to make resource allocation requests for traffic flowing from A to B along the "best" path. At some point, that path will run out of resources. As long as routing is separated from QoS, it will continue to favor this path, and attempts to reserve resources from A to B will fail, in spite of the fact that resources are available on the alternate path. The only way out of this situation is for routing to have some knowledge of resources and for QoS requests to be made over paths that are appropriate for those requests.

One way to think about the relationship between QoS and routing is as follows. In order to provide a QoS guarantee along a path between two nodes, we need to allocate some resources (e.g., buffer space, link bandwidth) along that path. Queuing is the set of mechanisms that provides control over local resources at each node on the path, while routing, by selecting the path, provides control over whose (local) resources are used.

7.5.2 Guaranteed Bandwidth LSPs

In Chapter 6 we saw how RSVP could easily be extended to distribute labels as part of the resource reservation process, thus allowing LSPs to be established with reserved resources. While this provides some advantages over the conventional use of RSVP to reserve resources, it does not address the relationship between routing and QoS. In the absence of some extra help from routing, RSVP PATH messages follow the "shortest" (lowest-cost) path toward their destination, and thus an LSP established in this way will also lie on the shortest path.

It should come as no surprise to learn that the extensions to RSVP described in Section 7.2.3 can be used when establishing an LSP with reserved resources. We call such an LSP a "guaranteed bandwidth LSP." Suppose, for example, that we wish to establish a reservation along a path from node A to node B, both nodes being in the same routing area. Before sending an RSVP PATH message from A to B, node A consults the link-state database and selects a path from A to B that meets the following constraint: it must have enough available bandwidth on every link to support the desired reservation. Upon obtaining such a path, A inserts an Explicit Route Object into the PATH message, thus ensuring that the LSP will be established along the selected path.

Note that this process does not guarantee that a reservation attempt will succeed, even if the constraint-based routing system is able to find a path from A to B meeting the stated constraint. For example, each node along the path needs to have enough buffer space to accommodate bursts for the reserved traffic flow, and a lack of buffer space at one node might cause admission control to fail even on a path that has enough bandwidth. Of course, you might avoid such problems by using both buffer space and bandwidth as constraints when selecting the path.

How is this process different from the application of constraint-based routing to traffic engineering? The pivotal difference is that traffic engineering does not require all the queuing machinery that is required to deliver QoS guarantees. When we establish a traffic engineering trunk between two points, it is not necessary to police the offered load entering the LSP or to dedicate any queuing resources to the trunk. To provide QoS guarantees on an LSP, however, does require policing at the LSP ingress, as well as appropriate scheduling of link resources and allocation of buffer space at nodes along the path. Thus, from a signalling point of view, establishing a traffic engineering trunk and setting up a guaranteed bandwidth LSP are similar processes; the difference lies in how we allocate resources and treat traffic at nodes along the LSP.

7.6 Summary

We have now seen one of the most important innovations enabled by MPLS: constraint-based routing. Constraint-based routing is a step beyond conventional IP routing because, in addition to minimizing some administrative metrics (like conventional routing), constraint-based routing also selects paths that satisfy one or more constraints. Typical constraints include the available bandwidth along the path and administrative constraints.

A constraint-based routing system is built from a number of components. The first is path selection, which we refer to as constrained shortest path first (CSPF). The second is a forwarding mechanism, for which we use MPLS. Third, an LSP setup mechanism that provides explicit route support is required; RSVP and CR-LDP are the two options for this component. Finally, we need extensions to link-state routing protocols such as OSPF and IS-IS to distribute information about the links regarding their ability to satisfy the constraints.

Constraint-based routing has a number of applications. Probably the most well recognized is traffic engineering—the ability to control how traffic is routed in a network in a way that optimizes network utilization. Another application is fast reroute, which is the ability to quickly respond to link or node failures by routing around them. Finally, we saw how constraint-based routing may be combined with QoS support to provide guaranteed bandwidth LSPs that are efficiently routed along paths that have the best chance of providing the QoS required.

7.7 Further Reading

The first RFC produced by the MPLS working group was on the subject of traffic engineering:

Awduche, D., et al., *Requirements for Traffic Engineering over MPLS*. RFC 2702, September 1999.

Like all RFCs, it can be found at

www.rfc-editor.org/rfc

Other documents describing RSVP extensions, CR-LDP, and extensions to IS-IS and OSPF can all be found as Internet drafts at the IETF Web site:

www.ietf.org

For basic information on link-state routing and SPF algorithms, we refer you to the introductory networking texts referenced in the Further Reading section of Chapter 1.

The concept of traffic trunks was introduced in

Li, T., and Y. Rekhter. *A Provider Architecture for Differentiated Services and Traffic Engineering (PASTE)*. RFC 2430, October 1998.

The December 1999 issue of *IEEE Communications Magazine* (vol. 37, no. 12) contains several interesting articles on MPLS traffic engineering:

Awduche, D., "MPLS and Traffic Engineering in IP Networks."
Ghanwani, A., B. Jamoussi, D. Fedyk, P. Ashwood-Smith, L. Li, and N. Feldman. "Traffic Engineering Standards in IP Networks Using MPLS."
Swallow, G. "MPLS Advantages for Traffic Engineering."

Virtual Private Networks

I n this chapter we look at how MPLS can be used for supporting Virtual Private Networks (VPNs). There are several approaches for supporting VPNs that use MPLS. Even though these approaches all use MPLS, it is important to understand that MPLS is just one of the components within each approach; that is probably the only thing these approaches have in common. While in principle it may be desirable to cover all of these approaches, to do so at a useful level of detail would probably require an entire book. Therefore, we have chosen to describe one specific approach in detail rather than giving a superficial overview of all these approaches. Nevertheless, many of the general principles of MPLS VPNs will become clear in this chapter.

We begin by clarifying the meaning of *VPN*. The term has been widely used and abused, and there is a great deal of confusion as to what it really means. Following this, we examine traditional VPN solutions based on Frame Relay, ATM, or IP tunnels, and we discuss the problems that these solutions are unable to address. The rest of the chapter describes one particular MPLS-based VPN solution—BGP/ MPLS VPN. As the name suggests, this solution is based on a combination of two technologies, BGP and MPLS. We look at the components of the solution, including such areas as security and Quality of Service.

Note that although we have tried to describe the solution in considerable depth, not all the details are covered in this chapter. Moreover, not even all the components are covered in this chapter. For example, while VPN Service Management is clearly an important component of a VPN solution, we don't cover it in this chapter at all.

8.1   What Is a VPN?

Consider a company that has a set of geographically dispersed sites. To interconnect computers at these sites, the company needs a network. The network is private in the sense that it is expected to be used by only that company. It is also private in the sense that the routing and addressing plan within the network is completely independent of the routing and addressing plans of all other networks. The network is virtual in the sense that the facilities used to build and operate such a network may not be dedicated just to that company, but could be shared with other companies that want to have their own VPNs. The facilities needed to build such a network are provided, at least partially, by a third party, known as a VPN service provider. The company that uses the network is known as a VPN customer.

Informally, we could say that a VPN is a set of sites that can communicate with each other. More formally, a VPN is defined by a set of administrative policies that control both connectivity and Quality of Service among sites.

It is quite natural that it is the VPN customer who sets up the policies that define that customer's VPN. With respect to who implements these policies, depending on the technology used, there could be a range of choices. For example, it should be possible to completely confine the implementation of these policies to the VPN service provider, so that the VPN customer could completely outsource the VPN service to the service provider. Likewise, it should be possible to distribute the implementation of these policies between the service provider and the customer.

With respect to the intersite connectivity, there is also a range of choices. At one end of the spectrum is complete mesh connectivity among all the sites, while at the other end of the spectrum is hub-and-spoke connectivity, where connectivity among the sites labeled as "spokes" occurs only through the site labeled as the "hub." Yet another example of intersite connectivity is when the sites are partitioned into two or more sets; in this case connectivity among sites within each set is a complete mesh, whereas connectivity between sites in different sets is indirect, only through a particular site.

While so far we've been talking about VPNs that span sites that belong to the same company, we see more and more cases where VPNs are also used to interconnect sites in different companies. The common name for the former is an *intranet* and for the latter is an *extranet*. The definition of a VPN given above applies to both cases. The distinction between the two cases is in who sets up the policies that define the VPN—in the case of an intranet it is a single company (or administrative entity), while in the case of an extranet it is a group of companies.

Our VPN definition allows a given site to be part of more than one VPN. For example, a particular site may be in a VPN associated with an intranet, and at the same time, it could also be in a different VPN associated with an extranet. In that sense VPNs could overlap.

Finally, we don't assume that a given VPN has to be confined to a single VPN service provider—facilities needed to build and operate a VPN could be provided by a group of VPN service providers.

8.2 Overlay Model

At the present moment the most common techniques for providing VPN services are based on the overlay model. With the overlay model, each site has a router that is connected via point-to-point links to routers in other sites. A site may have one or more such routers, which may be connected to all other sites or to only a subset of all other sites. The technology used to offer point-to-point links could be leased lines, Frame Relay circuits, or ATM circuits. We call the network that consists of these point-to-point links and the routers attached to these links a "virtual backbone." It is this virtual backbone that provides connectivity among sites.

To illustrate the overlay model, consider an example shown in Figure 8.1. In this example we have two VPNs, A and B. The "cloud" in the middle represents a VPN service provider. VPN A consists of three sites, Site 1, Site 2, and Site 3. Router R_{A1} at Site 1 is connected via either Frame Relay or ATM circuits to router R_{A2} at Site 2 and router R_{A3} at Site 3. Likewise, router R_{A2} at Site 2 is connected to router R_{A1} at Site 1 and router R_{A3} at Site 3. Thus, in VPN A we have a complete mesh of intersite connectivity. The Frame Relay or ATM virtual circuits are provided by the VPN service provider. VPN B also consists of three sites,

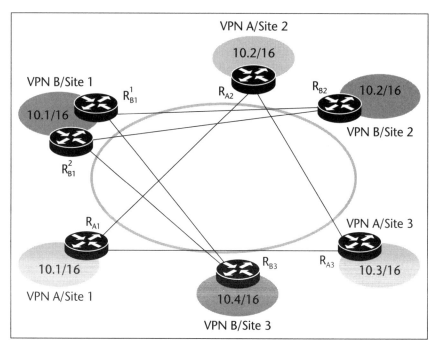

Figure 8.1
Overlay model—an example.

but the connectivity among these sites is hub-and-spoke, where Site 1 acts as a hub and Sites 2 and 3 act as spokes. Note that the hub site has not one, but two routers, R_{B1}^1 and R_{B1}^2, that connect that site to other sites. An advantage of using two routers instead of one is that it eliminates a single point of failure—if one of the routers crashes, the other one would still be able to provide connectivity. If there were only one router at the hub site, and if that router crashed, not only would the hub be unable to communicate with the spokes, but none of the spokes would be able to communicate with each other. Note that the address space used by VPN A is the same as the one used by VPN B—both use private address space, as defined in RFC 1918. There is no requirement for VPN A to use the same routing protocol as VPN B. For example, VPN A may use OSPF while VPN B uses RIP.

Although the VPN solutions based on the overlay model are predominant today, these types of solutions have several major problems that limit large-scale VPN service deployment based on such solutions. The first problem comes from the need for a VPN customer to design and operate its own virtual backbone. Design and operation of a virtual backbone assumes a certain minimum amount of expertise in IP routing, which is not that common. As a result, not too many companies could use a VPN service that requires each company to design and operate its own virtual backbone. In addition to requiring expertise in routing, this approach also requires customer expertise in IP QoS, Layer 2 QoS, and the mapping between IP QoS and Layer 2 QoS. This is because, while ATM and Frame Relay can provide QoS, this QoS is expressed in terms of Layer 2 parameters, not in terms of IP QoS. The decision on what traffic gets a particular QoS is made by the backbone routers, and these routers are assumed to be controlled by the VPN customers. Again, as with expertise in IP routing, the expertise in IP QoS and its mapping into ATM or Frame Relay QoS is not that common.

In an attempt to solve the first problem, VPN service providers offer what is known as a "managed router" service, whereby the service provider designs and operates a virtual backbone for each of its VPN customers. However, while solving one problem, this approach introduces another, as it requires a service provider to design and operate a virtual backbone for each of its VPN customers. This requirement makes it difficult for the service provider to offer services to a large number of customers (consider a service provider that has 100,000 VPN customers and therefore has to design and operate 100,000 different virtual backbones, one for each customer); it also makes the service rather costly to the service provider, as designing and operating a virtual backbone is a labor-intensive job. So the managed router service doesn't really solve the problem.

Inability to support a large number of customers is just one of the problems with the overlay model. The second problem comes from customers who have a relatively large number of sites (100 and more) and require complete mesh connectivity among these sites. For these customers a backbone router within a given site would require a routing peering with the backbone router in every other site. So, for a VPN of N sites, a backbone router would need $(N - 1)$ routing peerings. The problem with that number of peerings is precisely the same problem as running IP over ATM with the overlay model, as we discussed in Chapter 1.[1]

---

1. You may attempt to solve the problem of requiring a large number of peerings by using the Next Hop Resolution Protocol (NHRP). However, such a solution has a fatal flaw—it may create persistent forwarding loops. As stated in RFC 2332, "Operation of NHRP as a means of establishing a transit path across an NBMA subnetwork between

Yet another problem with the overlay model is the amount of configuration changes required when adding a new site to an existing VPN. For a VPN that requires full mesh connectivity among its sites, adding a new site involves changes to the configuration on all of the existing sites, as each one would need an additional point-to-point connection to the new site and an additional routing peering with the router in the new site.

A variation on the overlay model is the model where a service provider deploys routers that are capable of acting as "virtual routers." In this case a single router acts as a collection of virtual routers. A virtual router is functionally equivalent to a conventional router, except that it shares CPU, bandwidth, and memory resources with other virtual routers. A virtual router is connected to other virtual routers via point-to-point links. To reduce the number of point-to-point links required, you could multiplex several connections into a single leased line or Frame Relay circuit or ATM circuit, by introducing some form of a multiplexing header that is prepended to the packets exchanged between virtual routers. Each site has a router that is connected to a particular virtual router. In this case the virtual backbone is composed of such virtual routers and the links that interconnect them.

One advantage of using virtual routers is that it reduces the amount of physical equipment that a service provider offering the managed router service has to manage. This is because a single box could act as a collection of multiple virtual routers, where each virtual router is used by a given VPN. However, using virtual routers still doesn't eliminate the fundamental limitations associated with the overlay model that we discussed above. This should not be viewed as a surprise—after all, the use of virtual routers doesn't change the model; it just allows physical boxes (routers) to be replaced with virtual ones (virtual routers).

In addition to leased lines, Frame Relay circuits, or ATM circuits, you could also use GRE or IPSec tunnels as mechanisms to connect routers. However, since both GRE and IPSec tunnels act only as mechanisms to provide point-to-point connectivity among the routers, and

---

two routers will be addressed in a separate document." And with respect to the separate document that this sentence is referring to, the IESG reached the following conclusion: "After continued analysis, draft-ietf-ion-r2r-nhrp-03.txt is being withdrawn from RFC publication. The router-to-router algorithms have been shown to be restricted to a very small subset of possible configurations without keeping state on every router, which would not be practical. Given the small set of configurations, it is best to withdraw the draft." [e-mail from the ION Working Group chair Andy Malis to the ION mailing list on 8/2/1999]

do not change the overall model, VPN solutions based on either GRE or IPSec inherit all of the problems associated with the overlay model that we discussed above. Moreover, they introduce a few new problems.

Use of GRE tunnels introduces the problem of data spoofing. By sending packets to an IP address that represents the tail end of a GRE tunnel, it is possible to inject packets into a VPN, and sending such packets can be done by anyone, not just the router at the head end of the tunnel. One way to address this problem is by using packet filters. But that involves additional configuration complexity and is also error prone.

Another way to address the problem of data spoofing is by using IPSec tunnels instead of GRE. With IPSec the tail end of a tunnel could authenticate the sender, thus allowing only the packets being originated by the head end of the tunnel to be accepted, and rejecting all other packets. While the use of IPSec provides more robust protection against packet spoofing, this additional robustness has an extra cost associated with key management used by IPSec. Also notice that the use of IPSec as a tunneling mechanism between routers managed by a VPN service provider doesn't really offer VPN customers any benefits of IPSec, such as data privacy. This is because in this scenario the IPSec keys are managed by the service provider.

In the area of QoS, the best that could be accomplished with GRE or IPSec tunnels is to rely on IP Differentiated Services, as described in Section 6.2. However, it is not clear whether QoS based only on IP Differentiated Services is adequate for VPN customers, as VPN customers who use leased lines or Frame Relay or ATM are accustomed to QoS guarantees that are stricter than those that can be provided by IP Differentiated Services.

One of the claimed advantages of using GRE or IPSec tunnels over leased lines, Frame Relay, or ATM is the ability to extend the VPN service to anyplace connected to the Internet, rather than being limited by the scope of an ATM or Frame Relay network. In practice this advantage is limited by the fact that when a GRE or IPSec tunnel spans multiple providers, the providers at the end of that tunnel have little or no influence on the path taken by the tunnel. As a consequence, such key aspects of a VPN service offering as QoS and fault management are left largely undetermined. Therefore, a service provider that offers a VPN service based on GRE or IPSec tunnels is unlikely to be able to provide any guarantees on QoS and/or fault management, since both QoS and fault management would be beyond that provider's control. To put it differently, "The idea is to create a private network via tunneling and/or encryption over the public Internet. Sure, it's a lot cheaper than using your own frame-relay connections, but it works as well as sticking cotton in your ears in Times Square and pretending nobody else is around" (*Wired Magazine,* February 1998).

To summarize, the overlay model has certain fundamental properties that limit large-scale VPN service offerings based on that model. These properties are fundamental in the sense that they exist regardless of the particular technology used to build the site-to-site connections in this model.

8.3 The Peer Model

In the previous section we described VPN solutions based on the overlay model. In the rest of this chapter we describe a VPN solution that is based on a different model—the "peer" model. The major goal of this solution is to overcome the fundamental limitations associated with the overlay model. Specifically, this model aims at enabling VPN service providers to support very large-scale VPN service offerings (thousands to millions of VPNs per service provider), where most of the customers have little or no IP routing expertise, and to support a diverse population of customers, where some VPNs would consist of just a few sites, while others would have hundreds or even thousands of sites per VPN. At the same time, it aims at keeping the cost of offering the VPN service low.

The solution we describe is built around several key technologies:

- Constrained distribution of routing information
- Multiple forwarding tables
- Use of a new type of addresses, VPN-IP addresses
- MPLS

In the rest of this chapter we look at how these technologies, used together, provide a solution that meets the goals outlined in the previous paragraph.

To illustrate the peer model, consider the example shown in Figure 8.2. The middle cloud is a collection of one or more service providers that offer VPN services. Around the cloud we have sites that form VPNs. In this picture we show two Virtual Private Networks, A and B. A site is connected to a VPN service provider by a Customer Edge (CE)

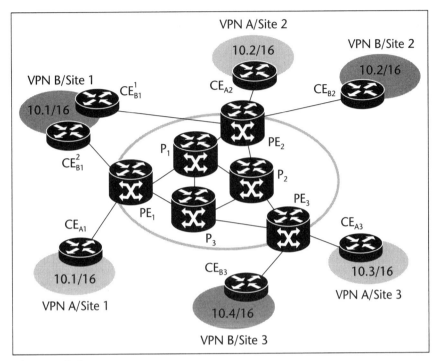

Figure 8.2
BGP/MPLS example.

router. A site may have one or more Customer Edge routers. For example, Site 1 in VPN B has two CE routers, CE_{B1}^1 and CE_{B1}^2, while Site 3 in VPN B has only one CE router, CE_{B3}. We also show a set of destinations reachable within each site (e.g., the set of destinations reachable within Site 2 of VPN A is covered by an IP address prefix 10.2/16).

On the service provider side, a CE router is connected to a Provider Edge (PE) router. Note that a single PE router may be connected to sites that belong to different VPNs; moreover, these sites may use the same IP addresses for destinations within the sites.[2] For example, PE_2 is connected to sites that belong to VPN A (Site 2) and VPN B (Site 2). In addition, both Site 2 in VPN A and Site 2 in VPN B use the same block of addresses, 10.2/16, for destinations internal to these sites. Also note that a site may be connected to more than one PE router. In the

---

2. IP addresses have to be unique within a VPN, but don't have to be unique across multiple VPNs. In fact, it is highly likely that multiple VPNs would use the same block of addresses, namely, the addresses specified in RFC 1918.

example above, Site 1 of VPN B is connected to PE$_1$ and also connected to PE$_2$.

The third type of router in this figure is the Provider (P) router, which does not connect to customer sites. We distinguish the P routers from the PE routers because they have more restricted functionality, as described below.

The reason for calling this a "peer" model is that, from the routing point of view, the service provider network acts as a peer of the customer networks, since the customer routers peer directly with provider routers. This is in contrast to the overlay model, where customer routers peer only with other customer routers over layer 2 links or IP tunnels provided by the service provider.

In the following sections we examine the individual components of the BGP/MPLS VPN solution, which is an implementation of the peer model. We begin with the constrained distribution of routing information.

8.4 Constrained Distribution of Routing Information

Recall that we defined a VPN by a set of policies that determine, among other things, connectivity among sites. Therefore, one of the mechanisms we need is a mechanism that can control connectivity among sites. The mechanism we use to accomplish this is constrained distribution of routing information. The reason why constrained distribution of routing information provides control over connectivity is because the flow of data is determined by the flow of routing information; therefore, constraining the flow of routing information constrains the flow of data.[3] Another way to put it is to say that connectivity and the flow of data are controlled by routing tables on the routers, and the content of those routing tables can be controlled by constraining the flow of routing information.

To understand how constrained distribution of routing information is used in the context of the BGP/MPLS VPN approach, let's first look at the distribution of routing information, which can be decomposed into five steps:

---

3. The use of constrained distribution of routing information to control connectivity is a fairly old and proven technique that has been used extensively in the Internet since the late 1980s.

1. The routing information is propagated from a customer site to the service provider. More precisely, the information is propagated from a CE router to the PE router to which the CE router is connected. There are several options for propagating this information, such as RIP, static routing, OSPF, or BGP.

2. At the ingress PE router, this information is exported into the provider's BGP.

3. This information is distributed within the service provider among the PE routers using BGP.

4. This step is exactly the opposite of the second step. That is, at the egress PE router, the routing information is imported from the provider's BGP.

5. This step is exactly the opposite of the first step. That is, the routing information is sent from the egress PE router to a site to a CE router. Again, there are several options for doing this, such as RIP, static routing, OSPF, or BGP.

To constrain distribution of routing information, we use the technique of route filtering based on the BGP *Community* attribute, where BGP Community essentially acts as an identifier that may be attached to an advertised route. At step 2, as a result of its local configuration, the ingress PE router attaches the appropriate Community attribute to a route, as the route is exported into the provider's BGP. At step 4, as a result of its configuration, the egress PE router uses the Community attribute carried by a route to control the importing of routes from the provider's BGP to a customer site (to a CE router).

Notice that there is a significant flexibility with respect to the granularity of the route filtering mechanism based on the BGP Community attribute. At one end of the spectrum, an ingress PE router could apply a particular BGP Community attribute to all routes coming from a particular site (i.e., from a particular CE router), while at the other end of the spectrum, the router could apply a distinct Community to each individual route. Flexible granularity of the route filtering mechanism enables flexibility with respect to the intersite connectivity within a VPN, as the connectivity is controlled by routing filtering based on the Community attribute. This, in turn, enables a service provider to use just one common mechanism to support VPN customers with diverse intersite connectivity policies.

Note that constrained distribution of routing information is performed in steps 2 and 4. Moreover, note that these two steps are handled by a service provider. Since the mechanisms we need to constrain the flow of routing information could be completely confined to the service provider, a VPN customer doesn't have to be involved in understanding and implementing these mechanisms. This, in turn, helps to accomplish the goal of being able to offer VPN services to customers who don't have significant expertise in IP routing.

To illustrate how constrained distribution of routing information is used in the context of BGP/MPLS VPNs, we look at the example shown in Figure 8.2 and examine the flow of routing information from Site 1 to Site 3 in VPN A. In the first step, the route for 10.1/16 is distributed from the CE router in Site 1 of VPN A, CE_{A1}, to a PE router that this site is connected to, PE_1. This distribution could be accomplished, for example, by RIP. In the second step, this route is exported into the provider's BGP, and as the route gets exported, the ingress PE router, PE_1, under control of its local configuration, attaches the appropriate BGP Community attribute to the route. In step 3, this route is distributed to other PE routers using normal BGP procedures. In step 4, at the egress PE router, PE_3, the route is imported from the provider's BGP. The importing is controlled by the route filtering that is performed (under control of its local configuration) by PE_3 and is based on the Community attribute carried by the route. Finally, in step 5, the route is distributed from PE_3 to the CE router, CE_{A3}, in Site 3 of VPN A. This distribution could be accomplished either by the same protocol, RIP, that we used in step 1 or by some other protocol, like OSPF or BGP.

Let's look at several important characteristics of the mechanism used by BGP/MPLS VPN to control intersite connectivity, as these characteristics have fairly significant implications on the scalability of the BGP/MPLS VPN approach. First of all, observe that within a given VPN, a CE router maintains routing peering just with its directly connected PE router, but not with CE routers in other sites of that VPN. This is a basic attribute of the peer model. For example, in Figure 8.2, CE_{A1} has a routing peering just with PE_1 but not with CE routers in other sites, CE_{A2} or CE_{A3}. As a result, the number of routing peers that a CE router has to maintain is constant and independent of the total number of sites within a VPN. That facilitates support of large VPNs with hundreds and thousands of sites per VPN, because the amount of routing peering that a CE route has to perform is independent of the total number of sites within a VPN. In contrast, when you want to have a full mesh of intersite connectivity with the overlay model, the need to have a complete mesh routing peering among all the sites means that the amount of routing peering grows with the number of sites, which, in turn, means that the scalability of the overlay model in the area of routing peering is inferior to the BGP/MPLS VPN approach.

Second, observe that in order to add a new site to an existing VPN, all a service provider has to do is appropriately configure the PE router that will be connected to the new site. More generally, the amount of configuration changes needed to handle addition or deletion of sites within a given VPN is constant and therefore is independent of the number of sites of that VPN. In contrast, when you want to have full mesh intersite connectivity with the overlay model, the number of such configuration changes is proportional to the number of sites (as adding a new site requires addition of a new Frame Relay or ATM circuit or a new IP tunnel to all other sites). Therefore, the scalability of the overlay model in the area of configuration management is inferior to the BGP/MPLS VPN approach.

Finally, observe that a PE router has to maintain only the routes for the VPNs whose sites are directly connected to that PE router (i.e., whose sites have CE routers connected to that PE router). Using the example shown in Figure 8.2, PE_1 has to maintain routes only for VPNs A and B. There may be some other VPNs, not shown in the figure, that have no sites connected to PE_1. Because sites of these VPNs are not connected to PE_1, PE_1 doesn't have to maintain routes for these VPNs.

One problem with using route filtering based on the BGP Community attribute is that this attribute allows at most 2^{16} different communities per service provider. This is because each community is 32 bits wide and is structured as a concatenation of 16 bits for the Autonomous System Number and 16 bits for local assignment. Since each VPN would require at least one distinct Community, it follows that if we use BGP Communities, a single service provider would be limited to at most 2^{16} VPN customers. To overcome this limitation, we introduce the concept of BGP *Extended Communities*. Semantically, Extended Communities are quite similar to plain Communities, so from the route filtering point of view there is little or no difference. The main new feature introduced by Extended Communities is the ability to support 2^{32} different Communities per service provider. This is accomplished by extending the size of the local assignment part from 16 to 32 bits. Note that since each Extended Community embeds the Autonomous System Number (just like a plain Community), and since Autonomous System Numbers are globally unique by virtue of assignment, it follows that each service provider can control local assignment on its own, while at the same time maintaining the global uniqueness of such assignments.

8.5 Multiple Forwarding Tables

Constrained distribution of routing information is clearly necessary, but not sufficient, to control connectivity. This is because a given PE router may have sites from different VPNs attached to it. If that PE router has just one forwarding table, then this table would have to contain all the routes for all these VPNs, therefore preventing per-VPN segregation of routing information. It would thus be possible for packets to be forwarded from one VPN to another, which is clearly not acceptable.

A solution to this problem is to require each PE router to maintain not one, but multiple forwarding tables. It is a combination of multiple forwarding tables and route filtering that allows per-VPN segregation of routing information and therefore control over intersite connectivity on a per-VPN basis.

In an extreme case, each site attached to a PE router would have its own forwarding table. That would happen, for example, when each site connected to a given PE is in its own VPN. However, when a PE router has several sites with common VPN membership (e.g., a set of sites that are in the same VPN), all such sites could share the same forwarding table.

A PE router uses its multiple forwarding tables to handle packets it receives from its directly attached sites. In the most simple case each customer port on the PE router is associated at provisioning time with a particular forwarding table. At forwarding time, the incoming port on the PE router determines which forwarding table the PE router would use to forward the packet.

Each forwarding table on a PE router is populated from two sources. The first source is the set of routes that the PE router receives from its directly attached CE routers. A forwarding table associated with a particular VPN would be populated by the routes the PE router receives from the CE routers that are connected to the PE router and that belong to that VPN. The second source is the set of routes that the PE router receives from other PE routers. For the second source of the routes, it is precisely the route filtering based on the BGP Community attribute, as described in the preceding section, that determines the routes the PE router would place in its particular forwarding table.

Let's take a look at some examples of how you could construct VPNs. The most simple example is where sites within a VPN require full mesh intersite connectivity. In this case, for this VPN we use just one community, which we'll call C_{closed}. At a PE router that has sites from that VPN connected to it, all the sites' routes are exported in the provider BGP with this community C_{closed}. Likewise, on all these PE routers, the routes that are imported into the forwarding table associated with this VPN are only the routes that have this community, C_{closed}. Using the example shown in Figure 8.2, if VPN A requires full mesh connectivity among its three sites, then the service provider assigns just one community for this VPN, $C_{VPN\ A}$. When router PE_1 exports the routes it receives from CE_{A1} into the provider's BGP, it exports them (under control of its local configuration) with BGP Community $C_{VPN\ A}$. Likewise, the only routes the PE_1 router imports from the provider's BGP into its forwarding table associated with VPN A are the routes that have Community $C_{VPN\ A}$.

Next, look at an example where a VPN requires hub-and-spoke intersite connectivity, where all the spoke sites could communicate with each other only via the hub site. In this case, we need not one, but two different communities. One community is associated with the hub, C_{hub}, and the other with the spokes, C_{spoke}. A PE router that has spoke sites connected to it would export into the provider's BGP the routes received from these sites with BGP Community C_{spoke} and would import from the provider's BGP into the forwarding table associated with that VPN only the routes whose community is C_{hub}. Likewise, a PE router that has the hub site connected to it would export routes received from these sites with BGP Community C_{hub} and would import into the forwarding table associated with that VPN only the routes whose community is C_{spoke}. These two simple examples illustrate just some of the ways connectivity can be controlled using Community attributes.

8.6 VPN-IP Addresses

So far we have described the mechanisms that allow us to control intersite connectivity on a per-VPN basis. But these mechanisms use BGP, and BGP, in turn, makes certain assumptions about IP addresses. Specifically, BGP assumes that IP addresses are unique. That assumption is clearly incorrect in the VPN service provider environment, where the same block of IP addresses (e.g., private addresses as defined in RFC 1918) could be simultaneously used by multiple VPN customers. So, in order to use BGP-based mechanisms, we need to figure out how to use BGP in an environment where IP addresses are no longer unique. An obvious solution to this problem would be to turn non-unique addresses into unique addresses. How? By creating a new type of address, which we call the VPN-IP address, and making sure that these addresses are unique.

By definition, a VPN-IP address is constructed by concatenating a fixed-length field, called a Route Distinguisher, with a plain IP address. What makes such addresses unique is the Route Distinguisher. A Route Distinguisher is structured in such a way as to allow each VPN service provider to create unique Route Distinguishers on its own, without the risk of the same Route Distinguisher being assigned by some other provider. By definition, a Route Distinguisher consists of three fields: Type (2 octets), Autonomous System Number (2 octets), and Assigned Number (4 octets). The Autonomous System Number field contains the Autonomous System Number of the VPN service provider. The assignment of the Assigned Number field is controlled by each VPN service provider on its own. In the most common case, a service provider assigns just one value to a given VPN served by the provider (but in some cases it may assign more than one value).[4] Since no two VPNs within a given service provider share the same Assigned Number, and since Autonomous System Numbers are globally unique by virtue of assignment, it follows that no two VPNs share the same Route Distinguisher. Since IP addresses are assumed to be unique within a VPN, and since no two VPNs share the same Route Distinguisher, it follows that VPN-IP addresses are globally unique.

From the BGP point of view, handling routes for VPN-IP addresses is no different than handling routes for plain IP addresses, as the BGP multiprotocol capability makes BGP capable of handling routes for multiple-address families. It is important to stress that the structure of VPN-IP addresses, as well as the structure of the Route Distinguisher component of VPN-IP addresses, is totally opaque to BGP—when BGP compares two VPN-IP address prefixes, it ignores the structure. In that sense we don't introduce any new mechanisms to BGP, but just reuse the existing ones. For example, such mechanisms as BGP Communities, route filtering based on the communities, use of BGP Route Reflectors, BGP Refresh, and so on, are as applicable to routes for VPN-IP addresses as to routes for plain IP addresses.

---

4. Note that there is no requirement for all the routes within a given VPN to have the same Route Distinguisher. Moreover, there are cases, like multiprovider VPN (as described in Section 8.11.3), where allowing multiple Route Distinguishers is advantageous.

Use of VPN-IP addresses is completely confined to a VPN service provider—a VPN customer (and, specifically, the customer's equipment) is unaware of VPN-IP addresses. Conversion between VPN-IP addresses and IP addresses happens at the PE routers. For each directly connected VPN, a PE router is configured (at the provisioning time) with a Route Distinguisher. When the PE router receives a route from a directly attached CE router, the PE router identifies the VPN that the CE router belongs to and, before exporting this route into the provider's BGP, converts the reachability information of this route from plain IP to VPN-IP by using the Route Distinguisher that is configured for that VPN. Likewise, when a PE router has to import routes from the provider's BGP, the PE router converts the reachability information of these routes from VPN-IP addresses to plain IP addresses.

At this point it may be instructive to compare the roles played by Route Distinguishers and BGP Communities. We have two separate problems, and corresponding to these two problems we have two separate mechanisms. The first problem is how to deal with globally non-unique addresses. To solve this problem, we introduce a new type of address, the VPN-IP address, and use Route Distinguishers to make such addresses globally unique. Thus, the Route Distinguisher is used to disambiguate IP addresses. At the same time, the Route Distinguisher is not used to constrain connectivity, as it is not used for route filtering. The second problem we need to solve is how to constrain connectivity. We solve this problem by constraining distribution of routing information, which is done by using filtering based on the BGP Community attribute. The BGP Community attribute, on the other hand, is not used to disambiguate IP addresses.

Note that while the same Route Distinguisher can't be used by more than one VPN, a given VPN may use multiple Route Distinguishers. (One example of this is multiprovider operations, as described in Section 8.11.3.) Likewise, while the same BGP Extended Community can't be used by more than one VPN, a given VPN may use multiple Extended Communities. (An example of this is a hub-and-spoke VPN, as we described in Section 8.5.) Therefore, in general, neither the Route Distinguisher nor the Extended Community identifies a VPN. This is consistent with the way we defined a VPN—as a set of *administrative policies* that control connectivity and quality of service among sites.

It is worth noting that VPN-IP addresses are carried only in routing protocols, not in the headers of IP packets. Thus, they are not directly used for the forwarding of packets. The task of forwarding packets is handled using MPLS, as described in the following section.

8.7 MPLS as a Forwarding Mechanism

So far we managed to figure out how to use BGP to construct all the necessary routes, even in the presence of nonunique IP addresses. However, the problem with using these routes is that their reachability information is expressed not in terms of IP but of VPN-IP addresses. And there is nothing in the IP header to carry these VPN-IP addresses. So how can we forward IP packets along these routes?

To provide forwarding of IP packets along the routes expressed in terms of VPN-IP addresses, we use MPLS. The reason MPLS enables us to do this is because it decouples the information used for packet forwarding (the label) from the information carried in the IP header. Therefore, we can bind LSPs to VPN-IP routes and then forward IP packets along these routes by using MPLS as the forwarding mechanism. Observe that since VPN-IP addresses are confined to the service provider, MPLS could be confined to the service provider as well.

To illustrate how the actual forwarding is done, first consider an example shown in Figure 8.3. Notice that from the MPLS point of view

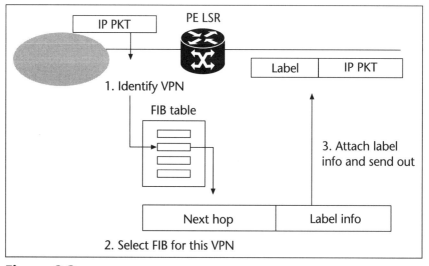

Figure 8.3
Label imposition at PE router.

the PE router is an edge LSR. That is, the PE router converts unlabeled packets into labeled ones and vice versa.

When a CE router sends an IP packet to its directly connected PE router, the PE router uses the incoming port (the interface on which the PE router receives the packet) to identify the VPN that the CE router belongs to and, more precisely, to identify the forwarding table (also called a *forwarding information base* or FIB) associated with that VPN.[5] Once the FIB is identified, the PE router performs normal IP lookup in this FIB, using the destination IP address in the packet. As a result of the FIB lookup, the PE router adds the appropriate label information to the packet and forwards the packet.

To improve the scaling properties of this approach, we employ a hierarchy of routing knowledge, similar to that discussed in Section 4.1.2. By using this technique, none of the P routers maintains any VPN routing information, which, in turn, reduces the routing load (i.e., the number of routes and the number of labels) on the P routers. To implement the hierarchy of routing knowledge, we use not one, but two levels of labels, where the first-level label is associated with a route to an egress PE router, and therefore provides forwarding from an ingress PE router to the egress PE router, and the second-level label controls forwarding at the egress PE router. The first-level label could be distributed either via LDP or, if a service provider wants to use traffic engineering, via RSVP or CR-LDP. The second-level label is distributed via BGP, as described in Section 5.4.4, together with VPN-IP routes.

Note that a VPN-IP route distributed via BGP carries as the next hop attribute the address of the PE router that originates the route, and that the route to that next hop address is provided via the provider's intradomain routing procedures. Thus, we may observe that it is the information carried in the next hop attribute that provides coupling between a provider's internal routing (intradomain routing) and the VPN routes (which, from a provider's point of view, are external routes).

To illustrate how we use the concept of the MPLS hierarchy of routing knowledge, consider an example shown in Figure 8.4. It shows two sites within a particular VPN, where each site is represented just by its CE router (CE_1 and CE_2). Both PE_1 and PE_2 are configured with the

---

5. Remember that, at the provisioning time, an interface that connects a PE router to a CE router is associated with a particular VPN or, more specifically, with a particular forwarding table on the PE router.

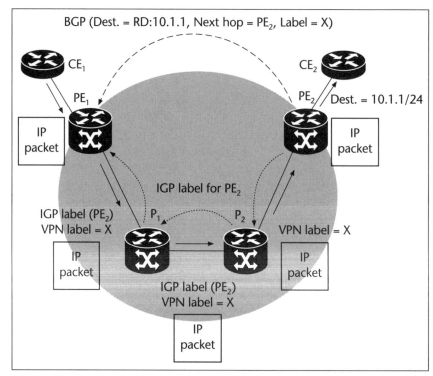

Figure 8.4
Use of two-level label stack.

appropriate Route Distinguisher to be used for that VPN, as well as with the appropriate BGP Community to be used when exporting routes into the provider's BGP and when importing routes from the provider's BGP. On PE_1 the interface that connects PE_1 to CE_1 is associated (at provisioning time) with the forwarding table of that VPN.

When PE_2 receives from CE_2 a route with reachability information 10.1.1/24, PE_2 converts the reachability information of that route from plain IP to VPN-IP addresses, attaches the BGP Community attribute, and exports this route into the provider's BGP. The next hop BGP attribute of this route is set to the address of PE_2. (Usually, this address is the loopback address of the router.) In addition to all the conventional BGP information, the route also carries a label that is associated with that VPN-IP route. This information is distributed to PE_1 using BGP (as shown by the dashed line). When PE_1 receives the route, PE_1 converts the route from VPN-IP to IP and uses it to populate the forwarding table associated with the VPN.

In addition, there is an LSP from PE_1 to PE_2, which is associated with a route to PE_2 and is established and maintained by either LDP or MPLS traffic engineering. Note that the route distributed via BGP carries, as the next hop attribute, the address of PE_2, and that the route to that address is provided via the provider's intradomain routing. So it is the address of PE_2 (carried in the next hop attribute) that provides coupling between the provider's internal routing (e.g., routing to PE_2) and the VPN routes (e.g., routing to 10.1.1/24). At this point the VPN forwarding table on PE_1 contains a route for 10.1.1/24 and a label stack, where the inner label is the label that PE_1 receives via BGP and the outer label is the label associated with a route to PE_2.

Now let's assume that CE_1 sends a packet with destination address 10.1.1.1. When the packet arrives at PE_1, PE_1 determines the appropriate forwarding table and then performs the lookup in that table. As a result of the lookup, PE_1 attaches two labels to the packet and sends the packet to P_1. P_1, in turn, uses the outer label when making its forwarding decision and forwards the packet to P_2. Since P_2 is the penultimate hop with respect to the LSP associated with a route to PE_2, P_2 pops the outer label before sending the packet to PE_2. When PE_2 receives the packet, it uses the label carried by the packet (the label that PE_2 distributed to PE_1 via BGP) to make its forwarding decision. PE_2 strips the label and sends the packet to CE_2.

To appreciate the scalability gain provided by the MPLS hierarchy of routing knowledge, consider the example of a service provider network that consists of 200 routers (both PE and P routers), which supports 10,000 VPNs, with each VPN having on average 100 routes. Without the use of the MPLS hierarchy of routing knowledge, each P router would need to maintain $10,000 \times 100 = 1,000,000$ routes. With the MPLS hierarchy of routing knowledge, each P router would need to maintain only 200 routes.

8.8 Scalability

"The only real problem is scaling. All others inherent are from that one. If you can scale, everything else must be working."

Mike O'Dell, Chief Scientist, UUNet
MPLS Conference, Nov 1998

We already discussed some of the scaling properties of the BGP/MPLS VPN approach in Section 8.4, where we observed that the amount of routing peering that a CE router has to maintain is constant and therefore independent of the total number of sites within a VPN, thus allowing support of VPNs with sites numbering in the hundreds or thousands. We also observed that the amount of configuration changes needed when adding or deleting a site is constant and therefore is independent of the total number of sites within a VPN.

Now let's take a look at the scaling properties with respect to handling routing information. First of all, by employing the MPLS hierarchy of routing knowledge, we keep all the P routers completely free of any VPN routing information. That is, P routers don't maintain any VPN routing information—the VPN routing information is maintained only on the PE routers.

Second, although a PE router has to maintain VPN routing information, it has to maintain only the routing information for the VPNs whose sites are directly connected to that PE router—it doesn't have to maintain routes for all the VPNs supported by a service provider. If the volume of VPN routing information on a particular PE router gets too high for that router, we can add a new PE router and move some of the VPNs from the old router to the new one.

Finally, let's look at how to handle BGP Route Reflectors.[6] To avoid a situation where a particular Route Reflector would be required to handle routing information for all the VPNs supported by a provider, we partition Route Reflectors among VPNs supported by the provider. This way one set of Route Reflectors, for example, contains routes for the first hundred VPNs, the second set of Route Reflectors contains routes for the second hundred VPNs, and so on. As a result, if the volume of VPN routing information maintained by a particular set of Route Reflectors gets too high, we can add a new set of Route Reflectors and move some of the VPNs from the old to the new set.

Note that there is no single component within a service provider network that is required to maintain all the routing information for all the VPNs supported by the provider. Consequently, the VPN routing capacity of the service provider network isn't bound by the capacity of any individual component, which results in virtually unlimited routing scalability.

---

6. BGP Route Reflectors are useful to eliminate the requirement of a complete mesh of BGP sessions among all the PE routers—with BGP Route Reflectors, a PE router would need to maintain BGP sessions with just a few Route Reflectors.

8.9 Security

Security is clearly an important component for any credible VPN solution. In the area of security, the goal of the BGP/MPLS VPN approach is to achieve security comparable to that provided today by Frame Relay or ATM-based VPNs. Specifically, the goal is to make sure that, in the absence of either deliberate interconnection or misconfiguration, packets from one VPN wouldn't be able to get into another VPN.

To see how we accomplish this goal, first observe that forwarding within a VPN service provider is based on label switching, not on traditional IP forwarding. Therefore, forwarding within the provider is not determined by the IP addresses carried in the packets. Moreover, observe that LSPs associated with VPN-IP routes originate and terminate only at the PE routers—they don't terminate in the middle of a service provider network, and they don't start in the middle of a service provider network. At a PE router, these LSPs are associated with particular forwarding tables, and the forwarding tables are associated (at provisioning time) with interfaces on the PE router. Finally, observe that these interfaces are associated at provisioning time with particular VPNs.

Therefore, when a PE router sends a packet to a CE router that belongs to a particular VPN, this packet has to arrive at the PE router either from another (directly connected) CE router or from some other PE router. In order for this to happen in the former case, both of the CE routers have to be within the same VPN and have to share the same forwarding table on the CE router. In the latter case, the packet has to be forwarded to the PE router via an LSP associated with a particular forwarding table, where the table is associated with the VPN at provisioning time via configuration. The LSP has to originate at some other PE; on that other PE, the LSP is associated with a particular forwarding table, and that table (via configuration) is associated with a particular VPN. On that other PE, in order for the packet to be forwarded via the forwarding table associated with the VPN, the packet has to arrive at that PE on an interface that is associated (via configuration) with that VPN. As a result, in the absence of misconfiguration, injecting the packet into a VPN could be done only through an interface on a PE router that is associated with that VPN. It therefore follows that packets cannot be maliciously or accidentally injected into some VPN to which the sender does not belong, just as in an ATM or Frame Relay network.

8.10 QoS Support

When we defined the term VPN in Section 8.1, we said that a VPN is defined by a set of administrative policies that control both connectivity and Quality of Service (QoS) among sites. In this section we look at the mechanisms that a service provider would use to implement the QoS aspects of the policies. This section uses material from both Chapter 6 and Chapter 7.

In the area of QoS, the challenge is to develop a set of mechanisms that supports QoS in a way that is flexible enough to support a wide range of VPN customers and scalable enough to support a large number of VPN customers. For example, a service provider should be able to offer its VPN customers multiple Classes of Service per VPN, where different applications within the same VPN would receive different Classes of Service. This way, for example, email would get one Class of Service while some real-time application could get a completely different Class of Service. Moreover, the Class of Service that a particular application would get within one VPN could be quite different from the Class of Service that precisely the same application would get within another VPN. That is, the set of mechanisms in support of QoS should allow the decision about what traffic gets a specific Class of Service to be made on a per-VPN basis. Moreover, not all VPNs have to use all the Classes of Service that a VPN service provider offers. Therefore, the set of mechanisms in support of QoS should allow the decision on which Class of Service to use to be made on a per-VPN basis.

Before describing specific mechanisms used by BGP/MPLS VPN to support QoS, we first look at two models that are used to describe QoS in the context of VPNs—the "pipe" model and the "hose" model.

In the pipe model a VPN service provider supplies a VPN customer with certain QoS guarantees for the traffic from one customer's CE router to another. In a sense you could represent this model by a "pipe" that connects the two routers, and the traffic that enters this pipe gets certain QoS guarantees. One example of the sort of QoS guarantees that could be provided with the pipe model is some guaranteed minimum bandwidth between two sites.

You could further refine the pipe model by making only a subset of all the traffic (e.g., only specific applications) from one CE to another CE able to use the pipe. The ultimate decision on what traffic could use the pipe is purely local to the PE router at the head end of the pipe.

Note that the pipe model is very similar (but not identical) to the QoS model that VPN customers have today with Frame Relay or ATM-based solutions. The essential difference is that with Frame Relay or ATM the connection is bidirectional, whereas the pipe model offers unidirectional guarantees. The fact that the pipe is unidirectional allows for asymmetry with respect to the traffic pattern, whereby the amount of traffic from one site to another may be different from the amount of traffic in the reverse direction.

As an illustration, consider the example shown in Figure 8.5, where a service provider supplies VPN A with one pipe that guarantees 7 Mb/sec of bandwidth for the traffic from Site 3 to Site 1 (to be more precise, from CE_{A3} to CE_{A1}) and another pipe that guarantees 10 Mb/sec of bandwidth for the traffic from Site 3 to Site 2 (from CE_{A3} to CE_{A2}). Observe that a given CE router may have more than one pipe originating from it (e.g., two pipes originate from Site 3). Likewise, more than one pipe may terminate at a given site.

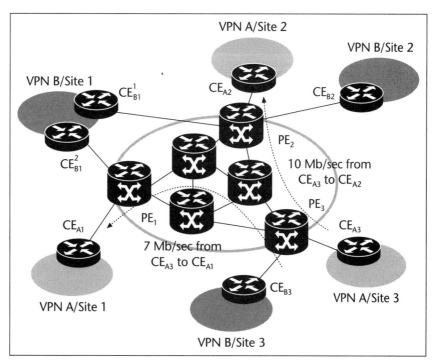

Figure 8.5
QoS pipe model—example.

One advantage of the pipe model is that it bears a great deal of similarity to the QoS model that VPN customers use today with Frame Relay or ATM. Therefore, it is easily understood by customers. However, the pipe model has several drawbacks as well. For one thing, it assumes that a VPN customer knows its complete traffic matrix. That is, for every site, the customer must know the amount of traffic that goes from that site to every other site. Quite often this information is not available and, even if available, could be outdated.

In the hose model, a VPN service provider supplies a VPN customer with certain guarantees for the traffic that the customer's CE router sends to and receives from other CE routers of the same VPN. In neither case does the customer have to specify how this traffic is distributed among the other CE routers. As as result, in contrast to the pipe model, the hose model does not require a customer to know its traffic matrix, which, in turn, places less burden on a customer that wants to use the VPN service.

The hose model uses two parameters, Ingress Committed Rate (ICR) and Egress Committed Rate (ECR). The ICR is the amount of traffic that a particular CE could send to other CEs, while the ECR is the amount of traffic that a particular CE could receive from other CEs. In other words, the ICR represents the aggregate amount of traffic from a particular CE, while the ECR represents the aggregate amount of traffic to a particular CE. Note that, for a given CE, there is no requirement that its ICR should be equal to its ECR.

To illustrate the hose model, consider the example shown in Figure 8.6, where a service provider supplies VPN B with certain guarantees of up to 15 Mb/sec for the traffic that Site 2 sends to other sites (ICR = 15 Mb/sec), regardless of whether this traffic goes to Site 1 or to Site 3 or is distributed (in an arbitrary way) between Site 1 and Site 3. Likewise, the service provider supplies VPN B with certain guarantees of up to 7 Mb/sec for the traffic that Site 3 sends to other sites in that VPN (ICR = 7 Mb/sec), regardless of whether this traffic goes to Site 1, or to Site 2, or is distributed (in arbitrary way) among Site 1 and Site 2. Similarly, the provider provides VPN B with certain guarantees of up to 15 Mb/sec for the traffic that other sites send to Site 2 (ECR = 15 Mb/sec), regardless of whether this traffic originates from Site 1 or Site 3, or is distributed (in arbitrary way) among Site 1 and Site 3.

Note that the hose model closely resembles the diff-serv model described in Section 6.2. This model supports multiple Classes of Service, with the services differing from each other in their relative performance characteristics; for example, one service might have lower

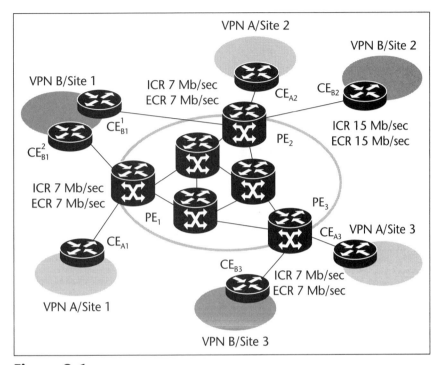

Figure 8.6
QoS hose model—an example.

packet losses than another service. For the services that require "hard" guarantees (e.g., guaranteed bandwidth), the pipe model is a better fit. Note that the pipe model is closer to the int-serv model described in Section 6.1.

The pipe and hose models are not mutually exclusive. That is, a service provider should be able to offer to a VPN customer a combination of the hose and the pipe models, and it should be up to the customer to decide which service to buy and which traffic should be getting a particular Class of Service.

To support the pipe model, we use guaranteed bandwidth LSPs, as described in Section 7.5.2. These LSPs originate and terminate at the PE routers and are used to provide guaranteed bandwidth for all the pipes from one PE router to another. That is, for a given pair of PE routers, there may be multiple CE routers attached to those PE routers that have pipes between them, and rather than using a guaranteed bandwidth LSP for each such pipe, we use a single guaranteed bandwidth LSP for all of them.

For example, in Figure 8.5 there may be one pipe for VPN A from CE_{A3} to CE_{A1} and another pipe for VPN B from CE_{B3} to CE_{B1}^2. To support these two pipes, we establish a single guaranteed bandwidth LSP from PE_3 to PE_1 and reserve on that LSP the amount of bandwidth equal to the sum of the bandwidth of the two pipes. When PE_3 receives a packet from CE_{A3} and the packet is destined to some host in Site 1 of VPN A, PE_3 determines under control of its local configuration whether the packet should receive the guaranteed bandwidth Class of Service. If so, then PE_3 forwards the packet along the guaranteed bandwidth LSP from PE_3 to PE_1.

Using a single guaranteed bandwidth LSP to carry multiple pipes between a pair of PE routers improves the scaling properties of the solution. This is because the number of such guaranteed bandwidth LSPs that a service provider has to establish and maintain is bound (from above) by the number of PE router pairs of that service provider, rather than by the number of pipes the VPN customers of that provider could have.

To support Classes of Service that fall into the hose model, a service provider uses Diff-Serv support with MPLS, as we described in Section 6.2.2. The service provider may also use MPLS traffic engineering, as described in Chapter 7, to improve network utilization while meeting the desired performance objectives.

The procedures by which an ingress PE router determines which traffic receives a particular Class of Service, regardless of whether that Class of Service falls into the hose or the pipe model, are purely local to that PE router. These procedures can take into account such factors as incoming interface, IP source and destination addresses, IP precedence, TCP port numbers, or any combination of the above. This gives a service provider significant flexibility with respect to control over what traffic gets a particular Class of Service.

Although a customer signs a contract with a service provider for a certain amount of traffic in a particular Class of Service, the customer may send traffic in excess of this amount. To determine whether the traffic is within the contract, the service provider uses policing at the ingress PE routers. For traffic that is out of contract, the provider has two options: either to discard this traffic immediately, at the ingress PE router, or to send the traffic, but mark it differently from the traffic that is in contract. With the second option, in order to reduce out-of-order delivery, both in- and out-of-contract traffic should be forwarded along the same LSP (as discussed in Section 6.2.2). The out-of-contract traffic is marked differently, and this marking affects the drop probability in case of congestion.

Within the service provider network, the P routers may use diff-serv PHBs for service differentiation. Note that the P routers need only maintain queuing state on an aggregate (e.g., per-PHB) basis, rather than on a per-VPN basis.

8.11 Advanced Topics

In this section we briefly cover several advanced topics related to BGP/ MPLS VPN. We first look at how a BGP/MPLS VPN service provider could offer VPN services to customers who are Internet Service Providers. Then we look at how a BGP/MPLS VPN service provider could offer VPN services to customers who are BGP/MPLS VPN service providers on their own. Finally, we look at how the BGP/MPLS VPN solution could be used in an environment where a given VPN spans multiple BGP/MPLS VPN service providers—multiprovider operations.

8.11.1 ISP as a Customer

Consider a VPN service provider that offers VPN services using BGP/ MPLS VPNs and a customer who is an Internet Service Provider (ISP). Such a customer may have several sites, where each site could be a Point of Presence (POP) or a regional network, and the customer wants to interconnect these sites using the VPN service offered by the service provider. For such a customer, the solution we have described so far in this chapter would require the VPN service provider to carry a full set of Internet routes (approximately 65,000 at the time of writing). It is true that only a subset of the service provider routers (or, more precisely, only the PE routers connected to the sites of that customer) would need to carry these routes. However, if several such customers had sites connected to a common PE router, this PE router would need to maintain a distinct forwarding table for each such customer, and each table would need to have a full set of Internet routes. That clearly presents a serious scalability problem for the PE router.

To enable service providers who use BGP/MPLS VPN to offer scalable VPN services to customers who are ISPs, we need to find some way to avoid requiring the service provider to carry all the Internet routes of these customers. To understand how we can accomplish this, observe that in the current IP routing architecture there is a clear distinction between internal (intradomain) routing and external (interdomain) routing. From the perspective of an ISP, the Internet routes are external while the routes to all the routers of that ISP are internal, with the number of internal routes being much smaller than the number of external routes. Whereas the ISP carries its Internet routes (its external routes) in BGP, the addresses carried in the next hop BGP attribute of these routes are the addresses reachable via the ISP's internal routing.

With the observations above in mind, for a customer who is an ISP we restrict the routing exchange between the CE routers of that customer and the PE routers of the BGP/MPLS VPN service provider to only the internal routes of that customer. Doing this allows a significant reduction in the number of routes that have to be maintained on the PE routers, thus making it practical to connect CE routers from multiple VPNs to a single PE router, even when each such VPN is an ISP and therefore has to carry a full set of the Internet routes.

Exchange of external routes among routers within each customer's site, as well as among routers in other sites, is accomplished by normal Internal BGP procedures.[7] Establishing Internal BGP sessions between routers in different sites is possible because routes to these routers are the customer's internal routes; therefore, intersite routing for these routers is provided by the BGP/MPLS VPN service provider.

Although exchanging just the ISP's internal routes between CE and PE routers solves the problem of routing load on the PE routers, it also introduces a new problem. Specifically, when a CE router of that ISP sends a packet to the PE router, this packet may be addressed to some destination in the Internet. But since we restrict routing information exchange between PE and CE routers to only the ISP's internal routes, the PE router has only the ISP's internal routes, but no Internet routes. So how can the PE router forward the packet? To solve this problem, we extend MPLS to the CE routers, which allows us to create LSPs from CE to PE routers that are bound to the routes associated with the addresses carried in the BGP next hop attribute. That is, when a PE router advertises routes to a CE router, it also advertises to the CE router labels associated with these routes. As a result, for all the Internet routes that the ISP has to carry, a CE router of that ISP has LSPs associated

---

7. Recall that the term "Internal BGP" is used to describe a BGP session between a pair of routers within the same autonomous system.

with the addresses carried in the BGP next hop attribute of these routes.

When a CE router constructs its forwarding table, it uses its BGP routing information to determine the address of the BGP next hop associated with each external route. For BGP next hops that are not in the same site as the CE router, the PE router connected to the CE router provides the CE router with both the routes to the BGP next hops and the labels associated with these routes. As a result, for each external route whose BGP next hop is not in the same site as the CE router, the CE router has a label that it should use when forwarding packets for that external route. When the CE router has to forward a packet to the PE router, and the packet has to be forwarded using an external route, the CE router places the label that should be used for that external route on the packet and sends the packet to the PE router.

To illustrate the approach above, consider the example shown in Figure 8.7, where a VPN service provider (SP) has a customer who is an ISP with two sites, Site 1 and Site 2, and where D1 and D2 represents two Internet routes that the ISP (or, to be more precise, router ASBR2[8]) received from some other router (not shown in the picture).

Let's first look at the routing information exchange. The routing information that CE_2 sends to PE_2 consists of the ISP's internal routes within Site 2, which includes a route to ASBR2. Within the SP this routing information is distributed to PE_1 following normal BGP/MPLS VPN procedures. As a result, PE_1 gets label L3, which is associated with the route to the VPN-IP address of ASBR2, ASBR2/VPN_ISP.[9] PE_1 also gets label L2, which is associated with the route to PE_2. PE_1 propagates the routing information associated with Site 2's internal routes to CE_1, together with the appropriate label binding information. As a result, CE_1 gets a route to ASBR2 with PE_1 as the next hop, and label L1 associated with this route. CE_1 then distributes this routing information within Site 1. As a result, every router in Site 1 gets a route for every destination internal to Site 2. Therefore, every router in Site 1 could establish a BGP (to be more precise, an Internal BGP) session

---

8. "ASBR" stands for *autonomous system border router.* This is the term used by OSPF to denote a router that connects one autonomous system with another.

9. We represent VPN-IP addresses as X/Y, where X is an IP address and Y is a Route Distinguisher. Thus, ASBR2/VPN_ISP represents a VPN-IP address, with ASBR2 being a plain IP address and VPN_ISP being the Route Distinguisher of that VPN.

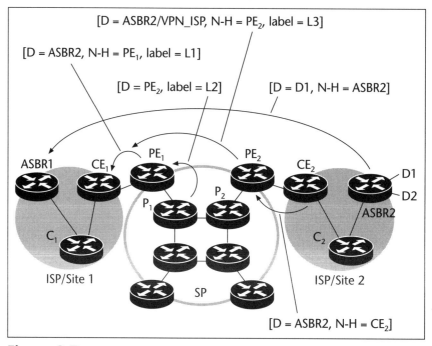

Figure 8.7
ISP as a customer.

with ASBR2.[10] These sessions are used to exchange the ISP's external routing information, including a route to D1.[11] As a result, every router within Site 1 has a BGP-learned route to D1, with ASBR2 as the BGP next hop of that route.

Now let's look at the packet forwarding. Assume that ASBR1 receives (from a router not shown in the picture) a packet destined to D1. Handling of the packet by ASBR1 and C_1 follows normal IP routing procedures. Since the BGP next hop of the route to D1 is ASBR2, and since ASBR1's next hop to ASBR2 is C_1, ASBR1 forwards the packet

10. In this example we assume a full mesh of Internal BGP sessions. The figure shows just one such session—between ASBR1 and ASBR2. In practice it is likely that, instead of a full mesh of Internal BGP sessions, an ISP would use BGP Route Reflectors, whereby each site would have one or more Route Reflectors.
11. Here we assume that within each site every router maintains all the routes, both internal and external. Alternatively, the ISP may deploy MPLS within each site (and not just at the routers that connect each site to the SP) and use the technique of MPLS hierarchy of routing knowledge to confine the external routes to its border routers only.

to C_1. When C_1 receives this packet, C_1 forwards this packet to its next hop on the path to ASBR2, which is CE_1. When CE_1 receives the packet, it sends the packet to its next hop on the path to ASBR2, which is PE_1. However, when sending the packet to PE_1, CE_1 also puts label L1 on the packet. When PE_1 receives the packet, PE_1 doesn't need to look at the destination address in the IP header (which is D1); PE_1 forwards the packet based on the label carried by the packet—L1. When PE_1 forwards the packet, PE_1 replaces L1 with L3, pushes label L2 onto the label stack, and sends the packet to P_1. P_1 forwards the packet based on its outer label—L2. At P_2 the outer label (the label associated with the route to PE_2) is stripped, as P_2 is a penultimate hop with respect to PE_2, and the packet is forwarded just with label L3 to PE_2. PE_2 uses the label carried in the packet, L3, to make its forwarding decision and sends the packet to CE_1. Before sending the packet to CE_1, PE_2 removes the label from the packet. Once the packet reaches CE_2, handling the packet within Site 2 follows normal IP routing procedures.

Note that from the customer's (ISP's) point of view, MPLS has to extend only to the CE routers. To prevent data spoofing, a PE router has to check that the packets it receives from a CE router carry only the labels that the PE router advertised to that CE router. These are the only extensions required to the BGP/MPLS VPN solution we have described so far. Moreover, other than plain MPLS support on the CE routers, the other mechanisms used by the BGP/MPLS VPN solution, such as VPN-IP addresses, are invisible to the customer.

8.11.2 BGP/MPLS VPN Service Provider as a Customer

Another possibility is that a BGP/MPLS VPN service provider could have customers who are themselves BGP/MPLS VPN service providers. To support such a customer, we need to figure out how to avoid requiring the first VPN service provider to carry all the VPN-IP routes of the VPN service providers who are customers of that provider.

Observe that from a BGP/MPLS VPN service provider point of view, all the VPN-IP routes are external routes, just like from an ISP point of view all the Internet routes are external routes. This similarity suggests that the same approach we used for handling customers who are ISPs (as described in the preceding section) could also be used for handling customers who are VPN service providers on their own.

The two main differences between the case where the customer is an ISP and the case where the customer is a BGP/MPLS VPN service provider are (1) in the former case the customer's external routes are IP

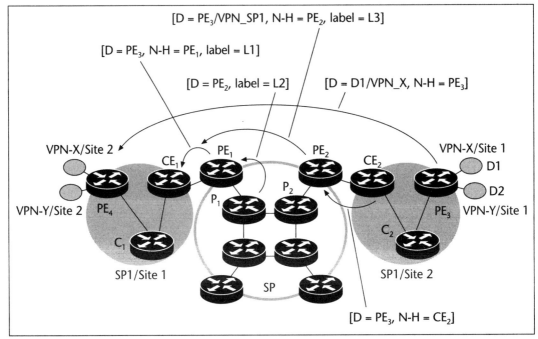

Figure 8.8
BGP/MPLS VPN Service Provider as a customer.

routes, while in the latter case the customer's external routes are VPN-IP routes, and (2) in the former case use of MPLS within each site is optional, while in the latter case it is required.

The example shown in Figure 8.8 is a small modification of Figure 8.7, where, instead of ASBR1 and ASBR2, we have PE routers (PE$_3$ and PE$_4$); in addition, the Internal BGP session between these two routers[12] carries VPN-IP routes (together with the appropriate labels) rather than IP routes, and all the routers within both Site 1 and Site 2 support MPLS.

8.11.3 Multiprovider Operations

So far we have considered the scenarios where all the sites within a given VPN are connected to the same BGP/MPLS VPN service provider.

---

12. In this example we assume full Internal BGP mesh between the PE routers of SP1. In practice it is likely that, instead of a full mesh, SP1 would use BGP Route Reflectors.

Now let's look at the scenarios where different sites within a given VPN are connected to different BGP/MPLS VPN service providers. Providing VPN services in such an environment is significantly more complex than in an environment where all the sites of a given VPN are connected to the same service provider. Among the challenges to consider are QoS in the multiprovider environment and Operational Support Systems (OSS) interworking. In the following we briefly outline how the BGP/MPLS VPN solution addresses the connectivity aspect in the multiprovider environment.

First, consider a scenario where a given VPN has sites connected to several BGP/MPLS VPN service providers that are not directly connected with each other, but rather use some other BGP/MPLS VPN service provider for transit traffic. Since the routing protocol used to carry VPN routing information by a service provider is BGP, and since BGP is an interdomain routing protocol, it follows that VPN routing information could be exchanged (using BGP) among providers that offer VPN services. And from the forwarding point of view, MPLS is not affected by the routing domain boundaries. The main problem with this approach is that the routers at the interconnect between the providers would need to carry VPN routing information, and the volume of this information may be fairly significant. To reduce the routing load on these routers, you could use multiple routers and partition the routing information among these routers.

An alternative to exchanging VPN routing information at the interconnect between the providers is to use the approach similar to the one we use when the customer is a BGP/MPLS VPN service provider on its own. From the transit service provider point of view, the other service providers that interconnect with each other using the transit provider form a single VPN, just like in the scenario where the customer of a BGP/MPLS VPN service provider is a single BGP/MPLS VPN service provider on its own. In the former case the sites of that VPN belong to different administrations (as each site is a separate service provider), while in the latter case the sites belong to the same administration (as all sites belong to the same service provider). The routing information that the transit service provider exchanges with these other service providers consists of routes to other service providers' internal destinations only, but not of VPN-IP routes carried by these other service providers, just like in the scenario where the customer of a BGP/MPLS VPN service provider is a BGP/MPLS VPN service provider on its own. The routing information exchange between the transit providers and the other providers could be accomplished via External

BGP, which will carry not just routes but labels for these routes as well.[13]

The main distinction between this scenario and the scenario where a service provider offers VPN services to a customer who is a BGP/MPLS VPN service provider on its own is that in the latter case the customer's external routes are exchanged among sites via Internal BGP (as all the sites belong to the same customer), while in the former case the customer's external routes are exchanged between customers (who are BGP/MPLS VPN service providers on their own) using External BGP (as different sites belong to different providers), and we need to use multi-hop External BGP (as these sites are not directly connected with each other).

To illustrate the difference, consider the example shown in Figure 8.8, but assume that instead of Site 1 we have BGP/MPLS VPN service provider SP1, and instead of Site 2 we have BGP/MPLS VPN service provider SP2, with SP providing transit service between SP1 and SP2. CE_2 would advertise (using External BGP) to PE_2 routes for SP2's internal destination (including a route to PE_3), as well as the labels for these routes. SP would distribute these routes to PE_1, and PE_1 would distribute these routes (using External BGP), as well as the labels associated with these routes, to CE_1. CE_1 would then distribute these routes within SP1, and SP1 and SP2 would exchange their VPN-IP routes using multihop External BGP. For example, if C_1 is a BGP Route Reflector in SP1, and C_2 is a BGP Route Reflector in SP2, then such a multihop External BGP could be between C_1 and C_2.

Observe that with this approach the transit service provider doesn't carry the VPN-IP routes of the other service providers, and therefore the routing load on any of the routers of the transit service provider doesn't depend on the amount of VPN routing information carried by the other service providers.

Yet another variation on the scenario above is when two BGP/MPLS VPN service providers are directly connected to each other. In this case the routers that interconnect these two providers exchange just routes associated with providers' internal destinations—these routers don't have to maintain any VPN-IP routes of the providers. Therefore, the routing load on these routers doesn't depend on the total amount of VPN routing information that each provider has to maintain.

---

13. Recall that the term "External BGP" is used to describe a BGP session between a pair of routers in different autonomous systems.

To illustrate routing information exchange between the two directly connected BGP/MPLS VPN service providers, consider the example shown in Figure 8.9, where we have two providers, SP1 and SP2, that are connected by a link between routers R_1 and R_2. Within each provider we have a BGP Route Reflector, RR_1 in SP1 and RR_2 in SP2. (In practice there would be more than one BGP Route Reflector within each provider.) The routing information exchanged at the interconnect between the providers (between R_1 and R_2) consists of the destinations internal to each provider. Thus, R_2 advertises to R_1 routes for PE_2, RR_2, and itself. Likewise, R_1 advertises to R_2 routes for PE_1, RR_1, and itself. The routing exchange between R_1 and R_2 is via External BGP, and this routing exchange is used to pass not just routes but the label binding information for these routes as well. So when R_2 advertises to R_1 a route for PE_2, R_2 also advertises to R_1 a label (L1) associated with that route. The VPN routing information is exchanged between BGP Route Reflectors within each provider. Thus, we have a multihop External BGP session between RR_1 and RR_2. Over that session RR_2 advertises to RR_1 a VPN route for D1 in VPN X (the reachability of this route is advertised as a VPN-IP address prefix), as well as a label (L2) associated with that route. From RR_1 this information is distributed to PE_1 (as PE_1 is a BGP Route Reflector client of RR_1). As a

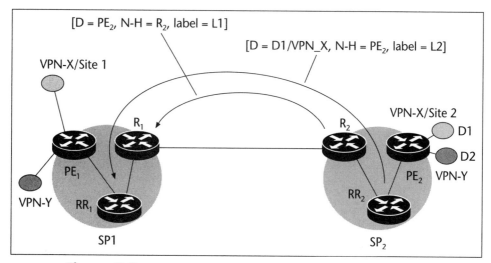

Figure 8.9

Multiprovider operations—interconnect between two BGP/MPLS VPN service providers.

result, PE_1 has all the routing and label binding information that is necessary in order to forward traffic from Site 1 of VPN X to Site 2 of that VPN. When PE_1 has to forward a packet to D1 in VPN X, PE_1 adds a stack of three labels to the packet, with L2 as the label at the bottom, a label associated with a route to PE_2 in the middle, and the label associated with a route to R_1 on top.

When two BGP/MPLS VPN service providers exchange VPN-IP routing information, they clearly don't have to exchange all the VPN routes—only the routes associated with the VPNs whose sites span both of these providers. Route filtering based on BGP Communities provides one way to filter out unneeded routes.

Since the procedures by which each VPN service provider assigns BGP Extended Communities and Route Distinguishers guarantees that such assignments result in globally unique Communities and Route Distinguishers, such assignments could be done by each service provider on its own. For a VPN that spans multiple service providers, each provider could on its own assign the Route Distinguisher that would be used to convert from IP to VPN-IP addresses for the routes coming from the sites of that VPN that are connected to that service provider. Likewise, each provider could on its own assign the Community attribute that would be attached to these routes when they are exported into the provider's BGP.

8.12 Summary

Let us briefly recap some of the key features of the BGP/MPLS VPN solution. First, the solution places no constraints on addressing plans used by VPNs. A VPN customer could use a private address, a globally unique address, or a globally nonunique address. In effect, a VPN customer could use whatever addresses it wants.

The solution also provides basic security that is comparable to that provided by Frame Relay or ATM-based VPNs. It is important to stress that this level of security is provided without incurring the overhead and complexity associated with the use of IPSec. Certain customers may have security requirements (e.g., data privacy) above and beyond what is provided by Frame Relay or ATM-based VPNs. For such customers, these requirements could be addressed by the customer's equipment, for example, using IPSec encryption between CE routers. And since IPSec is carried over plain IP, the use of IPSec by VPN customers is completely transparent to a VPN service provider.

In addition, the solution provides flexible and scalable support for QoS, whereby a VPN service provider can offer its customers a set of Classes of Service, with some Classes of Service that fall into the hose model and others that fall into the pipe model. There is a great deal of flexibility with respect to the policies that control which traffic gets a particular Class of Service. At the same time the mechanisms needed to implement such policies are confined to the service provider.

In the area of scalability, the solution could scale to very large VPNs with hundreds and thousands of sites per each Virtual Private Network, as well as to virtually unlimited numbers of Virtual Private Networks per service provider. The solution also allows a service provider to use a common infrastructure to offer both Virtual Private Network and Internet connectivity services.

Since connectivity between CE routers and PE routers is IP, and since we use MPLS within a service provider, the solution is link layer independent. A service provider could use any link layer technology (SONET, DSL, Frame Relay, ATM, leased lines, VLANs, etc.) to connect CE routers with PE routers, as well as to interconnect PE routers and P routers.

One important prerequisite for growing the VPN business is the ability to minimize the networking skill that is required by VPN customers. This is important because the more customers a service provider wants to serve, the less expertise each customer is going to have. The solution we described addresses this by allowing simplified operations and management for VPN customers. Specifically, a VPN customer doesn't need to operate its own backbone. Moreover, the solution lets VPN customers use fairly simple routing strategies. For example, a single-homed site could just use a default route for its inter-site connectivity. The solution simplifies VPN operations not only from the VPN customer's perspective but also from the perspective of the service provider. In today's environment, service providers use the concept of the managed router service to address the problem of inadequate networking skill of their VPN customers. While this concept certainly addresses the problem, it addresses it in a nonscalable and fairly expensive way, as it effectively requires the service provider to operate a separate backbone for each of its VPN customers. With the BGP/ MPLS solution, there is no separate backbone for each VPN customer. Therefore, there is no need for the service provider to operate a separate backbone for each VPN customer. That, in turn, results in improved scalability with respect to the ability of a VPN service provider to support a large number of VPN customers and lower cost to the VPN service provider.

The solution is also fundamentally recursive. That is, a VPN service provider could offer VPN services to customers who are not just enterprises but ISPs or VPN service providers on their own.

8.13 Further Reading

The white paper that describes a related approach to MPLS VPNs, IP Navigator MPLS, can be found at

www.ascend.com/docs/techdocs/ipnavwp.pdf

The BGP/MPLS VPN scheme is described in

Rosen, E., and Y. Rekhter. *BGP/MPLS VPNs*. RFC 2547, March 1999.

The following set of documents describes BGP:

Rekhter, Y., and T. Li. *A Border Gateway Protocol 4 (BGP-4)*. RFC 1771, March 1995.

Bates, T., R. Chandra, D. Katz, and Y. Rekhter. *Multiprotocol Extensions for BGP-4*. RFC 2283, February 1998.

Bates, T., and R. Chandrasekeran. *BGP Route Reflection: An Alternative to Full Mesh IBGP*. RFC 1966, June 1996.

Chandra, R., P. Traina, and T. Li. *BGP Communities Attribute*. RFC 1997, August 1996.

Further information on BGP can be found in any number of books, such as

Stewart, J. *BGP4: Inter-domain Routing in the Internet*. Addison-Wesley, 1999.

Halabi, B. *Internet Routing Architectures*. Cisco Press, 1997.

Concluding Remarks

At this stage we have explored some of the history and technical issues that led to the development of MPLS; we have seen how MPLS works; we have described the MPLS architecture, protocols, and standards; and we have examined the major application areas in which MPLS is currently being used. These applications include traffic engineering, fast rerouting around failures, support for quality of service, scalable virtual private networking, and simplified integration of ATM into IP networks. In these last few paragraphs, we will review the most important characteristics of MPLS and make some observations about the future of the technology.

The most significant technical characteristic of MPLS is that it decouples the information used to forward a packet from the information carried in the IP header. It does this by using labels, rather than anything contained in an IP packet, to make forwarding decisions. This simple fact has far-reaching consequences.

The use of labels to forward packets provides enormous flexibility in the deployment of new routing capabilities. It enables networks to employ routing paradigms other than the traditional hop by hop, destination-based paradigm of IP routing. This leads to the ability to perform traffic engineering, in which the flow of traffic can be flexibly controlled to move traffic from congested paths to paths with excess capacity. It also enables traffic to be quickly rerouted around failed links or nodes without waiting for reconvergence of routing tables among all routers in a network.

By attaching labels to packets, it becomes possible to support large-scale VPN services in which customers use overlapping (nonunique) IP addresses. Labels can be bound to customer-specific routes, so that the packets from one VPN customer are not routed to the network of another customer.

There is great flexibility in determining which groups of packets will share a common label and thus receive common treatment in the network. The decision of which label to apply is local to the LSR that imposes the label and thus may be made based on information that is available only at that LSR, such as the physical interface on which the packet arrived. Packets can receive different labels based on an infinite range of possible criteria. Thus, for example, a set of packets needing a particular QoS guarantee might all be given the same label. The determination of which packets receive that label and hence the QoS guarantee could be based on any available information, including information in the packet headers, the incoming interface, time of day, and so on. Thus, labels also provide an effective way of aggregating traffic, avoiding the need to perform complex classifications at every hop.

The flexibility of label switching is also conveyed by the "multiprotocol" part of MPLS. While much of this book has focused on applications of MPLS in which the labeled packets are IP datagrams, MPLS can quite reasonably be applied to other protocols. For example, work is under way at the time of writing to specify ways to carry both ATM and Frame Relay virtual circuits over MPLS label switched paths.

MPLS also provides a range of alternative ways in which labels may be carried. Today these include the shim header, which is used on most link types, and the VPI/VCI field of ATM cell headers. This enables a common set of control protocols to be applied to devices with different low level forwarding capabilities. The most notable benefit of this feature to date is the ability to integrate ATM switches into IP networks without many of the drawbacks of traditional IP over ATM models, since an ATM-LSR supports exactly the same control protocols as any other LSR.

Flexibility in the encoding of labels has interesting implications for future applications of MPLS. We have seen in ATM-LSRs that a device that doesn't recognize either IP headers or IP packet boundaries can nevertheless function effectively as an LSR in an MPLS network. Looking to the future, labels could also be represented by wavelengths (lambdas) in an optical cross-connect. Such a device has no notion of packets at all and yet could still function as an MPLS device using the same control architecture as other LSRs. This application of MPLS, known as *multiprotocol lambda switching,* is under development at the time of writing.

It should be apparent at this point that the future is bright for MPLS. It is solving a number of real-world problems in large production networks today. In the future we are likely to see new applications for MPLS that cannot be predicted today, as it is applied to new lower layer technologies, such as optical switching, and as new routing and control paradigms are developed to take advantage of the flexibility of labels. It is therefore appropriate to describe MPLS as more than just a new piece of technology—it is a powerful extension to the IP routing and forwarding architecture.

Glossary

AAL (ATM adaptation layer). A protocol layer that allows higher layer protocols to run over ATM virtual circuits. Of particular relevance is AAL5, which enables segmentation and reassembly of variable-length packets so that they may be sent as streams of cells on an ATM VC.

ARIS (Aggregate Route-based IP Switching). The name given to the label switching scheme invented at IBM, which associates labels with aggregate routes (e.g., address prefixes) in the common case. Also used as the name for the associated label binding distribution protocol.

ATMARP (Asynchronous Transfer Mode Address Resolution Protocol). The server-based protocol that enables IP addresses to be translated into ATM addresses.

BGP (Border Gateway Protocol). The predominant interdomain routing protocol used in IP networks.

BOF (Birds of a Feather). The name for a session at the **IETF** that is held prior to the formation of a working group to determine whether sufficient interest exists.

BUS (broadcast and unknown server). A server used in emulated LANs to provide broadcast service on a network such as ATM that does not natively support it.

CLP (cell loss priority). A bit carried in the header of an ATM cell indicating the drop priority of the cell.

Community attribute. An identifier carried in **BGP** that is associated with a route for route filtering purposes. May be used when building MPLS/BGP VPNs to identify routes that are to be imported into a **FIB** for a certain **VPN**.

Constraint-based routing. The process of determining suitable routes in a network subject to a variety of constraints, such as minimum available bandwidth, over the route.

CR-LDP (Constraint-based Routing Label Distribution Protocol). A set of extensions to **LDP** that enable constraint-based routing and QoS reservation in an **MPLS** network.

CSPF (constrained shortest path first). An extension of the shortest path first (**SPF**) algorithm, in which only the links that meet certain specified constraints are considered for inclusion in the shortest path tree.

CSR (Cell Switching Router). The name for a device implementing Toshiba's **label switching** scheme.

Differentiated Services (diff-serv). A QoS architecture developed in the **IETF** that divides traffic into a small number of classes and provides QoS to large aggregates of traffic.

DSCP (Differentiated Services Code Point). A 6-bit value carried in an IP header indicating the QoS treatment that a packet should receive.

EBGP (external BGP). A BGP session between routers in different autonomous systems. When a pair of routers in different autonomous systems are more than one IP hop away from each other, an external BGP session between these two routers is called multihop external BGP. See also **IBGP**.

ECN (explicit congestion notification). An experimental congestion avoidance mechanism for IP in which congestion is signalled from within the network to the communicating endpoints.

Edge LSR. A Label Switching Router (**LSR**) that first applies a label to a packet.

ERO (Explicit Route Object). An object carried in an **LSP** setup protocol (such as **RSVP** or **LDP**) to specify the sequence of hops that an explicitly routed LSP must traverse.

Extended Community Attribute. Similar to **Community Attribute,** but each Community is 64 bits, rather than 32 bits as with normal Community.

FEC (Forwarding Equivalence Class). A set of packets that can be handled equivalently for the purpose of forwarding and thus is suitable for binding to a single label. The set of packets destined for one address prefix in one example of an FEC. A **flow** is another example.

FIB (Forwarding Information Base). A forwarding table in a router.

Flow. Generally, a set of packets traveling between a pair of hosts, or a pair of transport protocol ports on a pair of hosts. For example, packets with the same value of <source address, source port, destination address, destination port> might be considered a flow.

Flow identifier. An object used in data-driven approaches (**CSR** and **IP Switching**) to define a **flow** to be label switched.

Forwarding. The process of transferring a packet from an input to an output on either a switch or a router.

GRE (generic route encapsulation). A form of IP-in-IP tunneling.

GSMP (General Switch Management Protocol). The protocol defined by Ipsilon to allow communication between an **IP Switch** controller and an ATM switch.

IBGP (internal BGP). A BGP session between routers within the same autonomous system. See also **EBGP**.

IETF (Internet Engineering Task Force). The major standards-setting body for the Internet and the IP suite of protocols.

IFMP (Ipsilon Flow Management Protocol). The **label binding** protocol for IP Switching, which an **IP Switch** uses to notify its neighbors that a **flow** has been selected for **label switching**.

IGP (Interior Gateway Protocol). A routing protocol used within a single domain, such as OSPF or IS-IS.

In band. Signalling information sent on the same channel (e.g., VC) as data.

Integrated Services (int-serv). A QoS architecture developed in the **IETF** that uses signaling to establish end-to-end QoS for application flows.

IP Switch. Defined in this book as a device implementing the Ipsilon approach to label switching. In other settings, it may sometimes mean any label switching device that uses IP control protocols or even any device that forwards IP packets (such as an IP router).

IP Switching. Ipsilon's approach to label switching. See **IP Switch**.

IPSec (IP Security). A set of standards to provide confidentiality and authentication of packets at the IP layer, which includes a tunneling mode that may be used to build encrypted, authenticated tunnels in a **VPN**.

ISR (Integrated Switch Router). The **ARIS** term for a Label Switching Router.

Label. A short, fixed-length identifier that is used to determine the forwarding of a packet using the exact match algorithm and that is usually rewritten during forwarding.

Label binding. An association between a label and an **FEC**, which may be advertised to neighbors to establish a label switched path.

Label switching. The generic term used here to describe all approaches to forwarding IP (or other network layer) packets using a label swapping forwarding algorithm under the control of network layer routing algorithms. Label swapping forwarding uses exact match and rewrites the label on forwarding.

LDP (Label Distribution Protocol). The protocol to distribute label bindings defined by the **IETF**.

LIS (logical IP subnet). A set of IP nodes connected to an ATM network that share the same subnet address and may thus communicate without the intervention of a router.

LLC/SNAP. A form of encapsulation that enables several higher layer protocols to be multiplexed onto a single datalink, such as an ATM VC.

Longest match. The forwarding algorithm most often used for IP forwarding, in which a (fixed-length) IP address is compared against the (variable-length) entries in a routing table, looking for the entry that matches the most leading bits in the address.

LSP (label switched path). A path that is followed by a labeled packet over several hops, starting at an ingress **LSR** and ending at an egress LSR.

LSR (Label Switching Router). The general term for a device that implements **label switching**, as defined above.

MARS (multicast address resolution server). A device used in ATM networks to enable IP multicast to be mapped onto ATM point-to-multipoint VCs.

MPLS (Multiprotocol Label Switching). The name of the **IETF** working group responsible for **label switching**, and the name of the label switching approach it has standardized.

MTU (maximum transmission unit). The largest packet size that can be transmitted on a datalink without fragmentation.

NHRP (Next Hop Resolution Protocol). A protocol used to enable cut-through paths to be established between logical IP subnets on an ATM network.

OSPF (open shortest path first). A popular link-state routing protocol.

Out of band. Signalling information sent on a channel (e.g., VC) different from that on which data is sent.

Overlay model. An approach to building a virtual network in which a set of devices (e.g., routers) is interconnected across another network using virtual connections such as ATM virtual circuits or tunnels. In a **VPN** context, each customer site is connected to other customer sites using VCs or tunnels, forming a "virtual backbone." See also **peer model.**

Peer model. An approach to building a **VPN** in which the customer sites form a peering relationship with the VPN provider network rather than connecting to other customer sites using a virtual backbone.

PHB (per-hop behavior). The externally visible behavior of a router that defines the QoS treatment of a group of packets in the diff-serv architecture.

PHB scheduling class. A group of **PHB**s that share an ordering constraint, such that packets with different PHBs in the class must not be misordered.

PIM (protocol independent multicast). A multicast routing protocol being standardized in the **IETF.**

Port. (1) A physical interface to a switch or router. (2) An identifier used by transport protocols to distinguish application flows between a pair of hosts.

RED (random early detection). A congestion avoidance mechanism that drops a small percentage of packets arriving at a router queue when the average queue length exceeds a threshold.

Refresh reduction. A set of extensions to **RSVP** designed to reduce the overhead of maintaining unchanged state.

RFC (Request for Comment). A document in a series maintained by the **IETF**, which includes all Internet protocol standards.

Route distinguisher. An identifier used in BGP/MPLS VPNs to ensure uniqueness of address prefixes among **VPN**s when multiple VPNs use the same address space (e.g., address space defined in RFC 1918).

Route target. An **Extended Community** that identifies a group of routers and, in each router of that group, a subset of forwarding tables maintained by the router that may be populated with a **BGP** route carrying that extended community.

RSVP (Resource Reservation Protocol). A protocol for reserving network resources to provide Quality of Service guarantees to application flows, which is also used to establish forwarding state for explicitly routed **LSP**s.

Soft state. State that will time out (be deleted) if not periodically refreshed; it may also be explicitly deleted, but does not need to be.

SPF (shortest path first). The common routing algorithm used by link-state routing protocols, such as OSPF and IS-IS; also known as Dijkstra's algorithm.

Tag. Another name for a label, used in Cisco's Tag Switching.

TCP (Transmission Control Protocol). The widely used reliable byte stream delivery protocol.

TDP (Tag Distribution Protocol). Cisco's **label binding** distribution protocol.

TFIB (Tag Forwarding Information Base). The data structure used in Tag Switching to hold information about incoming and outgoing tags and the associated **FEC**s.

TSR (Tag Switching Router). The Tag Switching term for an **LSR**.

VCI (virtual circuit identifier). A field in the ATM header used to identify the virtual circuit to which a cell belongs.

VPI (virtual path identifier). A field in the ATM header used to identify the virtual path to which a cell belongs.

VPN (Virtual Private Network). A group of sites that, as the result of a set of administrative policies, are able to communicate with each other over a shared backbone network.

Bibliography

Awduche, D. "MPLS and Traffic Engineering in IP Networks." *IEEE Communications*, December 1999.

Awduche, D., et al. *Requirements for Traffic Engineering over MPLS*. RFC 2702, September 1999.

Bates, T., R. Chandra, D. Katz, and Y. Rekhter. *Multiprotocol Extensions for BGP-4*. RFC 2283, February 1998.

Bates, T., and R. Chandrasekeran. *BGP Route Reflection: An Alternative to Full Mesh IBGP*. RFC 1966, June 1996.

Blake, S., et al. *An Architecture for Differentiated Services*. RFC 2475, December 1998.

Braden, R., S. Shenker, and D. Clark. *Integrated Services in the Internet Architecture: An Overview*. RFC 1633, June 1994.

Braden, R., L. Zhang, S. Berson, S. Herzog, and S. Jamin. *Resource ReSerVation Protocol (RSVP): Version 1 Functional Specification*. RFC 2205, September 1997.

Brodnik, A., S. Carlsson, M. Degermark, and S. Pink. "Small Forwarding Tables for Fast Routing Lookups." In Proceedings of ACM SIGCOMM 97, Cannes, France, September 1997.

Chandra, R., P. Traina, and T. Li. *BGP Communities Attribute*. RFC 1997, August 1996.

Chandranmenon, C., and G. Varghese. "Trading Packet Headers for Packet Processing." In Proceedings of ACM SIGCOMM 95, September 1995, 162–173.

Comer, D. *Internetworking with TCP/IP. Vol. 1: Principles, Protocols and Architecture*. 3rd ed. Englewood Cliffs, NJ: Prentice Hall, 1995.

Davie, B., P. Doolan, and Y. Rekhter. *Switching in IP Networks: IP Switching, Tag Switching and Related Technologies*. San Francisco: Morgan Kaufmann, 1998.

Davie, B., and J. Gibson. "Enabling Explicit Routing in IP Networks." In Proceedings of Globecom '98, Sydney, Australia, November 1998.

Deering, S., D. Estrin, D. Farinucci, V. Jacobson, C. Gung Liu, and L. Wei. "An Architecture for Wide-Area Multicast Routing." In Proceedings of ACM SIGCOMM 94, London, September 1994.

Estrin, D., et al. *Protocol Independent Multicast-Sparse Mode (PIM-SM): Protocol Specification*. RFC 2368, June 1998.

Feldman, N., and A. Viswanathan. *ARIS Protocol Specification*. IBM Technical Report TR 29.2368, March 1998.

Garcia-Luna-Aceves, J. "A Unified Approach to Loop-Free Routing Using Distance Vectors or Link States." *Computer Communications Review* 19, no. 4, September 1989.

Ghanwani, A., B. Jamoussi, D. Fedyk, P. Ashwood-Smith, L. Li, and N. Feldman. "Traffic Engineering Standards in IP Networks Using MPLS." *IEEE Communications,* December 1999.

Halabi, B. *Internet Routing Architectures*. Indianapolis: Cisco Press, 1997.

Heinanen, J. *Multiprotocol Encapsulation over AAL5*. RFC 1483, July 1993.

Huitema, C. *Routing in the Internet*. Englewood Cliffs, NJ: Prentice Hall, 1995.

Jacobson, V. "Congestion Avoidance and Control." In Proceedings of ACM SIGCOMM 88, September 1988.

Katsube, Y., K. Nagami, and H. Esaki. *Toshiba's Router Architecture Extensions for ATM: Overview*. RFC 2098, April 1997.

Laubach, M. *Classical IP and ARP over ATM*. RFC 1577, January 1994.

Li, T., and Y. Rekhter. *A Provider Architecture for Differentiated Services and Traffic Engineering (PASTE)*. RFC 2430, October 1998.

Lin, S., and N. McKeown. "A Simulation Study of IP Switching." In Proceedings of ACM SIGCOMM 97, Cannes, France, September 1997.

Luciani, J., D. Katz, D. Piscitello, B. Cole, and N. Doraswamy. *NBMA Next Hop Resolution Protocol (NHRP)*. RFC 2332, April 1998.

Moy, J. *OSPF Version 2*. RFC 2328, April 1998.

Nagami, K., et al. *Toshiba's Flow Attribute Notification Protocol (FANP) Specification*. RFC 2129, April 1997.

Newman, P., T. Lyon, and G. Minshall. "Flow Labelled IP: A Connectionless Approach to ATM." In Proceedings of the IEEE Infocom, March 1996.

Newman, P., T. Lyon, and G. Minshall. "IP Switching: ATM under IP." *IEEE/ACM Transactions on Networking* 6, no. 2 (April 1998):117–129.

Newman, P., G. Minshall, T. Lyon, and L. Huston. "IP Switching and Gigabit Routers." *IEEE Communications,* January 1997.

Paxson, V. "End-to-End Routing Behavior in the Internet." *IEEE/ACM Transactions on Networking* 5 (October 1997): 601–615.

Perlman, R. *Interconnections: Bridges and Routers.* Reading, MA: Addison-Wesley, 1992.

Peterson, L., and B. Davie. *Computer Networks: A Systems Approach.* San Francisco: Morgan Kaufmann, 2000.

Ramakrishnan, K., and S. Floyd. *A Proposal to Add Explicit Congestion Notification (ECN) to IP.* RFC 2481, January 1999.

Rekhter, Y., B. Davie, D. Katz, E. Rosen, and G. Swallow. *Cisco Systems' Tag Switching Architecture Overview.* RFC 2105, February 1997.

Rekhter, Y., B. Davie, E. Rosen, G. Swallow, D. Farinacci, and D. Katz. "Tag Switching Architecture Overview." In *Proceedings of the IEEE* 82, no. 12 (December 1997): 1973–1983.

Rekhter, Y., and T. Li. *A Border Gateway Protocol 4 (BGP-4).* RFC 1771, March 1995.

Stewart, J. *BGP4: Inter-domain Routing in the Internet.* Reading, MA: Addison-Wesley, 1999.

Swallow, G. "MPLS Advantages for Traffic Engineering." *IEEE Communications,* December 1999.

Waldvogel, M., G. Varghese, J. Turner, and B. Plattner. "Scalable High Speed IP Routing Lookups." In Proceedings of ACM SIGCOMM 97, Cannes, France, September 1997.

Index

About the Authors

Bruce Davie works at Cisco Systems, Inc. in Chelmsford, Massachusetts, where he is a Cisco Fellow. He completed his Ph.D. in computer science at the University of Edinburgh, Scotland, in 1988 before joining Bell Communications Research (Bellcore) in Morristown, NJ. He has been with Cisco Systems since 1995 where he leads a group working on the development of Multiprotocol Label Switching and Quality of Service capabilities for IP networks. He is the author of numerous journal articles and RFCs, and the coauthor of *Computer Networks: A Systems Approach,* Editions 1 and 2 (Morgan Kaufmann Publishers, 1996, 2000). He is an active member of both the Internet Engineering Task Force and the End-to-End Research Group.

Yakov Rekhter works at Cisco Systems, Inc., where he is a Cisco Fellow. He is one of the leading designers of Tag Switching, BGP/MPLS VPNs, and MPLS Traffic Engineering. He is also one of the leading designers of Border Gateway Protocol (BGP). He is the author or coauthor of many RFCs, as well as numerous presentations, papers, and articles on TCP/IP and the Internet.